Luminos is the Open Access monograph publishing program
from UC Press. Luminos provides a framework for preserving and
reinvigorating monograph publishing for the future and increases
the reach and visibility of important scholarly work. Titles published
in the UC Press Luminos model are published with the same high
standards for selection, peer review, production, and marketing as
those in our traditional program. See www.luminosoa.org

The publisher and the University of California Press Foundation gratefully acknowledge the generous support of the Constance and William Withey Endowment Fund in History and Music.

Open Access publication was made possible through generous support from the Knights of Vartan Fund for Armenian Studies and the National Association for Armenian Studies and Research (NAASR), and from Birkbeck, University of London.

Everyday Cosmopolitanisms

Everyday Cosmopolitanisms

Living the Silk Road in Medieval Armenia

Kate Franklin

UNIVERSITY OF CALIFORNIA PRESS

University of California Press
Oakland, California

Suggested citation: Franklin, K. *Everyday Cosmopolitanisms: Living the Silk Road in Medieval Armenia*. Oakland: University of California Press, 2021. DOI: https://doi.org/10.1525/luminos.109

Library of Congress Cataloging-in-Publication Data

Names: Franklin, Kathryn J., author.
Title: Everyday cosmopolitanisms : living the Silk Road in medieval Armenia / Kate Franklin.
Description: Oakland, California : University of California Press, [2021] | Includes bibliographical references and index.
Identifiers: LCCN 2021012048 (print) | LCCN 2021012049 (ebook) | ISBN 9780520380929 (paperback) | ISBN 9780520380936 (epub)
Subjects: LCSH: Trade routes—Caucasus—History. | Silk Road—Description and travel—History. | Silk Road—History, Local. | Armenia—History—428–1522.
Classification: LCC DS329.4 .F74 2021 (print) | LCC DS329.4 (ebook) | DDC 956.6/2013—dc23
LC record available at https://lccn.loc.gov/2021012048
LC ebook record available at https://lccn.loc.gov/2021012049

30 29 28 27 26 25 24 23 22 21
10 9 8 7 6 5 4 3 2 1

CONTENTS

ILLUSTRATIONS

FIGURES

MAPS

Let me be the first to tell you that I am a romantic when it comes to travel. I love motor court hotels, grand old train stations, and the scene in parking lots outside old Soviet termini where microbuses are loading, where the best shawarma is sold next to cemetery flower arrangements and bottles of cognac. Over a few years of being an archaeologist, I have spent a lot of time in transit spaces—sleeping on a pile of luggage in western Ireland or on an overnight bus in coastal Peru, waiting for a train in the middle of the night under a single lamppost in the open steppe near Russia's border with Kazakhstan, or hailing a ride on the Aparan-Yerevan highway, and then spending hours pressed against patient riders as the microbus jolted down the mountainside to the city.

But I can date the moment I became a romantic about medieval travel in Armenia. In 2008 I was standing at the site of the Talin caravanserai, an enormous ruin on the Gyumri-Yerevan highway, on the western shoulder of Mount Aragats. At the time I was a guest. I been brought to the caravan inn through the hospitality of the archaeological team led by Jean Pierre Mahé, and I was hosted (with infinite patience and kindness) by Hamazasp Khachatryan and Larisa Yeganyan of the Shirak Regional Museum. Despite being extensively ruined, with its walls robbed of their ashlars and vaulted architecture lying in chunks on the plain, the caravanserai was impressive. It was a large building and—as the team of architects and archaeologists discussed—it had been enlarged during its use-life to hold even more people, animals, bales of goods. In the more recent past it had been converted into a corral, with a gate made from wire and a giant metal *S* plundered from a long-gone road sign. Standing near the remains of a campfire in the shadow of the east wall, I reflected that this was a place to which I could connect many of the questions I had about social life in medieval Armenia, and in particular about how places on the slope of Aragats encountered a broader world. A few miles south of the caravanserai, I scaled the castle wall of the Zak'arid fortress at Daštadem; from this aptly named castle it is impossible not to feel romantic. With the mountain at your back you gaze imperiously over ruined medieval villages and cascading slopes receding into the haze of the Ararat plain. Later in the Shirak Museum, Hamik pulled off the shelf Harutyunyan's *Caravanserais and Bridges in Medieval Armenia* and I learned that the South Caucasus contained not just one caravan inn like Talin but a whole network of places built for a traveling world.

I feel so insanely lucky that I was able to turn this romantic curiosity into a doctoral research project, primarily thanks to the endless hospitality, patience, and volunteerism of my friends and colleagues in the Republic of Armenia. A few weeks after visiting the caravanserai at Talin, I went to participate in the Institute of Archaeology and Ethnography's excavations at Dvin, having been invited there by Gregory Areshian. It was at Dvin that I first met my future colleagues and collaborators in the medieval department in their element, excavating the houses, streets, and halls of that great city, and sharing coffee, fruit, and stories under a mulberry tree in the medieval moat. I am so grateful to have had that time to learn from Aram Kalantaryan, who shared his astounding knowledge and his library. At Dvin I also met Frina Babayan, who later became my collaborator at Ambroyi, and my friend. Frina taught me so much about the culture of medieval archaeology in Armenia, filling my endless ignorance at the same time that she ceaselessly fed me with aladi, perashki, and peaches. And none of this work would have been possible without Ruben Badalyan, who was infinitely patient but, more importantly, so wonderfully curious, that he went out on a limb for my medieval project in 2011. Of course, Ruben was prodded by Adam T. Smith, my doctoral advisor, who first took me to Armenia and who talked through the caravanserai project in the field while washing dishes or while drinking beer after work, as we bounced up hills in the project van or while paying the Aparan hospital for stitching me up after a fall into my own *hetaxuzaxor* (trench).

I must also thank a cavalcade of colleagues and friends at the Institute, starting with Pavel Avetisyan, whose continued faith in my work is an ongoing source of inspiration, admiration, and gratitude. I have been blessed by a group of friends and colleagues in Armenia, who have made my research not only easier but frequently an incredible pleasure. Thanks to the *jahelner* of the Institute of Archaeology and Ethnography. Diana Mirijanyan took me under her wing at Dvin when she had so much else to do. Hasmik Hovhannisyan indulged me in late-night wine-fueled conversations, and Levon Aghikyan showed me some of the best dive bars in Yerevan. Thanks to Roman Hovsepyan for being a good friend as well as collaborator. I am so grateful for the patient advising of Husik Melkonyan and Gagik Sargsyan, and I thank Boris Gasparyan, Aghavni Zhamkochyan, Nura Hakopyan, and Garine Kocharyan for their ongoing collegial support. Thanks as well to Project ArAGATS 2011, my colleagues in the field and workroom, and friends around the dinner table.

As my doctoral research expanded into a larger scale project at Arai-Bazarǰuł, I expanded my community of friends and colleagues working at that site. I must thank Mr. Edik Petrosyan and his family—especially Gevorg and Petik—for their generosity, hospitality, and help with my work in Arai from 2011 through 2014. Tasha Vorderstrasse opened my eyes to other ways of thinking about Armenia in larger context, and was an amazing co-conspirator. But most of all I need to thank Artur Petrosyan and Andranik Sargsyan for so much: comradely work, humor, homemade meals, and the hospitality of their houses and families—but even more, for being rock-solid guys who saved my ass time and time again, and made me laugh about it afterward. And I am grateful to the folks of the Kasakh Valley and Aragatsotn, whose names I didn't always learn but who gave me directions, drove me up mountains in Ladas, invited me in for coffee, and helped me get on the road again.

At the University of Chicago, I must thank the other members of my doctoral committee: Kathy Morrison, Francois Richard, and Shannon Dawdy. I have to thank Kathy in particular for being a true mentor, for continuing to show me the kind of feminist academic I want to be in addition to teaching me how to research and write, and above all, for treating me like an adult and a colleague. There is a community of folks in Chicago who were in the trenches of grad school with me, some of whom remain close friends and all of whom I have to thank, in particular: Elizabeth and Bryan Fagan, Maureen Marshall, Michelle Lelievre, Melissa Rosenzweig, Maddie McLeester, Emily Hammer, Brian Wilson, Matthew Knisley, Alan Greene, Jim Johnson, Estefania Vidal-Montero, Hannah Chazin, Rebecca Graff, Mary Leighton, Josh Cannon, Mudit Trivedi, and Ani Honarchian. Amanda Logan was a bright light in some dark days and continues to fuel so many of my best ideas with Malört. The entire crew in the CAMEL Lab at the Oriental Institute deserves a credit for listening to me talk through this book in its early stages, but I have to thank Tony Lauricella in particular for joining me in righteous (often bourbon-fueled) rants about SF and imagined landscapes. I am also grateful to the wider network of archaeologists working on Eurasia for their friendship and welcome, first and foremost Claudia Chang, who has been the fairy godmother to my work from early on, and who shares my deep love of bazaars and textiles. Thanks also to Tekla Schmaus and Michelle Negus-Cleary for much-needed sisterhood. I set out on this book project thanks to the encouragement of Michael Frachetti and was helped in the rocky early stages by Asya Graff's generous reading. The book's argument was honed in conversations in Durham and Chiangmai with my SSRC Transregional Research Junior Scholar: InterAsian Contexts and Connections Fellows cohort, hosted with flair by Prasenjit Duara and Enseng Ho. I feel really lucky that Alice Yao introduced me to Eric Schmidt, who had to cheerlead to get this book where it is. Khodadad Rezakhani and a second, anonymous reader improved this work immensely: thank you both.

In London, I thank the new colleagues who are quickly becoming old friends, and upon whom I foisted a first draft: Matthew Champion, Lesley McFadyen, Rebecca Darley, and Kat Hill. In Aberdeen, Josh Wright provided comments, support, and whiskey. I am also grateful to my students, at Chicago, SAIC and Birkbeck, for letting me think in their company; in particular the students of my Travels in Armenia class at Chicago, my Anthropology and Science Fiction classes at SAIC, and the students from my Silk Road and my Imagined Landscapes classes at Birkbeck.

I'd like to think that my obsessions with the Middle Ages, speculative fiction, and feminist theory are a source of amusement to my family; in any case, they have borne me through the last decades "with sacrifice and love." My dad raised me to love sci-fi, local food, and divey bars, while my mom taught me to love architecture and cooking, to notice small details, and ask questions. Most of my professional life has been lived in pale imitation of my aunt Patricia, who is still the coolest person I know, and the most generous. Thanks to my brothers, Jon and Joe, and my sisters, Mariana and Libby, for calling me on my bullshit—and thanks to Harry for being the best at being a dog the world has ever seen.

I don't really know how to thank Astghik Babajanyan, who has become my collaborator, confidant, and dear friend. Thanks, *aziz jan*, for reminding me not to panic, for teaching me how to cook and to read pottery, and, most importantly, for showing me how to work every day with joy and grace, as well as infectious humor. Likewise, I would not have had the heart to write this book if Tyson Leuchter hadn't lent me a chunk of his.

Finally, in a persistently romantic move to acknowledge my own situatedness, I want to express gratitude to the places where I thought through this work. I personally believe that imagination is inextricable from the places that co-constitute it, and so I realize that the places where my conversations happened were sometimes as influential as the interlocutors (especially when I was talking to myself): the porch at New Smyrna, Brockwell Park, the 59, 18, and 6 buses, and the Wolverine Line. I will always love the ghost that haunts good bars in Chicago. Some in particular I have thought in, and with: the L&L, Skylark, Delilah's, Simon's, Long Room, Kasey's, and Jimmy's. The front porch at Ando's house, with the sunset lighting up Arai Ler beyond the highway; the bench under the grapevines in Astghik's *bak* in Zeytun.

This work was made possible through support from the Wenner Gren Foundation, Project ArAGATS, the American Research Institute of the South Caucasus, the Oriental Institute at the University of Chicago, and the Social Sciences Research Council.

NOTE ON TRANSLITERATION

This book uses the Hübschmann-Meillet-Benveniste (HMB) system for Armenian. The exception to this is in the case of person and place names that now have alternative conventional transliterations, such as Ghafadaryan, Aragatsotn, Kasakh Valley.

ա	a	ի	i	յ	y	տ	t
բ	b	լ	l	ն	n	ր	r
գ	g	խ	x	շ	š	ց	cʿ
դ	d	ծ	c	ո	o	ւ	u
ե	e	կ	k	չ	čʿ	ւ	w
զ	z	հ	h	պ	p	փ	pʿ
է	ē	ձ	j	ջ	ǰ	ք	kʿ
ը	ə	ղ	ł	ռ	ṙ	և	ew
թ	tʿ	ճ	č	ս	s	օ	ō
ժ	ž	մ	m	վ	v	ֆ	f

1

The Silk Road, Medieval Globality, and "Everyday Cosmopolitanism"

Sitting in the shadow of the north wall of the ruined caravan house (*karavanatun*) at Arai-Bazarǰuł on a clear day in summer, one can see four mountain peaks. To the west above Aragats, the tallest mountain in the Republic of Armenia, clouds catch and gather, threatening to descend and change the day from sun to hail in minutes. To the northeast, the stooping shoulder of Tełenis hefts a load of radio antennas and cell towers above the Tsaghkunyats range. To the southeast, roads heading toward Lake Sevan pass behind the green slopes of volcanic Arai Ler. Due south from where the now collapsed doorway of the *karavanatun* would have opened onto the mountain road, the double peaks of Ararat appear over the horizon of the Kasakh Valley as it falls away toward the plain of the Araxes River below. The caravan inn, now a solitary ruin in a hay field, sits far out on the shoulder of Mount Aragats. Unlike the medieval villages, forts, and churches which still remain in the Kasakh Valley, tucked on mountain slopes and into the curves of riverbanks, the caravan house occupies the center of the view, sitting atop a rise in the surrounding wheat fields, which affords a sense of expansive proprietorship to the shepherds, harvesters, and archaeologists who rest in the shade of the ruined wall. Sitting there, drinking coffee from a shared jam jar, one's eyes follow the trailer-trucks, marked with Turkish and Iranian names, as they roll north- and southward through the Kasakh Valley (now a primary route of the international transit trade through Armenia) and disappear behind the mountains. Conversation under the wall frequently turns to the world beyond the horizons. There is a solid consensus that Soviet shovels still beat the newer Chinese ones for quality, and everyone in the village has a brother, a father, or a husband who is currently working in Russia or Uzbekistan in construction. In Aparan, up the valley, one woman remembered traveling to Moscow as a little girl and standing in the crowd to see Stalin's embalmed corpse. And all the older passing shepherds remember when, during

1

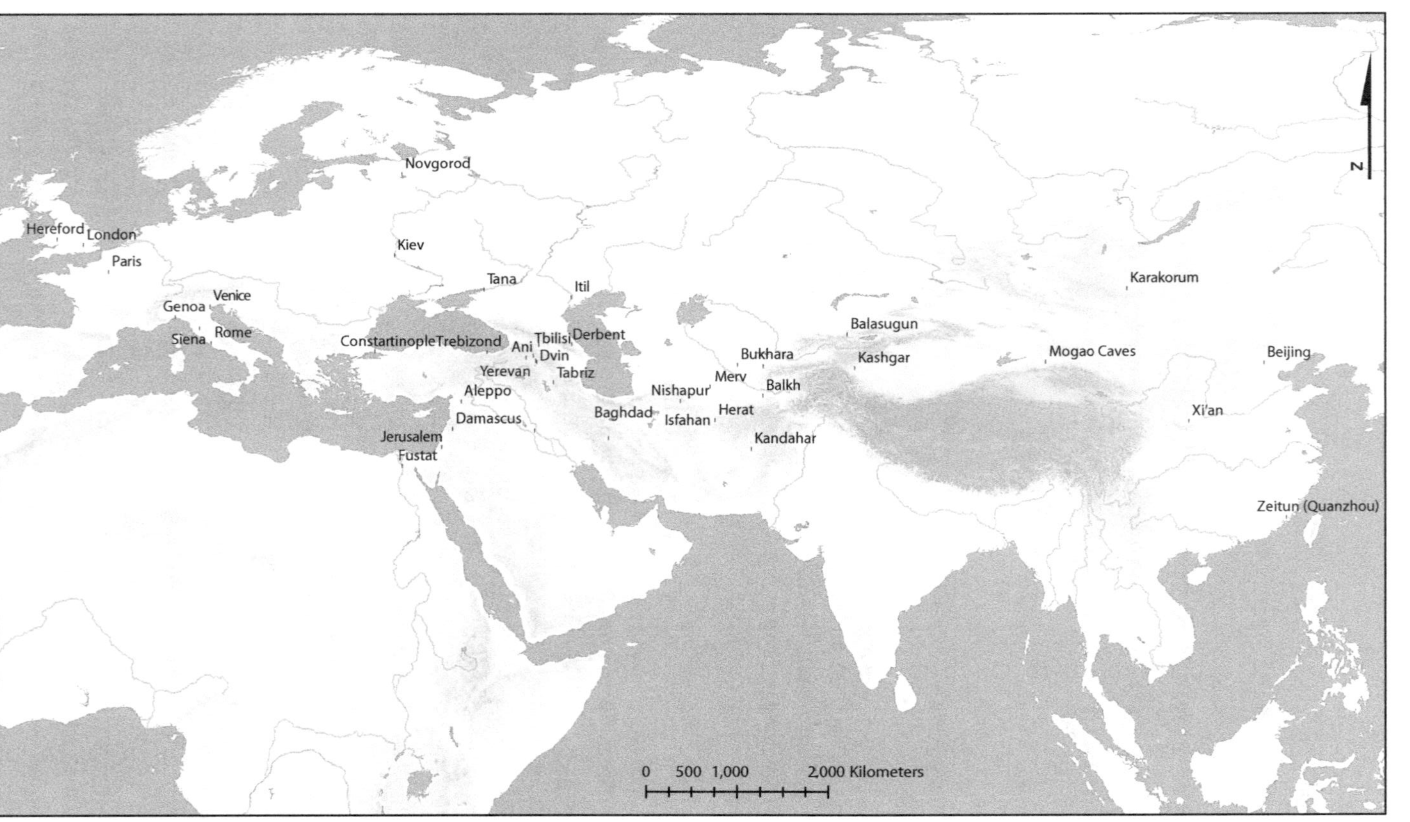

MAP 1. Eurasia with some of the major sites referenced in the text. Map created by the author. (Data sources for the maps are: https://ace.aua.am/gis-and-remote-sensing/vector-data/; www.diva-gis.org/documentation; https://earthexplorer.usgs.gov.)

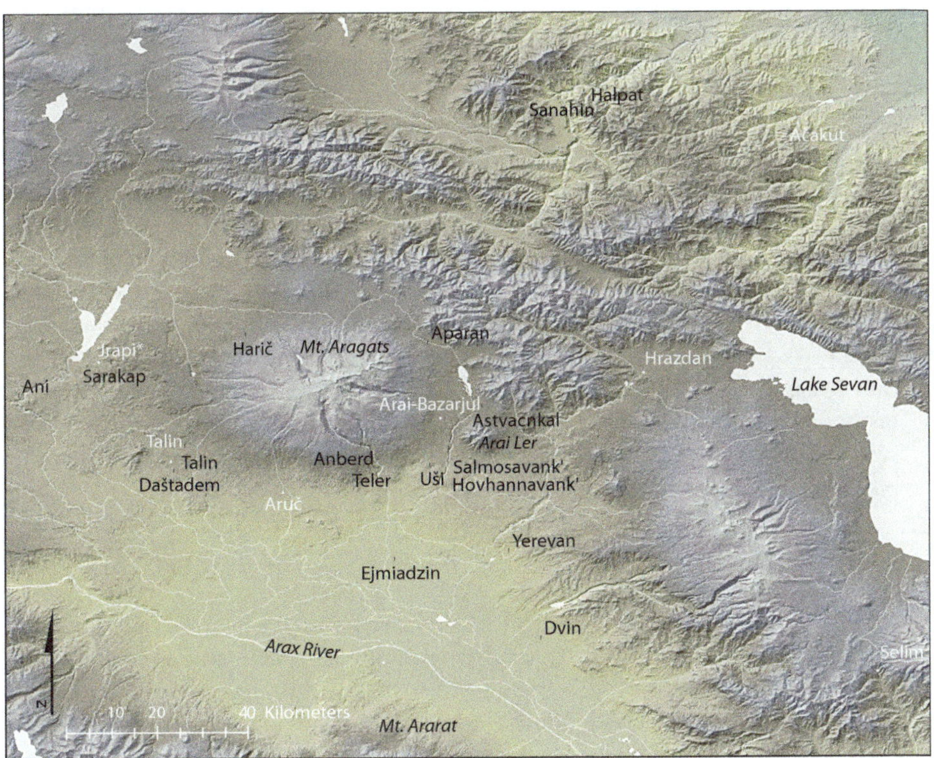

MAP 2. The central valleys of highland Armenia, with sites mentioned in the text. Map created by the author. Placenames in white denote caravanserais.

the period of *kollektivizatsiya* (collectivization), Soviet tractors dug up the hillside and uncovered bread ovens, gleaming red clay jars, coins, and human bones. These relationships, material, actual, intimate and remembered, tie the village people at Arai-Bazarjuł into the world—even as the stones in the *karavanatun* wall (and in the walls of their houses) tie them to a medieval time when a village here sat along the edge of a highway traveled by caravans, kings, Mongols, merchants, and slaves: one of a number of routes and networks now called the *metaksi čanaparh*, or Silk Road (see maps 1 and 2).

This book is the product of nearly a decade of thinking about medieval (tenth through fifteenth centuries a.d.) *cosmopolitanism*, or the practices of imagining the multiply scaled worlds within which one is situated, and of dwelling (acting, dreaming, making) within those worlds.[1] Specifically, I investigate ideas of cosmopolitanism connected to the modern concept of the Silk Road, and how our understandings of medieval worlds are dependent on scales of doing, perceiving, analyzing, and imagining. I am interested in the connection between the practical cultural experiences of thinking oneself in relation to a broader world containing topographies of difference and distance, and the grand bundle of phenomena linking sites and subjects in Eurasia—travel, trade, encounter, and cultural transformation—which, since the nineteenth century, has been referred to as the medieval "Silk Road." This catchy modern phrase ties up many directions of research, and—as I will explore in the next chapter—a lot of baggage as well. In particular, I agree with Khodadad Rezakhani that the idea of a singular east-to-west highway privileges western desire as an engine of global history, neglecting the cosmopolitan imaginations, agencies, and labors of people in the worlds in-between.[2] In writing about the Silk Road, I shall frame it as an intersection of phenomena in need of explanation, not as an explanation in itself. Most critically, I will abjure assigning "the Silk Road" historical agency: the Silk Road does not bring, impact, influence, transport, carry, or enable. But I, like many of my colleagues, appreciate the (qualified) usefulness of the Silk Road as a way of bracketing zones of interaction and influence, routes of exchange, spheres of shared culture, topographies of taste and desire, and linked cosmopolitan worlds. In a similar mode, the Silk Road can be used to provide a number of framings at different scales for the peoples, places, and material cultures discussed in this book.

A space of roads. The most common representation of the Silk Road is as a line, or a series of lines, stretching east-west across the middle of Eurasia. The lion's share of discussion has focused on the central and eastern stretches of these lines, connecting Transoxiana to western China; for more than a century our Romantic vision of Sogdian merchants, wandering Buddhist monks, and nomad armies has been framed within the Romantic narratives of the imperial explorers and adventurers who "discovered" these landscapes and looted their antiquities.[3] But these were not the only roads. In the high Middle Ages, Armenia was situated at a crisscrossing of mountain routes connecting a number of regions to form commercial and political relationships. One route ran north and west, to the Black Sea port of Trebizond, a major entrepot for Italian traders and a gateway to the Mediterranean. Other routes went north through Tbilisi and Derbent, through the lands of the Khazars to the valley of the Volga, thence northward to Novgorod, eastward across the steppe, or westward to the Baltic. Routes east from the highlands ran through cities such as Tabriz, Rayy, and Nishapur, then into the deserts and mountains of Central Asia.[4] Southwestern roads through Byzantine and Seljuk Anatolia connected the Ararat plain with Aleppo and the Eastern Mediterranean, with Jerusalem and Mecca. Of course, the routes did not stop there: maritime and overland routes of travel tied medieval Eurasia together in networks of reconfiguring integration, from the North Sea to the north coast of Africa, to the dynamic sea lanes of the Indian Ocean.

Caravans. The Silk Road is also a shorthand for the endeavors of medieval travel through Eurasia. Historians will frequently point out that most people traveled very short distances, and most merchants carried relatively few goods.[5] People did tend to travel in groups in the Middle Ages, whether a cavalcade of crusaders or a band of pilgrims. The term *caravan,* from the Persian *karvan,* is widely used to describe a group of travelers, usually accompanied by an armed escort; it is also a component within the most common term for medieval and later roadside inns, called *caravanserais* (caravan halls). The specific practices of caravans varied from region to region and through history, as well as depending on who was traveling (whether a band of pilgrims, merchants, or a royal emissary). By the seventeenth century, for example, silk caravans through Persia could contain a thousand beasts, and were protected by road guards.[6] Of course, hundreds of miles of the Silk Roads were also pilgrimage routes: the thirteenth-century merchant and traveler Ibn Battuta described traveling with other Muslims to Mecca along the hajj route in a caravan big enough to merit a guard of hundreds of horsemen and archers.[7] Women traveled in the Middle Ages—as artisans, pilgrims, merchants, musicians, emissaries, brides, and slaves—even if they left fewer written accounts of their movement.[8] The nonhuman composition of caravanserais also varied, but included some combination of horses, donkeys, oxen,[9] camels, and frequently dogs. Though, according to the geographer Ibn Hawqal the donkeys of Armenia were famous in the tenth century, we have reason to believe that all kinds of caravans passed through Armenia. The camels in Armenia were also apparently famed in the tenth century, and a fragment of a high medieval stamp-impressed wine jar excavated from Armavir, in the Ararat plain, is decorated with a procession of laden camels.[10]

Silk Road stuff. As is demonstrated by myriad museum exhibitions, the span of the Silk Road is also sensed in things. These included, at any given time, many of the key commodities of the medieval world: foodstuffs and spices, medicines, perfumes, beads and ornaments, plants and animals and their parts, precious metals, gems, paper, oils, beeswax and honey, furs, wine, books and texts, building materials, human relics, vessels of crystal, metal, wood, and ceramic, and enslaved peoples. And of course, textiles: linens, cottons, woolens, silks in raw and woven forms, dyestuffs, tapestries, tents, carpets, and clothing. Though it is a commonplace to point out that silk was only one of many commodities transported along the Silk Road, it is difficult to overemphasize to a modern audience how important textiles were for the construction of global medieval cultures, and medieval politics at world scales. Developing scholarship, including commodity-biography approaches,[11] demonstrates the role of textiles in integrating political performance, embodied cosmology, continent-spanning political economies, and revolutionary technologies. Transported textiles from China have been found in the northern Caucasus, while tartan-wrapped mummies have been discovered in the sands of the Tarim Basin;[12] and gold-twined silk draped precious objects, sublime spaces, and powerful, beautiful human bodies everywhere in-between.

Roads, journeys, and things. Already, it is apparent that to imagine the Silk Road requires thinking across scales. Synthetic volumes on the history of the Silk Road dance across these scalar jumps: for instance, Frances Wood's *Silk Road* ranged from the life span of a silk worm, to the swath of nineteenth-century Great Game geopolitics, to the fall of molded draperies on a single Chinese terracotta sculpture.[13] I am convinced that these scalar jumps, mediated by travel accounts, objects, and landscapes, are not only necessary for us to think the medieval Silk Road; they are also key to the ways that people in the Middle Ages could imagine a global cultural world in the space of their daily lives.

THE WORLDS OF OUR STORIES

What was the Silk Road experience *like*, in the span of one day spent traversing the Kasakh Valley, part of a single journey from the coast of the Mediterranean to Mongol Karakorum? From the history written in the late thirteenth century by the monastic historian Kirakos Ganjakec'i, we know that one of the medieval travelers along the Kasakh road was Het'um (also Hethum or Heyton), the king of Armenian Cilicia.[14] In 1254 a.d. Het'um traveled eastward to Karakorum to pay homage and declare his fealty to the Mongol khan, Möngke. Ganjakec'i's narrative—and mine as well—brackets a period of transition in Armenia and the broader region, as relationships of power and identity were reorganized and reoriented to accommodate Mongol rule; Ganjakec'i was himself a captive of the Mongols. Having journeyed north and east from the Mediterranean coast, Het'um departed the Seljuk city of Kars and traveled further east and north. Entering once more into lands ruled by Christian kings, and where perhaps more Armenian was spoken than Turkic, Het'um passed counterclockwise around the southern slope of volcanic Mount Aragats. Based on archaeobotanical data, we know that in the medieval period this was a landscape of fields, woodlands, and fruit orchards crossed by marshy streams; perhaps to his right-hand side Het'um might have seen the plain of Ararat patched in fields of wheat, barley, and millet.[15] By traveling this way along the mountainside, Het'um entered the administrative realm of the Vač'utyans, a newly founded dynasty of Armenian princely women and men. The Vač'utyans and their contemporaries are referred to in historical sources as *mecatun išxanner* (great, or noble, princes). This term is understood by twentieth-century historians to refer specifically to this class of princely folk who bought their hereditary estates with cash earned from trade. At the time of Het'um's travels the material power of the Vač'utyans was in a process of repositioning, situating their dynastic power as locally stable even as the hierarchy above them and borders around them shifted.

Perhaps passing the night with his retinue at the newly built *karavanatun* at Aruč, the traveling king would have been informed by the local managers of that road inn about new construction projects throughout Aragatsotn, directed by old Vač'e, his wife Mamaxatun, their son K'urd, and K'urd's wife Xorišah Mamikonyan. At this point on the highland road, farms and gardens to either side of the highway would be part of the hereditary lands given (or perhaps sold) to Vač'e Vač'utyan by his patrons the Zak'aryans.[16] The road inn and its associated buildings were part of this local power infrastructure, a location for the collection of fees and taxes on the goods transported on the roads, as well as a point for charitable provision of food and shelter to travelers and pack animals. A few years before Het'um's passage, these fees would have ultimately swelled the coffers of the

Georgian Bagratids; his journey intersected with the effective transition of power whereby the Ilkhanid Mongols surmounted the local hierarchy within which the Vač'utyans and Zak'aryans (as well as other families throughout the highlands, and emirs through Anatolia) acted as administrators. Perhaps as he entered the *karavanatun* at Aruč, Het'um may have even seen an inscription attesting to this fact on its entrance, decorated in the same style as the Seljuk *hans* he had avoided or entered in disguise on his way up through Anatolia.[17]

Rounding the peak of Aragats toward the medieval river town at Ashtarak, medieval travelers on the mountain road may have noted the new domes of the monastery of Tełer rising above the high horizon: this church was completed in a.d. 1221 and endowed by Mamaxatun Vač'utyan in her own memory and that of her husband Vač'e in 1232.[18] Taking the northern fork toward Aparan and Lori a few miles later, a traveler in Het'um's time may have remarked on the likewise newly renovated monastery of St. Sarkis at Uši, perched on the shoulder of the left-hand hills with a commanding view of the valley below.[19] The encounter of these medieval travelers with the Aragatsotn landscape was, perhaps, informed by differential knowledge that the revenues they paid in hostels and at the gates of cities along the route went to pay for these new buildings they passed on the road, and that such revenues along with yields from farms supported the people living and working inside those buildings. Other travelers may have had different associations with this route. Today, the road that climbs between Ashtarak and Uši, passing near the Vač'utyan-era monasteries of Hovhannavank' and Sałmosavank', is renowned by Armenians, especially in the summer. In June and July the already-narrow road is crowded with stalls selling produce from the nearby gardens: cherries, apricots, melons, and jewel-toned sheets of sticky fruit leather waving in the breeze from passing cars. Travelers in the Middle Ages may, like their early modern and modern counterparts, have been led up the road by senses other than the visual, including the smells of dung fires and cooking that promised a hearty meal at the next stop.

Climbing the northbound road between the peaks of Aragats and Ara, Het'um would have passed a lofty stone caravan hall standing just west of the road on the mountain's shoulder, surrounded by the wooden roofs and smoking chimneys of a village. Het'um himself passed by this hall, as his stopping point was the castle of the Vač'utyan princes at Vardenut. The history you are currently reading will, however, join other medieval travelers in turning off the road here, looking back out on the medieval Silk Road world from inside the high stone doorway of the caravan hall, framed by the mountains of the Kasakh Valley (see fig. 1).

The carefully negotiated relationship between Het'um and Möngke Khan was a small but emblematic part of transmutating sociopolitical landscapes of high medieval Eurasia. In order to situate the stories of the Kasakh Valley, and thus of this book, I will briefly tell some perhaps familiar tales of the Middle Ages that intersect and entwine in the space (central Armenia) and time (thirteenth and fourteenth centuries) of our stories.[20] I will start with an arbitrary benchmark. In the second half of the eleventh century the Caucasus was invaded in several waves

FIGURE 1. A view of the Kasakh Valley from the ramparts of a Bronze Age fortress on the slope of Mount Aragats, facing southeast toward Mount Ara (Arailer). Foreground: remains of a Yezidi transhumant pastoralist campsite with a corral. The Arai-Bazarjuł caravanserai is just beyond the brown protruding hill in the center-left of the figure. Photo by the author.

by groups of Turkic peoples from Central Asia and the Iranian plateau. These culminated with the Seljuk invasions in the 1060s, which conquered the capital city of Ani and organized Armenia within Seljuk administration.[21] Under Malik Shah (r. 1072–92) in particular, patterns of taxation and land tenure in Armenia were reorganized according to expanding Seljuk models. The Seljuk period entailed a continuation of the fragmentation, which had begun under hostile Byzantine administration, of the dynastic landscape in Anatolia and the South Caucasus into small, mutually antagonistic princedoms and emirates.[22] For the next several centuries, Armenian political leaders (princes, heads of dynastic families, and ecclesiastical leaders) would navigate loyalties with neighboring rulers of multiple faiths. As will be discussed in later chapters, the Seljuk period also had a profound influence on artistic and architectural styles in Armenian-speaking communities.[23]

In 1070–71, waves of Seljuk invasions washed over Jerusalem, turning what had been a regional and Eurasian conflict into a Mediterranean and then European one. Within five years of the call to arms at Clermont in 1095, European Christians had established the first crusader kingdoms within the Levant. Through the following century, the Eastern Mediterranean was reconfigured as a colonial contact zone which knotted together far-flung cultures and political configurations, from the Baltic to North Africa to the Indian Ocean. The Fourth Crusade (1202–4) temporally corresponded with the capture of the Armenian highlands by the Georgian Bagratids. Taking advantage of a violent Byzantine transfer of power, Queen Tamar's expansion reorganized the political landscape from Constantinople to the southeastern Black Sea.[24] In 1204 Constantinople was taken and plundered by the Venetians and opportunistic crusaders, who set up a relatively short-lived Latin kingdom. The Georgian Bagratids established the Byzantine-Georgian empire of Trebizond, expanding as well into the Seljuk territories of the South Caucasus (including the Kasakh Valley).[25] The resulting political reconfiguration further connected the cities of the Caucasus with the Black Sea coast, as well as with the Eastern Mediterranean, manifesting in a period of trade and dynamism in the early thirteenth century.

The territorial expansion of Mongol clans under the leadership of Genghis Khan in the third decade of the thirteenth century shifted political tectonics and global imaginaries across Eurasia. The initial conquest of Khwarezmia in 1219–20 disrupted political landscapes stretching from Transoxiana to the Iranian plateau.[26] The ramifications of this expansion had a ripple effect on the Caucasus, as an advance wave of Mongol armies chased fleeing Khwarezmian leaders as far as northern Armenia; these forces looted the locals before returning to the steppe.[27] In Christian Europe, the "discovery" of the Mongols resulted in an effective collision of worlds. As Maurizio Peleggi memorably put it,[28] from a Eurocentric perspective "the sudden irruption of the Mongol armies in Eastern and Central Europe in the winter of 1240–1 can be seen as the reversal of Columbus landing in Haiti in October 1492."[29] But, as in Sahlins's framing of the arrival of Cook in Polynesia,[30] the Mongols were received into preexisting European categories for *others*, and into expectations of how such others would act. As Peleggi himself observed, the Mongols were slotted into descriptions of the pagan hordes Gog and Magog, recorded by early medieval apocryphal sources as having been walled behind distant mountains by Alexander the Great.[31] Genghis himself was viewed through a lens polished by tales of Prester John, the fabled Christian king in the east, which had been circulating in western Europe for more than a century by this point.[32] The casting of the Mongols as potential allies in the crusades, if not as messianic Christian figures, motivated exploratory dispatches to the Mongol court over the later thirteenth century. The most famous of these emissaries, William of Rubruck, crossed the path of King Het'um on his journey, and weaves mentions of Prester John into his account of the Uighurs and other peoples subject to the khan.[33] It is with a degree of historian's schadenfreude that I imagine the European reception of the general Mongol response to these envoys: gracious pleasantries, and frank requests for continued tribute from the kings of the west to the ruler of the world.[34]

The Mongols invaded highland Armenia in 1236; these events are recounted with horror by the cleric eyewitness Kirakos Ganjakec'i, who opens the chapter on the "Tatars" in his circa 1240 *History* by stating simply: "this is the end of time."[35]

Ganjakec'i and many of his contemporaries understood the Mongol invasions to be a fulfilment of twelfth-century prophecies which foresaw the apocalypse as ushered in by a "nation of archers" let loose from behind the Gates of Darband (a clear parallel to the more widespread belief described above).[36] Within a few decades, Armenian historians had become more circumspect. In his late thirteenth-century *History of the Nation of Archers*, Grigor Aknerc'i (d. 1335) framed the conquest thus: "the wise princes of the Armenians and Georgians realized that it was God Who had given [the Mongols] the power and victory to take our lands, [and] they went to the T'at'ars in submission and promised to pay taxes."[37] At the turn of the fourteenth century, the bishop Step'anos Orbelyan described the conquest of Baghdad, Jerusalem, and the Levant by Hulagu Khan in 1258–59: "In all this, Hulagu displayed unmeasurable bravery. Because he greatly loved Christians, all the nations of believers willingly submitted and gave him active assistance."[38] This shift in tone reflects a shift in historical circumstance. By the 1299 date of Orbelyan's *History of Syunik* the highlands had been integrated within the Mongol Ilkhanate. Princes and religious leaders—including Step'anos and his princely kin—traveled to the Mongol center to negotiate mutual political relationships. At the same time, technologies of power—raiment, symbols, and powerful objects and substances— moved across Central Asia and the Mediterranean, drawing diverse political cultures into shared material and symbolic worlds. Beginning with Mahmud Ghazan Khan's conversion in 1295, the Ilkhanids were officially Muslim; their political culture for the next several decades combined aspects of Central Asian and Islamic cultures as well as Persian influences. The latest inscriptions discussed in this book come from around 1330; interestingly, a few years later Ambrogio Lorenzetti supposedly completed *The Martyrdom of the Franciscans* in the church of San Francesco in Siena, a fresco depicting a Mongol warrior as one among an assembly of eastern national types. Peleggi presented this fresco as a demonstration of the "domestication" of the Mongols within the Mediterranean imagination: by this point the Mongols are merely exotic foreigners, rather than inhuman others.[39]

This narrative of conquests and reconfiguring borders of control is only one way to tell the story of the Eastern Mediterranean and wider world in the thirteenth and fourteenth centuries—and it floats at a particular scale, above the frames of individual human lifetimes or the breadth of major journeys.[40] Even so, this story of political shifts still truncates the broader world of interactions, rumors, desires, and exchanges within which these peoples and places were tangled: what we now might call the Silk Road worlds. It also barely considers the space or scale of imagination, of what dreams crusaders had of the lands beyond mountains, or how highlanders in the Caucasus dreamed of mythical places like Venice, Karakorum, or Jerusalem. My concern with situated experience of the Silk Road at different scales is in part methodological: how do archaeologists talk about the Silk Road from the scale of our excavated assemblages, from landscapes, from architecture? But I am also challenged by historical and archaeological approaches to the Silk

Road as a premodern parallel to modern "cosmopolitanization" in the context of globalization: the processes of making universal culture through the transcending of local traditions. If we are to draw this comparison we must draw as well from postcolonial and feminist critiques of globalization's mechanics across perceived scales, and in particular of the presumed opposition between a cosmopolitan, impactful, modern global, and a traditional, parochial, impacted local—or in Doreen Massey's terms,[41] the presumed opposition between the space of the local and the time of global history.

THE WORLDS OF THE SILK ROAD: SPACETIME AND COSMOPOLITANISM

The Silk Road is a scalar problem in time as well as space: the span of the Silk Roads has been plotted on geologic time scale,[42] but also in the close encounters between individual people. As you read this book you will notice that my use of the phrase *the Silk Road* is conceptual rather than concrete. As an archaeologist, I have walked the paths and stood on the bridges that were trod by people and animals in the Middle Ages. I know that routes are real, physical places. On the other hand, as both an archaeologist and a historian I know that the "Silk Road" represents much more than a mappable set of land (and sea!) routes, many of which were seasonal, meandering, subject to infrastructural and political vagaries and kept open by the labor of pastoralists. While mapping out the locations of "Silk Road things" like scraps of silk, stringed instruments, or Chinese porcelains may create a dot-matrix map of apparent connections and points of hand-off, the mapping of human imaginaries and understandings is not as straightforward. As demonstrated by Eva Hoffman, exchange of cultural ideas in the Middle Ages was a slippery process happening at multiple scales at once;[43] thinking about roads is just part of the question. Much of the extant, engrossing, varied literature on the Silk Road explores the art and artifacts that enable us to re-create links across space and time.[44] Alternately, analyses like Valerie Hansen's *Silk Road* or numerous works by Susan Whitfield use textual and archaeological evidence to track the movement of ideas as well as materials, images, and cultures.

My project in this book messily overlaps with the work that precedes it. My data come from Armenia, a region privileged in the medieval period as well as in the twenty-first century to be considered both the center of the universe by its inhabitants and the edge of nowhere by nearly everyone else. Most importantly, my question centers on the sharing, not of precious objects, religious ideas, or particular traded goods, but of *spacetimes*, which I will gloss throughout the book as *worlds*. Each of my chapters is an engagement with the question of Silk Road worlds at different scales of encounter, but these scales are roughly nested inside one another and feed back into each other in tangled loops. My primary interest is in understanding how medieval people, participating to different extents and with varying degrees of agency, imagined a world that was tied together through shared culture—what we from our modern perspective could call a Silk Road ecumene, perhaps—even as they were situated in particular, plural worlds. What did the Silk Road world look, feel, or taste like to them—and did people in a medieval place such as Armenia think of themselves as on the edge or in the center of that world? At stake in this interrogation is the historical applicability of *cosmopolitanism*, a term usually reserved for urban, western, male, literate, global, modern subjects, to those "local" persons situated along the Silk Road as well as those moving along it in journeys of transcendental encounter.[45]

The concept of *spacetime* ties this book together, allows me to think about a plurality of Silk Road worlds, about the making of them, and about how such world(ing)s enabled a shared cultural cosmos within which to be or act cosmopolitan was to coexist with difference at multiple scales. Spacetime is not my own word; however, I will use it to "tie ties" and to "world worlds" (to draw from Haraway) in ways that pull tools from disparate theoretical projects in order to think and write the scales of everyday and cosmopolitan, to knot together the multiple temporal and spatial worlds involved in this story.[46] Many of these tools are words, which I will endeavor to use consistently, even as I attempt to stretch and recontextualize them.

Across numerous writings but most notably in her 1986 book *The Fame of Gawa*, Nancy Munn explored the ties that hold the world together for the Gawans, one of the many communities which made up the Papua New Guinean "Kula ring." As a world in motion and an object of long-term anthropological study, the Kula ring is very similar to the Silk Road and posed for Munn many of the same challenges of scale and simultaneity. In particular, Munn was interested in the forces (values) which mediated the situating of the Gawans in relation to each other and to the outside world, and that carried their efficacy, their *fame*, across space and time. She conceptualized this process of value creation and transformation in terms of individual and group ability to "extend or expand intersubjective *spacetime*— a spacetime of self-other relationships formed in and through acts and practices."[47] Spacetimes are produced in action and interaction, maintained in thought, memory, and practice. Critically, Munn demonstrated that things and people can also be spacetimes, loci for the construction of potential, the putting-in-motion of futures; gardens, meals, gifts, canoes, human bodies. Running through Munn's work is a driving assertion that events and practices don't happen "in space and time"; rather, they create spacetimes as they happen.[48]

These created spacetimes in turn are happenings; a spacetime is the world of possibilities for actions, thoughts, dreams within it. This idea of setting as an agent in action, of space and time as participants in happenings rather than the parameters of what happens, resonates with the idea of the *chronotope* (time-space), a significant concept within literary criticism. The chronotope was formulated by Mikhail Bakhtin, most famously in his 1937 *Forms of Time and of the Chronotope in the Novel*. In proposing the chronotope as an analytical term in literature, Bakhtin drew on conversations within science and mathematics; the inextricableness of space and time and their nonneutrality in events are of course central to quantum physics. As Bakhtin put it: "time, as it were, thickens, takes on flesh, becomes artistically visible; likewise, space becomes charged and responsive to the movements of time, plot and history."[49] Playing with this idea, Bakhtin explored the nonneutrality of place within the action of classical Greek story forms. Bakhtin's *romance time* is thus a different, alien world from the everyday world the reader inhabits, as is *adventure time*. While Bakhtin posited these chronotopes in the context of ancient Greek narratives, their significance is in the power they still have, their potencies as worlds we occupy when we tell stories. As Bakhtin explored, adventure time is the world we visit whenever we watch an action movie; if you have ever wondered why the hero always arrives just in time no longer how far they had to travel, or why crucial pieces of information are always delivered at the last possible moment, then you have wrangled with adventure time. These chronotopes have been honed over centuries of dreaming and writing and, as I will explore, they enclose our histories of fact as well as our fictions.[50]

The aim in exploring the making of spacetimes is not to argue that the world is whatever we write or make it to be. But human actions—from the "prosaic" routines of everyday life to momentous journeys, great loves, heroic feats—happen in worlds that are imagined as they are lived. This brings me to arguments from philosophies of science which assert the importance of human beings in all of this, and in particular of human perceptions (desires, imaginings, ideas, plans, schemes) mediated by embodied experiences. The body-shaped spacetimes of human beings are crucial for locating their action in the world, and their ability to make the worlds that situate that action, their power. Human bodies interact in cyborg ways with worlds of material culture,[51] with landscape, with architecture, with the worldbuilding *apparatuses* that Karen Barad defined as "material (re)configurings or discursive practices that produce material phenomena in their differential becoming."[52] Our things are spacetimes, our spacetimes have bodies. The last tool I will add to my kit is an argument made by Elizabeth Grosz: that spacetimes are made by people with bodies, and those bodies are gendered in the (nonbinary) sense of being *different*. The practices of knowing worlds—whether the world of events observed by science, or the worlds of human action researched by archaeologists and historians—are rooted in bodily difference: they are not recording the same world from different perspectives, but are making different worlds. This last tool is therefore a simple idea with ramifications for what stories we tell about the Silk Road and how we tell them: the necessity of according different situated subjects the "possibility of a different space-time framework."[53]

These different bodies are the mediators of the varying scales of worlds and world-making which make up the Silk Road of this book—and critically, situate imagination of those worlds and the place of human beings within them. To give a brief illustration: the medieval Hereford *mappa mundi* is an effective example of how embodiment mediates multiple scales of dwelling and of imagining the world(s) one is in. The Hereford map is a large (especially for its time, ca. 1300) map of the world, drawn in black, red, and gold ink on a single sheet of vellum, square on the sides and pointed at the top as an artifact of the body of the calf from which it was skinned. The map follows the "TO" mapmaking format, locating Jerusalem in the bullseye center of a circular world divided into two continents (Europe and Africa) downward and one (Asia) above. At the top of the map sits Christ; at the margins roam monstrous and miraculous creatures. The British Isles are located in the bottom left-hand corner of the map, and Hereford is visible as a town enclosure sketched alongside a schematic Wye River. That is, Hereford is *almost* visible; despite the overall incredible preservation and clarity of the Hereford map, the drawing of Hereford itself has nearly been wiped away.[54] Just imagine: years of medieval people looking at the map, and physically locating themselves by resting a fingertip on top of their city. Think of the work of literal indexicality that is achieved by pointing with an (index) finger at the spot on the map, and creating a line with your body from your finger to your feet, planted in the "real" Hereford—and situating that real space in turn within a world ringed by a wheeling zone of miracles and monsters. The map therefore is only a world "in itself" to the extent that it is read, touched, and understood by a human with their own embodied memories, habits, knacks, and knowledges. The world of the Silk Road was just as contingent on the capacities of embodied human perception to mediate its multiple spatiotemporal scales.

This question of edges and centers is important, as it raises the further question of the eligibility of medieval people living in on-the-road places like Armenia to participate within an emergent subject position in the history of the Middle Ages: that of *cosmopolitanism*. The quality of cosmopolitanism, or the state of being a citizen of the world, has a long philosophical pedigree dating back to the ancient Greeks. Cosmopolitanism is concerned with a person's capacity to be of a place, but also of the world—conceived frequently, modernly, by writers like Immanuel Kant or Hannah Arendt, as a *single* world of universal human values.[55] To be or become cosmopolitan, a person must transcend (overcome, rise above) their parochial worldview—and movement through the world is generally the first and best way to do this. Hence the early modern European enthusiasm for the Grand Tour, a hobby of the young and wealthy who traveled to the Mediterranean and the Middle East in order to experience the transcendental benefits of culture and history, and come back transformed (or at the very least, reassured of the superiority of their own culture).[56] The idea that one must travel to transcend, that there is a salutary effect of traveling, on the spirit and soul, is a modern idea with medieval roots. Yet standard genealogies of cosmopolitanism start with the Enlightenment, presuming something modern about the mobility and reach of Europeans at the expense of increasingly circumscribed colonial "locals."[57] Postcolonial debates over the form that a nonwestern cosmopolitanism might take move on the fulcrum of power inherent in a mobility at the expense of another's rootedness, of transcendence bought at the price of another's immanence.[58] These critiques are empowered by feminist tools for breaking down the binaries which reserve an Enlightenment cosmopolitan universalism for the Enlightenment's own universal, masculine, mobile, deterritorialized subject. Such tools include Pollock et al.'s *cosmofeminine*, signifying "an argument for situated universalism that invites other universalisms into broader debate based on a recognition of their own situatedness,"[59] which helps me think through intimate, embodied, and everyday medieval cosmopolitanism*s* (with intended emphasis on the *s*).

This postcolonial critique echoes concerns of ongoing conversations among medievalists, eager to resolve the apparent contradiction of "medieval cosmopolitanism" by thinking through the ways that people in the Middle Ages imagined their categorical others.[60] A central issue in these discussions is the role of medieval travel literature in evoking a world delineated in difference, traversed by a cosmopolitan subject, and understood as part of a single, orderly Creation. The idea that *travel enlightens* is frequently backed up with the accounts of travel and encounter, delight and wonder, which were written by medieval merchants, pilgrims, and adventurers—some of which will be discussed in the following chapters. One effect of this long backward gaze of modern cosmopolitanism is the idea that, if there were cosmopolitan, enlightened people in the "dark ages" of the medieval period, then these people were cosmopolitan by virtue of their mobility or their urbanity: to be cosmopolitan you either traveled or lived in a city and let the world come to you on the backs of people and/or animals. Archaeological use of the term cosmopolitanism usually deploys it as an aesthetic, to describe the harmonious blending of features from multiple, potentially antagonistic, cultures within an object, assemblage, or site. But cosmopolitanism as it continues to be explored is not an ethos exclusive to cities, or to urban "tolerance," even as it continues to shape debates over the relation between urban and state sovereignties. As Derrida explored at the end of the last century, defining cosmopolitanism in ethical rather than aesthetic terms requires that we define it as *hospitality*. This means contending with the politics of cosmopolitanism-hospitality as extending beyond state-situated tolerance (or intolerance) to the sovereignty entailed in hospitable care extended by the "local" to the "global."[61]

Building in part from debates over cosmopolitanisms of the present, I have long been dissatisfied with the exemplar of medieval cosmopolitanism being Marco Polo, or even Ibn Battuta—men whose accounts of travel were so marvelous that they have survived the centuries. If cosmopolitanism means to frame your actions and selfhood within a world (which for you is also *the* world), then cosmopolitanism in the Middle Ages (and in the present) might be messier, may entail transcendent encounters in unpredictable spaces, and in a diversity of bodies. Critically for a historical archaeology of the Silk Road, not all or even many of these persons leave a written account for us to find. Even more complex a barrier to "finding" the evidence for these lives and cosmoplitanisms is the long, durable resistance in history and archaeology to considerations of spacetimes other than that of romantic adventure as places to go and look for worldly cosmopolitics. Chief among these other spacetimes is the so-called local world of everyday life, of domestic work, and of routine maintenance.

EVERYDAY COSMOPOLITANISM AS A FEMINIST PROJECT IN SPACETIMES

In reconstructing the places and landscapes of the Silk Road in Armenia, I became increasingly aware that the Silk Road itself is itself a spacetime, an imagined topography that constrains our perceptions of the people we think of as living in it or moving through it. This imagined landscape that shapes archaeological thought about Silk Road societies is narrative and gendered. I want to be clear up front: this is not a book about "finding women" along the Silk Road, but an uncoupling of our historical idea of the Silk Road from the narrative projects established by patriarchal norms. In a summary reflection of her interrogations of embodied, oppositional paradigms within geography, Doreen Massey asserted that our work as feminists "involves not only working on gender but also, and I think in the end perhaps even more importantly, it involves confronting the gendered nature of our modes of theorizing and the concepts with which we work."[62] The Silk Road landscape is narrative because our imagination of it privileges written accounts (stories) and in turn the subjectivities of the protagonists of those stories. It is gendered because the protagonist of the standard Silk Road narrative is global, mobile, and male, and the landscape of Silk Road travel is a spacetime of *his* cosmopolitan transformation through encounters with exotic local peoples and natures.

One of my goals here is to make this persistent story-space more visible and more strange; chapter 2 is a grappling with the Silk Road as a narrative spacetime of western imagination. One of the challenges confronting a critical archaeology of the medieval Silk Road is the paradox of reconstructing medieval landscape, conceived (following Bender) as "time materializing."[63] This paradox lies in the fact that, as the "medieval" is that place and time when parts of our recognizably modern world were being licked into shape, it is also the period when many of our ways of representing and imagining space-time were enhanced: the map, the collection, and most important for this book, the travel account: a polysemous progenitor to now-distinct genres including the archaeological survey report, the ethnography, and the adventure novel. I am keenly interested in the ways that narratives of medieval travel shaped our modern imaginary of Silk Road landscape as a spacetime of male adventure, a series of transformative encounters *oriented* from west to east.

This imagined landscape of materialized time matters for our reconstructions of medieval lives defined in their relation to the Silk Road, because the chronotope of adventure is narratively defined in opposition: to the everyday life of routines and rituals, of nature's seasons, of maintenance tasks, of home.[64] And if adventurous journey-space is the chronotope of stories with traveling male agents and protagonists, then this space of small politics, of daily meals and seasonal schedules, is a feminized space—the space of return.[65] The co-construction of gender and the space-time of the everyday has also been observed within feminist critiques of geography and of "everyday history" as disciplines that construct the everyday as a female domain even while excluding it from spaces of power and historical event. As effectively summarized by Massey, our modern categories for thinking space are shaped by long-standing cultural oppositions which map onto one another, such that we struggle to not think about the world as divided into global/dynamic/historical/transcendent/*male* on the one hand and local/static/eternal/immanent/*female* on the other.[66] As observed by Dorothea Wierling, this opposition relegates the feminine to the everyday, and cordons off both within the realm of pre- or noncultural nature.[67] Within archaeology, critical interventions in the study of past politics and economy demonstrated that to "reveal" overlooked mechanisms of past social transformation, it is first necessary to scrap gendered categorizations of production, politics, and work, and of the spacetimes in which they occur. Elizabeth Brumfiel's work systematically dismantled presumptions about what constitutes ancient politics; examining the role of work done by women within the Aztec Empire, she demonstrated that any distinction between domestic economy and political life was a baseless hindrance to good history.[68] Likewise, Francesca Bray's work on political ideologies of labor in Imperial China emphasized the centrality of women's weaving within a system of production which bulwarked the coherence of not just the state, but the cosmos.[69] For my approach to the Silk Road, what is especially important about these feminist approaches to craft—and to the worlds that craft makes—is that they illuminate the political significance, not just of women, but of the cosmofeminine spacetimes ignored by archaeologists and historians as outside the realm of economics, politics, and history.

The seemingly fixed centrality of the transformative encounter to our idea of cosmopolitanism is deep at the heart of my analysis of these narrative spacetimes as dialectical and gendered. The opposition between transcendent subjects and alienated, objectified *others* is an old question in feminism: Simone de Beauvoir initially stated the "problem of feminine destiny" as whether women would be subjects in their own histories, or objects in the lives of others.[70] Our repeated reliance on the narrative spatiotemporal opposition between a Silk Road space of cosmopolitan masculine transcendence and a local medieval everyday therefore privileges male heroes and manly stories—and furthermore privileges male, mobile subjects who left written accounts over the characters who are outside the landscape materialized in written history. These people and their spaces are written but do not always write, and are vulnerable to being evacuated out of the literary space of the Silk Road we think we already know, due to the scale at which we tell the Silk Road story.

All of this matters because this book is ultimately about spacetimes, about shared worlds, and about the question of who participated in the making of them and dwelled within them. I want to shift our thinking to the embodying capacity of writing and the cosmological power of built spaces, as well as to the agencies of everyday objects and the activities of "ordinary" people. In my orientation to thinking about how global culture in the Middle Ages worked I am motivated by writings which argue that matter and space, including bodies and the possibilities of embodiment, *matter* for thinking society and history.[71] Throughout the book I am therefore urgently curious about what happens to the subject (rather than the hero) of a Silk Road history if my account centers on the making and living of worlds. In this sense then my worlds are a bit like Karen Barad's *apparatuses*, described above. Such an articulative view of mattering in the world is posthuman, not in the sense that humans aren't important, but in that we step away from the view that (male, universal) human subjects are the privileged architects of reality, history, spacetimes. So this book will be centrally, tenderly concerned with the doings of people, including some "big men": princes like Vačʻe Vačʻutyan and Tigran Honencʻ, and big-world-makers like Marco Polo and Ibn Battuta. But what happens to our appreciation of these medieval humans if we submerge them in the worlds they co-constructed, if we take seriously Barad's assertion that "determinately bounded and propertied human subjects do not exist prior to their involvement in natural cultural practices"?[72] Then, I hope, the medieval world of the Silk Road becomes plural, and the making of it/them a multiscalar, tentacular question. The rest of this book is me asking this question from the perspective of the Kasakh Valley Armenia, working from scale to slippery scale.

In chapter 3 I start to pick apart the high medieval narrative of Armenia and reweave it as a regional world constructed in spaces and practices. In particular, I examine the construction of architectural spaces as situated in landscape, and constitutive of the embodied selves of Armenian builders. Ultimately, this chapter will look at the concern for, and intersection of the space-body-building of medieval Armenian politics with, the spaces of production, hospitality, of seasonality and working rhythms—in short, of everyday life. In chapter 4 I consider world making in medieval Armenia at the scale of a single landscape, the Kasakh River Valley of Aragatsotn. The medieval Kasakh Valley was shaped both by practices of mobility as well as through projects profoundly concerned with locally emplaced power. The Kasakh Valley that we visit in this chapter was also made through historically layered storytellings, by medieval patrons in epigraphic projects, by patriotic Armenian historians, and by generations of archaeologists. I myself figure among these latter; in this chapter I also consider the way that medieval life in the Kasakh Valley was detected and reconstructed through my own archaeological surveys. Part of what appears in archaeological study of the material landscape of the Kasakh Valley are the spaces made and inhabited by medieval people who did not "build worlds for others to live in," in the literal, monumental sense of princely patrons, but who nonetheless made and dwelled in material spacetimes which contained both the Kasakh Valley and the Silk Road world. Reflecting over the traces of these people raises the question of the lifeways that both situated and enabled acts of princely dedication and political memory, which are commonly glossed as *everyday* in contradistinction to the eventual realm of construction and inscription.

These everyday spacetimes are also the domain of the people who live along the road, who appear in travel accounts of the Silk Road as either helpful hosts, enticingly exotic others, or alien antagonists. If we allow the Silk Road to be an adventure story with a protagonist, then the inhabitants of medieval everyday spacetimes "along the Silk Road" are doubly vulnerable to the time tricks that affect everyday or quotidian spaces. The medieval as a landscape, a time-materializing, is frequently conjured as a long everyday in opposition to the arrow of modernity's progress.[73] Even as modernity is performed as that which leaves the stasis of the Middle Ages behind in sources as diverse as Fernand Braudel and Arthur C. Clarke, medieval time is materialized as seasonal, cyclical, and flexible in opposition to the rigid and progressive clock-time of capitalist modernity. So there is an aggravated tendency, in imaginaries which inform research, to consign the local nonprotagonists of the medieval Silk Road to an endless quotidian to the side of the road walked by the traveler, who by virtue of his encounters with such others becomes more modern and more of a cosmopolitan world-subject.

To world the everyday medieval otherwise is to try to step outside of these determinist loops. In chapter 5 I look at the caravanserai or road inn; a hybrid Silk Road space, an apparent chimaera of linear travel-time and the small worlds of local politics. Medieval caravanserais are attaining a new level of global visibility recently, after the movements starting in the mid-1980s to develop Silk Road heritage and tourism in Central Asia. In addition to generally being visually prepossessing buildings, caravanserais are physical manifestations of the intangible modern associations with the Silk Road: long camel journeys, exotic adventure, the display of power and wealth, the footprints of "lost" cultures. Popular images of caravanserais are also emblematic of the challenges to reconstructing their social role; we frequently see them as picturesque, isolated ruins beside a dusty road, without another building (let alone a village) in sight. Speaking from experience, this perception of caravanserais has been produced in part by some creative camera angles on the part of travelers and archaeologists, editing out the other people, spaces, and activities that might spoil the romance.

Ultimately, what brings me back to the space-time of the medieval caravanserai is the question of scales. Caravanserais must work in multiple scales, that of the route network and that of this day's stopping place, this particular building; they demand that we think in multiple scales as well. They challenge the cherished opposition between local and global—as with Latour's railroad, the spaces between caravanserais are "continuous paths that lead from the local to the global, from the circumstantial to the universal, from the contingent to the necessary, only so long as the branch lines are paid for."[74] Indeed, what medieval caravanserais make unavoidable is thinking about the importance, the indispensable essentialness, of hospitable cultures in making the worlds of the Silk Road by "paying for" those local connections. Hospitality is a shifted framework for writing a history of the medieval Caucasus, where scholarship has for a long time been concerned with tracing borders back through linear, genealogical time. You may notice that I do not spend much time debating the details of the "identity" of the Armenians I write about. I am more interested in their doings, in the practices which were shared by people and which constructed worlds of mutual intelligibility, than in running down the moments of performed difference which can be perceived from a modern perspective as antecedent to modern nation-states. There are plenty of histories that do this already. In short, I am interested in what people were doing, rather than who they were; I will endeavor to delineate spacetimes in practice which created worlds of mutual regard and legibility for their practitioners. However, I will use the term *Armenian* to refer to folk who wrote (or commanded others to write) in Armenian, who endowed Christian churches, and who were identified as such in medieval Armenian histories. Similarly, the ethics of hospitality are frequently taken for granted as a functionalist aspect of Near Eastern and Central Asian Muslim politics. I try to move beyond this Orientalist assumption and look at hospitality as a power-laden way of captivating subjects in spacetime, and as a practice of making worlds.

Chapter 6 is the closest encounter with hospitable world-making on the Silk Road, a mattering at the smallest scale afforded by archaeological and historical data. In this chapter there are few named characters, as I try to center on the apparatuses of hospitality constructed in cooking and eating, in comfort making in the space of the caravanserai and in adjoining, conjoined village spaces. Ultimately the very slipperiness of these medieval multiscalar engagements may reveal the entire linear framework of scales as wobbly. The spacetimes produced in serving, eating, and remembering food are not scaled-down versions of the continent-spanning worlds written in a textual account according to some metric by which a grain of carbonized barley is smaller in scale than an illuminated copy of Marco Polo's *Travels*. Apparatuses enclose and construct apparatuses, worlds make worlds, world builders are themselves built. As I discuss in the final chapter, for me this shift in thinking about the Silk Road is important as well as useful, in addition to being more interesting in the story it ultimately may help me tell. I would like to construct these multiple cosmopolitanisms of the everyday as an antidote to the airless, scorched-earth story of the universal subjects of Kantian cosmopolitanism or global capitalism. I have tried to take seriously the implications for archaeological and historical writing of a commitment to storytelling, of a situating of subjectivity (mine) in the making of worlds in the medieval past. The result, this book, is an attempt to show the mechanics of my making sense of the medieval Silk Road everyday in Armenia, including the space-time contractions of metaphor, and, where possible, the interventions of caring "locals."

2

———

The Silk Road as a Literary Spacetime

It matters what matters we use to think other matters with; it matters what
stories we tell to tell other stories with; it matters what knots knot knots,
what thoughts think thoughts, what ties tie ties. It matters what stories
make worlds, what worlds make stories.
—DONNA HARAWAY (2016)

In conversations among themselves, historians and archaeologists frequently
repeat that "the Silk Road" is a made-up place. Of course, the mountain roads
of the Caucasus and the Tian Shan, the crossings of the Black and Caspian Seas,
the oases and caravan inns of Central Asia, and the markets of India and China
all were "real"; we have archaeological and textual evidence of the people who
traveled along these routes and dwelled in these places. Archaeologists have dug
oases in the Tarim Basin, at Samarkand and in the Murghab Delta, uncovering
material evidence for travel; meanwhile, historians have demonstrated the cultural transmissions between east and west in language, art, music, dance, food,
and dress. Still, articles about the Silk Road will frequently begin with the same
observation, that no one thought of a "Silk Road" until 1872, when the geographer
Baron Ferdinand Freiherr von Richthoven wanted a metaphor to describe the connections of trade, especially but not exclusively in silken textiles, that tied Europe
and the East together for almost two millennia.[1] He chose *der Seidenstrasse*, the
Silken Road, and the metaphor stuck. A first reason for this is perhaps the sheer
Orientalist romance of the term: how luxurious to walk the desert on roads of silk!
A second reason, however, is the inherent power of metaphor as a literary device.
The phrase *the Silk Road* prompts us to imagine the Eurasia of the past in a particular way, with very particular social dynamics, because it compels us as readers,
listeners, and writers to insert ourselves in the knotty literary landscape that has
been created around travel in Eurasia over the past twenty centuries. In particular,
I am interested in the shape, the chronotopography (if Bakhtin will permit me),
of some of the medieval accounts of travel, strange lands, and strange peoples and
natures that make up part of what Robert Edwards called "medieval cosmopolitan

21

imaginaries,"[2] and which formed the foundations of ongoing practices of imagining medieval and modern Eurasia.

Medieval accounts of traveling, travelers, and foreign lands to the East play an important role in the reconstructed western history of literature, and of a particular modernist narrative about the progressive development of scientific thought. According to this narrative, part of what marked the transformation from antiquity or medieval-ity to modernity was a shift in the ways that people (primarily in Europe) described the world and made arguments about the "nature" of it.[3] From a modern perspective, medieval accounts of travel and the world encountered through travel contain mutually incompatible forms of evidence: travelers valorized information both on the basis of empirical observation ("I saw this with my own eyes and thus it is true") and also on the basis of wonderment ("I have not seen this, but people tell me it happens and it is marvelous, so I write it down here"). Seeing an opposition between fact and marvel as two different and incompatible ways of understanding the world is supposed to be part of being a modern, scientific, as opposed to a medieval, superstitious person.[4] To crib from Latour's argument about cultures of science, medieval accounts of marvels are framed as cultural "errors of identification," while modern science is successful objective observation of natural "truths."[5]

A traditional position within the history of science is that as our culture has become more scientific, we have left wonderment behind—a consensus about scientists today is that they are supposed to argue things because they are observed facts, not because they are astounding marvels (though take a look through many publications and you will see a drive to do both, especially in archaeology). Literary historians argue, however, that there is a genealogical relationship between the following modern practices of writing worlds: travel writing, ethnography, archaeological accounts, natural histories, and speculative- or science-fiction stories.[6] All of these forms of writing about encounters with other worlds—whether the world of the ancient past, of other cultures, or of other planets—have a "common ancestor" in the medieval travel narrative. Critically, however, genres like archaeology and ethnography are supposed to be solidly on one side of the science vs. wonder divide, while travel writing and science fiction are somewhere on the other.[7] One key metaphorical technique that links these apparently disparate world-makings together is *allegory*, a complex symbolic labor by which characters, places, or events stand in for "real" things in the world—and a technique falsely used to characterize the exclusive epistemology of medieval or otherwise "premodern" peoples.[8] Allegory, like all metaphor, is slippery, and depends on webs of cultural context that historians work hard to reconstruct. Critically, within hypothetically deterritorializing or decentering projects of world-making, allegory works to bring the subject back to the reader, to the reader's homeworld. You may know this technique from science fiction: writers like Le Guin, Vonnegut, and Atwood lean hard on allegorical fantasy as a critique of a mystified or naturalized reality. Allegory is also fundamental to the world-making of ethnography, both in the ways that practices or beliefs are read as "total social facts" and in the implicit or explicit invitation to reflect back from the foreign to the familiar.[9] In medieval accounts of strange lands, creatures, and people, the reversal of wonder (i.e., the traveler's reflection of "but then what is normal to us would be wondrous to them") is part of an allegorical dialectic which recenters the reader even as their world expands.

There are interesting consequences to presuming a clean break between science and wonder, fact and imagination, matter and metaphor. One of them is a general presumption that part of what made the Dark Ages (a term most medievalists abhor) so "dark" was the fact that people learned about their world through indiscriminate combinations of empirical facts and marvelous fictions. A long-running trend in historical study of the Silk Road is therefore to try to weed out the facts from the fantasies, and to adjudicate which historical sources are the most "reliable" as accounts of the Silk Road world.[10] I will start this book's exploration of historical accounts of the Silk Road with two assertions: First, that to presume that there was a real Silk Road that medieval writers were describing with greater or lesser accuracy is not always the most useful approach. Rather, and second, we need to approach the medieval Silk Road world as medieval people did, as a spacetime built in imaginations, perceptions, allegorical metaphors and wonderful dreams. This is not to argue that any given written account of medieval Eurasia is more important for understanding "what really happened" than the wealth of material evidence. Instead, what I am trying to unravel is the ways that material investigations of the Silk Road in the West have always already been shaped by the ways that that world (and the smaller worlds that made it up) was written about, read about, and imagined.

For instance, there are interesting patterns in the ways that medieval travelers wrote about the landscapes and creatures they encountered, patterns that crystalize into a *topology*, or structuring understanding, of the relationships between things in the world. When these topologies multiply across literary projects, they bloom into a topos, or a spatial trope, a tenacious influence on the way that writers create certain places and worlds so that their readers can find their way around. The first pattern is that a travel account with a first-person eyewitness narrator was a tropic way of organizing written descriptions of wonder as well as of fact.[11] Part of the pleasure of experiencing a tale of wonder was linked to reading (or hearing) the embodied experience of someone encountering it, of being entranced, amazed, or terrified.

A second pattern is that, over the course of the Middle Ages, a topography of difference was drawn up in European imaginations.[12] According to this prevailing cultural imaginary, marvels lived in the East. This was argued from two perspectives: first, that in the unexplored realms of the Orient there were more monsters, miracles, and marvels; and second, that what was "marvelous" to travelers from the West was quotidian for peoples dwelling in the East.[13] These and other patterns became the warp threads of western ideas, not just about wonder, but also about the world, and the people, animals, and super/natural phenomena within it. These structuring tropes and patterns congealed over time into a chronotope, or space-time, imagined in writing, reading, and telling, parts of which were only later given the name the Silk Road.

If we examine medieval travel narratives of what we call the Silk Road as literary spacetimes, as imagined worlds that medieval people lived within and which continue to shape our perceptions of Eurasian landscapes, then we must approach the combination of eye-witnessed evidence and wondrous half-truths and full legends which make up these accounts as a unified field of metaphorical world-building. What I mean here is, instead of the critical question being "which of these sources is the most accurate?" the question becomes "what kind of world is being written here? What are its topographies—of power, of danger, and of desire and delight?" Considered this way, the spacetime of the Silk Road emerges as a mechanism through which medieval people situated themselves within a world, rather than a description of a preexisting "reality." The historian Peter Jackson framed this mechanism as a way of making sense of human difference, which mediated the medieval European encounter with the Mongols and other peoples of the wider world, all of whom came into increasing contact in the High Middle Ages.[14] Jackson drew on a system of literary cartography posited by Robert Bartlett for the thirteenth-century historian Gerald of Wales; Bartlett described the writing of commentators like Gerald as situating especially medieval European Christians at the center of concentric circles of familiarity and difference. The center circle of civilization was surrounded by a conceptual zone of barbarism: people who live in foreign, unorthodox, or more primitive ways. As Jackson described it, the third and furthest circle was "the abode of the marvelous, the alien, and the monstrous";[15] a world with which, Jackson argued, Europeans had no direct contact before the thirteenth century. Within this framework, thirteenth century and later literary accounts of the worlds beyond the southern and eastern rims of the Mediterranean represent the labor of Europeans to pin newly encountered people and places within the marvelous and monstrous imagined landscape of that third ring. An effect of this was to make alien peoples and places comprehensible in cosmological terms, even if they were not made "familiar." Thinking about the Silk Road as a literary landscape also means that archaeologists can (and should) think about histories of the Silk Road in literary terms, as stories that have heroes and villains and, most importantly, which cohere in important ways as a genre and which do the work of literature in creating spaces and times—a written world of a peculiar shape.

Let's look briefly at a very few famous examples of medieval Silk Road travelers. First, I will introduce the Silk Road travel account as a kind of literature, a genre that has familiar, repeated structures, by looking at a handful of well-known accounts. Then I will narrow my examination to looking at how Armenia and the Caucasus in particular have been constructed as written worlds over the last two millennia. Ultimately my goal for this chapter is to show how certain forms of encounter with medieval Armenia and medieval Armenians—by travelers, historians, and archaeologists—have been themselves engagements with literary spacetimes. This examination is a necessary step in a critical archaeology of the Silk Road in Armenia, itself a storytelling of medieval life using texts, objects, buildings, and landscapes; I will explore the ways that historical sources, and analyses of material culture, and even reconstructions of landscapes have been framed within Silk Road spacetimes.

In addition to the myriad historical documents about life in various places in ancient and medieval Eurasia, from the Cairo Geniza to the thousands of records recovered from the Dunhuang caves, we also have numerous sources specifically about the *road*, about the experience of traveling from place to place along one branch or another of what would eventually be called the Silk Road. Looking at these road accounts as a body of literature is important to the task of thinking in critical terms about life on the Silk Road; taken in aggregate, accounts of travel between Europe and Asia have shaped the parameters for talking about that world. Working as a literary genre over the last few centuries, medieval and early modern narratives of travel became foundational to the ways we imagine distance and difference. Further, they established the literary *dramatis personae* for stories of the Silk Road—both the characters it was expected to meet, as well as the character of the protagonists (and villains) of the journey-as-story. The question of the stock characters of the Silk Road story is important when we consider the politics of medieval cosmopolitanism, and of reconstructing not just who *was* but who *could be* a protagonist in a Silk Road story.

THE TRAVELER AS EMBODIED PROTAGONIST

A first step in reconfiguring perspective on histories of the Silk Road is thinking of the narrators of Silk Road travel tales as literary protagonists, as personalities who shape and are shaped by the events they describe. This means, on the one hand, thinking critically about the embodied perspectives of travelers, situating narrative description within the moving, seeing, tasting, and remembering body of a traveler. On the other hand, this requires that we think about the performance of traveler-as-persona, and especially of how the writers of travel accounts and geographies in the medieval period wrote their personae as endowed with particular forms of embodied expertise, authority, and integrity—all of which added veracity and authority to their written world. A fantastic and early example of this literary performance appears in the *Best Divisions for Knowledge of the Regions*, a geography written in the tenth century by the Arab scholar al-Muqaddasī. In this work, al-Muqaddasī set out to fill what he saw as a critical gap in knowledge of the world: the roads, stopping places, and character of cities which tied the lands of the caliphate together into an intelligible social whole.[16] In the *Divisions* al-Muqaddasī described not only cities and their inhabitants, but also infrastructure, customs, and even archaeological ruins. Critical to my purpose, al-Muqaddasī also presents a perfect example of the development of the travel writer who is an authority on his subject due to the experience of traveling, and therefore to a kind of worldly knowledge and experience that is contained within the exceptional mobile body of the traveler. Al-Muqaddasī parallels the knowledge compiled and contained in the written text with the experience collected within his authoritative, singular self. Read how al-Muqaddasī boasts of the breadth of his experience on the road, basically laying out his resume as a trustworthy source:

> Besides, I have had my share in all that commonly falls to the lot of travelers, with the exception of begging and the commission of a grievous sin. I have attended lectures in law and ethics; practiced asceticism and devotion, lectured, in my turn on law and ethics; preached from pulpits; cried the hour of prayer from minarets; offici-ated as Imam in masjids; delivered public discourses . . . frequented schools; pro-nounced special prayers in assemblies; spoke in meetings; swallowed *harisah* with Sufis, *tharid* with the monastics, and *aṣidah* with seamen.[17] I was driven in the night from mosques; have wandered in solitudes and lost my way in the deserts; was, for a time, earnestly bent on devotion; and have, at other times, openly acquired ill-gotten wealth. I have associated with the devotees of the mountain of Lubnan; mixed with persons in authority for some time; owned slaves; and carried things on my head in baskets. I was very near drowning on several occasions, and have, a number of times, been plundered in predatory attacks on our caravans. . . . I have been confined in prisons and arrested as a spy; have witnessed the fighting of ar-Rum in vessels of war and the striking of bells in the night; have bound books for hire; paid for water with my songs; traveled in litters and on horseback; walked through hot winds and snows; lodged in the precincts of royal courts among noblemen and lived in the midst of ignorant persons in the weavers quarters.[18]

Consider the breadth of experiences covered in this excerpt, as well as the span of distance and the variety of spacetimes: nights and early mornings, tops of min-arets, decks of ships, dangerous roads and holy places, rough seas and deserts. Each phrase is a small story, the intimation of a gripping tale—or perhaps a story of edifying tedium—that al-Muqaddasī could tell. Especially remarkable in this passage are the points of inflection, when al-Muqaddasī shifts from relating his credentials as a respected man of piety, to recounting the variety of his experi-ences on the road. This demonstrates al-Muqaddasī as a very particular kind of able traveler, who is apparently equally at home doing manual labor and owning laboring people, working a trade and stealing. Of particular significance for the latter parts of this book are al-Muqaddasī's invocations of foodstuffs in order to mark social difference. He demonstrates his ability to be "at home" with a variety of peoples by describing sharing their meals: *harisah*, the favored humble meal of

Sufi brothers,[19] *tharid*, the festival broth of devout Muslims, and *aṣidah*, the meal of simple sailors. His appreciation of this diverse—but also devout—menu frames al-Muqaddasī as the consummate *cosmopolitan* in the sense discussed in the last chapter. He is a citizen of the world, at home everywhere, and specifically comfortable in the attitudes and comforts of a body that labors, that experiences heat and cold, that hungers for both humble and elegant dishes. The rest of his geography, then, is backed up by the authority of this cosmopolitan, embodied subject to faithfully report on the nature of the world in all its wonder.

Next I want to look at two European travel accounts from the thirteenth through fourteenth centuries, at the height of the Mongol era. Marco Polo and the author known as John de Mandeville wrote equally influential accounts of travels from Europe to the Mongol court and beyond. Marco Polo is the more famous of the two, in part because his story is thought to be more factual and accurate.[20] As discussed above, my interest in introducing these two geographies is not to compare which one of them more correctly describes the "real" world of the medieval Silk Road; rather, I want to think about some of the mechanics through which Marco Polo and John de Mandeville *constructed* that world through the writing of their historically influential accounts.

Marco Polo's *Travels*, also known as the *Description of the World*, is, most basically, an account of the lands of the East by a Venetian merchant traveling to the court of Kublai Khan and onward to China and Southeast Asia in the later decades of the thirteenth century. Debate surrounding Marco Polo as a historical figure and author abounds, but there is general agreement that the *Travels* was coauthored with a romance storyteller, Rustichello of Pisa. The *Travels* is a motley collection of literary references, tropes, and *mirabilia*, as well as "factual" events and phenomena that Polo claims to have witnessed himself. The prologue casts the work as a romance, the travels of a youth to a faraway land where he finds his fortune and then voyages across land and sea with a beautiful and exotic princess, Kököchin. But the greater part of the *Travels* is a listing of marvelous lands, peoples, creatures, things, and events. Armenia plays a significant role in the *Travels*, implicated in the opening declaration of the truthfulness of the subsequent narrative: "*it is true* that there are two Armenias"—a declaration which is paired and also contrasted with the declarative mode of the rest of the book: "and yet *I tell you.*"[21] The formulaic-ness of these and other declarations which punctuate the text—"let me tell you . . . and what more can I tell you of it? . . . And why am I telling you of this at such length?"—suggest the status of the *Travels* not as a scientific report but as a romance, similar to the Arthurian sagas of travel, sudden misfortune, and grace regained, of which Rustichello was a practiced and popular author.[22]

Why does it matter whether Marco Polo's account was one kind of writing or another? The literary historian John Larner extensively reviews the debates surrounding the text of the *Travels*, the character of Polo's authorship, and, critically, the categorization of the book as a work of literature. According to Larner, a recurring theme within these debates is the opposition between Polo as a reliable eyewitness who really saw the things he described, and the romantic liberties taken by Rustichello of Pisa in order to produce a palatable account for western readers. But who is the true author of the tales of the *Travels*? Where do Marco Polo's facts leave off and Rustichello's fantasy begin? Larner cogently argues that such questions essentially bark up the wrong tree,[23] and that ultimately what matters for the history of knowledge of the east in the west is not the identities of the authors, but the influential book itself and the form it takes. To ask these questions about texts like the *Travels*, then, is to ask what kind of written world they were.[24] What kind of *spacetime*? If the *Travels* fit into known genres, then was it familiar to its readers and listeners as a spacetime within which actions took place, lessons were learned or unlearned, and fortunes won and lost? To look archaeologically at works like Marco Polo's *Travels* means thinking about them as crafted things, and also as spaces constructed from metaphor and trope, from the time and distance of narrative action. As archaeologists we are interested in the literary genre question insofar as it helps us understand Marco Polo's (and Rustichello's) writing as a built space in which to think, act, and live. From this perspective, then, it matters that the literary space of Silk Road travel is closely related to the literary spaces of courtly romance, eastern adventure, and perhaps even Chinese courtly performance.[25] It also matters more what actual shape that world takes—and on this point as well, John Larner made a fantastic observation specifically related to the "route" of Marco Polo across Eurasia. Much of the *Travels* is written as an itinerary, with different sections opening as if describing the movement of a traveler from one place to the next, following the movement of a reader between paragraphs: "The traveller who leaves this city [Yazd] to proceed further [east] rides for seven days over a plain."[26] "When the traveller leaves this city [Chagan-nor] and travels north-northeast for three days, he comes to a city called Shang-tu."[27] "After leaving the river [Brius] the traveller continues westwards for five days, through a country with numerous cities and towns which breeds excellent horses."[28]

This itinerary carries readers west to east and back again, traveling through the world of the book, even though they are not frequently reminded of the travels of Marco Polo's own body. Larner argues that this linear itinerary[29]—reproduced in countless maps by ambitious historians over the last few centuries—does *not* represent the actual path traveled by Marco Polo. Rather, the linear description is as it appears: a narrative frame, a device for storytelling, an organizational scheme for otherwise disjointed observations drawn from the genres of travel and adventure. As Larner later writes, "There is no description here of the route of the Polos through Asia; the route is just the means by which Marco and Rustichello lead their readers from West to East and then back from East to West, *the route of the narrator through his book*."[30] The ultimate outcome of the narrative and metaphorical forms deployed in the *Travels*, according to Larner, is the production of a singular, coherent space within its pages: " the cumulative effect . . . would have been to give the medieval reader an extraordinary vision of a *whole hitherto unknown world* of cities engaged in trade and commerce set within the east."[31] The spacetime of this wonderful world, traversed along a linear itinerary in the mind of the reader, is a critical legacy of the *Travels*—it is the spacetime we step into when we set ourselves the task of imagining the medieval Silk Road. The spacetime of the *Travels* is particular to its protagonist: a capable, persuasive, and male traveler who is on an adventure. Marco Polo always arrives on time, always escapes—until of course, the arrest and imprisonment which provide both the beginning and end of his story. To say that Marco Polo's itinerary is a fiction is not to cast it aside in favor of better, more accurate histories—rather, let us continue our examination of other fabrications of Silk Road travel, other created landscapes of Eurasia. These created or imagined spacetimes continue to shape the topography of thought about the Silk Road and about places along it, like Armenia, and about the world of the Middle Ages.

In the introduction to his nineteenth-century translation of *The Book of Marvels and Travels*, by John de Mandeville, Malcolm Letts is compelled to comment on the *genre* of the work he has transcribed: "the book sets out to be a guide to the Holy Land, but it soon becomes apparent that its main purpose is not to guide or instruct, but to entertain."[32] The account left by an author calling himself John de Mandeville, composed around 1360, tells of travels to the east; however, the scholarly consensus is that Mandeville's tale is *not* an eyewitness account but a compilation of wondrous tales of the Orient drawn from various sources. Other than the *Travels of Marco Polo* itself, accounts freely plagiarized by Mandeville include the descriptions of John de Plano Carpini, who traveled through Armenia to the court of the Mongol khan in 1245, and whose journey was then described in Vincent de Beauvais' 1264 *Speculum mundi*. Mandeville also drew on the published account of Het'um, the Cilician Armenian king mentioned in the previous chapter, and on the account of William of Rubruck, both of whom traveled across the Caucasus as emissaries to the Mongol court.[33]

Mandeville baffled modern geographical historians like Letts with an apparently irreconcilable combination of facts and marvels.[34] The *Book of Marvels* interweaves routine travel itinerary and geographic descriptions with tales of transformation, miracles, and of the Christian king in the east, Prester John.[35] For instance, if we go looking for an eyewitness account of fourteenth-century Armenia within the *Travels*, we must reconcile John de Mandeville's straightforward account of Armenia as a kingdom west of Persia that "was sometime divided into four kingdoms" with Mandeville's description, a few paragraphs later, of a "truly marvellous" region in Abcasia: "and this region is entirely covered in darkness so that it has no light by which one can see, and nobody dare go into this region because of the darkness. Nevertheless, people from near that region say they can sometimes hear men talking, horses whinnying, and cocks crowing, and they know well that people are living there, but they don't know what kind of people."[36]

This description is not only evocative, but it has a literary pedigree as well. Already by the Middle Ages the tale of a land of darkness had a long lineage; centuries before, Herodotus cited a dark land in the realm of the Scythians where the Amazons would meet their lovers. The dark land featured in the *Alexander Romance* of the early Middle Ages, a text that generated topoi which circulated widely through Eurasia, inspiring episodes in travel accounts like that of Ibn Battuta, and scenes in epics such as the tenth- or eleventh-century *Shahnameh* (Book of Kings) of Firdowsi, which in turn influenced numerous accounts such as the early fourteenth-century *Compendium of Chronicles*, by Rashid al-Din.

Mandeville conveyed a maplike understanding of places known to us to be "real," and commented on the spherical form of the earth, *and yet* described impossible wonders clearly drawn from literature—therefore constituting an aporia in the history of scientific thinking. According to the mid-twentieth-century editors of Mandeville, the passage of time and the ultimate triumph of science relegated Mandeville's account to "the shelf with the Arabian Nights Entertainments and the fairy tales."[37] Paul Smethurst takes a revisionist approach to the genre of Mandeville's *Travels*, arguing that the frustration that the *Travels* spurs in modern audiences—the questions of whether it is trying to be accurate, trying to entertain, or even whether it is openly plagiaristic or deceptive—indicates not the failure of Mandeville's account as science but, rather, the inadequacy of our modern categories. Reflecting on the willful inconsistencies of the account, Smethurst argues that Mandeville's *Travels* is instead a *postmodern* text[38]—that is, an effective rejection of the schemas of knowledge and ordering power sustained by categorization such as fiction/nonfiction, science/fantasy.

Smethurst's interpretation of *The Travels* opens another question: how can a medieval (premodern) text be postmodern? In a generous and literary reading of Mandevilles *Book*, Karma Lochrie defines it as a cosmopolitan utopia which decentered the west.[39] My own reading calls into question the opposition between medieval and modern ways of writing the world, and especially the opposition between allegorical and empirical ways of knowing. Soon after leaving India, Mandeville digresses in a discussion of the shape of the earth and the possibility of circumnavigation. He tells an anecdote of a man who "went so far in his travels by land and by sea that he found an island where he heard people speaking his own language."[40] Mistaking his own country for the most foreign land of all, the man turns around and takes the long way home. This section is delightfully polysemous; even as Mandeville demonstrates his "modernity" by moving from a circular to a spherical map of the world, he resolutely deploys that map as a metaphor for the ways that a traveler, encountering strange or monstrous others, reflects on (returns to) his own home-world. Others are revealed to be selves; science does the work of allegory.

So, instead of asking *how modern* these texts were, we might ask: *What did they make?* What kinds of written worlds, what sorts of *apparatuses*, are these?

What are their topographies of power and possibility? Mandeville's account is a marvelous world, which, like later cabinets of curiosity, served to create an authoritative account of wondrous places, people, and occurrences, and as a book, could itself circulate and delight.[41] Just as a cabinet of curiosity is not just a box of things, the travel account is different from a natural history in that the wonders in it are integrated by the eyewitness, and its spacetime is unified by the mobile subject of the traveling narrator. Like Marco Polo and Rustichello's *Travels*, and like al-Muqaddasī's *Divisions*, Mandeville's world is organized as a journey, with each landscape and wonder within it encountered by a mobile traveling subject. In contemporary accounts, where the personality and the body of the subject are brought more to the fore, this motif of encounter (surprising, terrifying, confusing, delightful) is underscored as a way of drawing the reader into a shared sense of the wonder of the Silk Road.

The Encountering Body

The sensation of encounter, both with strangers and with the limits of one's own known and familiar world, are clearly present in the travel account of Ibn Battuta, one of the most famous travelers from this period. Ibn Battuta's *Rihla* is full of startling encounters with difference—especially in Eastern Anatolia and the Caucasus, where Ibn Battuta travels between Christian, Muslim, and Mongol worlds. In a parallel to Marco Polo's *Travels*, Ibn Battuta is tasked with escorting the pregnant Khatun Bayalun, a young wife of Sultan Uzbeg, the khan of the Golden Horde, on a journey to visit her Christian family in Constantinople, where she plans to give birth to her first child. The repetition of this structure, beyond stressing the constrained ways that women could be imagined as mobile in the Middle Ages, further demonstrates the reliance of Silk Road travel narratives on the tropic forms of medieval romance. As I have mentioned, gendered bodies are not incidental characters in Silk Road stories. One of the effects of figures like Kököchin (the princess in the *Travels*) or Khatun Bayalun is to provide an alluring and intimately approachable embodiment for the otherness of the cultures encountered by the protagonist—indeed a body that is literally under his control and care.[42] The exotic bodies of these princesses, in their foreign compliance, illustrate the agentive subjecthood and relative structural freedom of Silk Road protagonists, those who travel and tell their own stories.

In Ibn Battuta's account, however, Khatun Bayalun demonstrates the role of bodily comportment in the performance of political and spatial agency. Ibn Battuta describes the process by which Bayalun tracks the distance traveled from her husband's *ordu* through transformations of her bodily and everyday practice. Moving westward, she leaves behind her portable (tent) mosque and resumes bodily habits of her own culture, drinking wine and eating pork.[43] This episode demonstrates both the necessity of thinking about bodies and their appearance when we think about medieval travel, and also the significance of women—as brides, mothers, daughters, and patrons in their own right—in knitting together disparate cultures in the Middle Ages. Having escorted the Khatun to her home city of Constantinople, Ibn Battuta recounts yet another moment of embodied encounter, of confrontation but also of inversion, which hinges upon his own mobile body. Until his arrival in the Christian city, the mode of the narrative has been that of following Ibn Battuta's traveling self as he encounters marvels scattered in the world, including meteors, lands of darkness, and strange customs and foods. We are reminded of al-Muqaddasī, as in Constantinople Ibn Battuta's body itself becomes the marvel. The traveler recounts his (possibly invented) encounter with the old king Jirjis, a devout Christian described as wearing a hair shirt. Upon hearing that in his travels Ibn Battuta has been to Jerusalem, the king reacts with wonder:

> The king asked about me, then stopped and said to the Greek [Ibn Battuta's companion, denoted using the general term for a Christian] who knew the Arabic tongue: "Say to this Saracen . . . 'I clasp the hand that has entered Jerusalem and the foot that has walked within the Dome of the Rock and the great church called Qumamah, and Bethlehem.'" And so saying he put his hand upon my feet and passed it over his face. I was amazed at their belief in the merits of one who, though not of their religion, had entered these places.[44]

In this moment Ibn Battuta's body is itself a marvelous object, capable of transmitting grace through its contact with holy places. Thinking back to the example of the Hereford *mappa mundi*, Ibn Battuta's body in this episode works in the same indexical mode. The king is able to "touch" the holy sites of Jerusalem through the powers of extension possessed by a mobile body. This moment in Ibn Battuta's account demonstrates another critical aspect of the Silk Road as a literary place. Travelers in literary accounts of the Silk Road are on adventures, and like other literary adventurers they are changed by their encounters. The case of Ibn Battuta shows that by the fourteenth century the idea of an encounter that shapes the self was not so much western as globally "modern." This close link between the exquisite experience of travel (which can be described) and the production of an exquisite self through traveling (which is unique, and authorizes the travel narrative) carries over from the medieval period into modern ways of thinking the mobile, cosmopolitan self, and of thinking literary landscapes like the Silk Road that exist to transform the traveler.

HOW TO BE A SILK ROAD PLACE: MEDIEVAL ARMENIA AS FAMILIAR AND FARAWAY

The discussion of literary landscape in this chapter has brought us to the point at which, when we describe a place as "along the Silk Road," we understand that historical imagination of such places is necessarily shaped by the literary topographies of Silk Road stories. How, then, have these stories shaped historical encounters with Armenia? How was Armenia, a mountainous place between Europe and Asia, constructed as a literary landscape by medieval travelers? I want to start here, constructing the view of Armenia from the road—or, rather, from a road-shaped literary imaginary—so that I can depict the Armenia of travelers' accounts as a place with familiar landmarks and topographies. Again, neither of these Armenias is more "real" than the other: they both had and have material ramifications for people living in Armenia and outside it. But my overall project with this book is to explore the multiple imagined worlds—literary *and* material—which intersected in the lives of people in Armenia in the medieval period. A first step is looking closely at how Armenia and Armenians were encountered in writing, and constructed as characters within the literary landscape that the western tradition imagines as the Silk Road.

So when we ask what kind of place Armenia was in the thirteenth through fifteenth centuries we need to look in the shared spacetime between written and material worlds, where medieval people dwelled, constructing and inhabiting intersecting bodily, spatial, and cosmological worlds.[45] As I move from classical and medieval travel accounts to narratives from later centuries and then up to the recent past, I will draw attention to the construction of Armenia, not only in place, but in time as well. As discussed earlier in this chapter, the Silk Road is a central concept used for imagining our place, not just in a spatial world, but within a linear timeline. A fascinating tendency in travel narratives is for the peoples and places of the Silk Road passed by a traveler to map onto the passage of time, between "long ago" and now, between a "dark ages" and a civilized modernity, or between a time of credulous allegory and modern science.

In considering the layered literary-historical construction of the Caucasus, I must briefly sojourn even further back in time than the Middle Ages, to the landscapes of Greek (mis)adventure. Xenophon's late fifth-century b.c. *Anabasis* is the narrative of an army of Greek mercenaries stuck in Persia after a sudden shift in the landscape of war. Their journey to reach the Black Sea coast is a Romantic saga, as the Greeks pass through mountain valleys inhabited by sometimes friendly, sometimes hostile, but always unsettling mountain-dwelling natives such as the Carduchians. Xenophon describes their entry into the Caucasus: "Thus the Greeks bivouacked for that night in the villages, while the Carduchians kindled many fires round about upon the mountains and kept shouting to one another."[46] The Carduchians, unlike the Greeks, are very much in their element in the mountains, and in fact appear as *elemental* to the mountains in Xenophon's account, an affective melding of humans and geology that seems to be one of the lasting legacies of the *Anabasis*. This short excerpt also suggests the complexity of the Caucasus landscape, which is not only visually prepossessing, but also delineated in strange and frightening sound. A climax of sorts occurs when the Greeks, nearly out of supplies, must pass through a territory populated by mountaintop fortresses, and made impassable by the local people hurling boulders down from their forts and crushing the Greek soldiers.[47] The Greeks besiege a fort until the inhabitants run out of stones to throw—only to be horror-stricken at the sight of the mountain people throwing themselves and their children off the battlements instead, in an uncompromising, insensate human rockfall. But Xenophon also observed the peoples of the Caucasus in their own context, describing their particular way of living: "The houses here were underground, with a mouth like that of a well, but spacious below; and while entrances were tunneled down for the beasts of burden, the human inhabitants descended by a ladder. In the houses were goats, sheep, cattle, fowls, and their young; and all the animals were reared and took their fodder there in the houses."[48] In the context of the *Anabasis* this description serves to further root the peoples of the Caucasus within their landscape: humans and animals dwelling together within a stony earth, all reduced to the status of wild nature.

Travel accounts from the thirteenth and fourteenth centuries (and medieval histories like that of Kirakos Ganjakec'i or Step'anos Orbelyan) show that in this period Armenia and the Caucasus were dynamic landscapes through which people were constantly mobile in the undertaking of projects of politics and social life—and these projects in turn were integral to maintaining an imaginable, operable world within which all these people were acting. But here I will move from discussing the practice and politics of writing/making worlds to the cosmopolitanism of acting, of getting things done, within these made worlds. Counter to Romantic notions of globalized "nonplace," just because the world was connected doesn't mean it was seamless or coherent for the people moving through it, even those who were hypothetically skilled at writing and acting.[49] Cosmopolitanism was (and is) messy, and sometimes painful.[50]

The high medieval travel account of Friar William of Rubruck is contained within a letter addressed to his patron, King Louis IX of France. As described in the last chapter, the appearance of the Mongols at the eastern edge of European Christian awareness of the world spurred wonder and hope that the Mongols might be enticed to side with Christendom in the apocalyptic conflicts of the crusade wars. Rubruck was one of a series of Franciscan friars dispatched on missions to the khans, seeking political alliance and the symbolic conversion of the Mongols. Rubruck himself traveled a winding route through the Caucasus and over the steppe to the court of Möngke Khan at Karakorum, the capital of the Mongol world in the mid-thirteenth century. As Rubruck moves farther north, away from lands where he feels more "at home"—for instance, like the cities of Erzinjan and Ani in Armenia—his narrative is marked by discomfort, displeasure, and disgust. Traveling among Mongols, sharing their food, and observing their customs, Rubruck writes a litany of complaints back to his patron: about the cold, dirt, manners, and of course the food and drink. He only slowly learns to enjoy kumiss, the fermented mare's milk drunk with relish by the Mongols, and is generally overwhelmed (or at least his account is) by experiences of cultural mistranslation and alienation.[51] His complaints make Rubruck a reluctant cosmopolitan. He struggles to work outside of the cultural frameworks in which he is situated, and for that reason his mission to "convert" Möngke Khan is in many ways an embarrassing failure, and also a demonstration of the real ways that medieval human subjects were themselves structured by worlds even as they wrote them.

In 1255, on his return journey along the Caspian shore and through the Caucasus, Rubruck was hosted by an Armenian prince whom he calls Sahensa. This prince was almost certainly Šahnšah,[52] the son of Zak'are Zak'aryan, an Armenian-Georgian general who was instrumental in the Georgian Bagratid seizure of territories in central Armenia from the Seljuks in the late twelfth century.[53] Resting at the home of Šahnšah in the city of Ani, Rubruck recounts: "It was his father, named Zacharias, who acquired this territory, plucking its Armenian population out of the Saracen's grasp. . . . I took food with Sahensa, and was shown considerable respect by him, his wife, and his son, Zacharias, a fine looking and sensible youth who asked me whether you [King Louis IX] would be willing to retain him if he joined you."[54] This episode shows us several things. First, it foreshadows the (disastrous) uprising of the "sensible youth" Zacharias Zak'aryan against the Mongols a few years later. Second and more interestingly, this description effectively casts the Armenians—princes of large cities, embroiled in complex politics of their own—as accessory characters in William of Rubruck's own journey. Šahnšah and his family appear in this narrative because they are hospitable to Rubruck, and potentially supportive of his patron's political interests. Ultimately two things are downplayed in Rubruck's account: both the political world that he passes through in Armenia (and which continues after he leaves), as well as the importance of hospitality in places like Armenia in producing a coherent world for travelers in the thirteenth century to move within.

I want to conclude this chapter by looking at the ways that classical and medieval techniques of writing about travel and about Armenia have carried through subsequent periods. This is an important question, as layered medieval and early modern accounts of this region continue to shape the imaginaries of novelists, directors, travelers, and bureaucrats, as well as historians and archaeologists.

In the early modern period (sixteenth to eighteenth centuries), overland routes through Armenia as well as developing maritime routes formed the basis for a globalism produced by traveling people, who maintained and enhanced the taste for and access to foreign goods through their descriptions of foreign places.[55] The overland routes from India to Persia and through the Caucasus and Anatolia during this period were maintained largely by networks of Armenians centered at New Julfa, Isfahan. This suburb of consummate merchants was described by a number of European travelers during this period, including the Russian Fedot Kotov,[56] the Frenchmen Jean Baptiste Tavernier and Jean Chardin,[57] and the British emissary Sir Thomas Herbert,[58] all of whom (among many others) traveled during the reign of the Safavid Shah Abbas I and his successors, in the seventeenth

FIGURE 2. A detail from Jean Chardin's 1672 engraving of Yerevan. Note the inclusion of a tiny Noah's Ark atop Ararat in the background on the left. WikiCommons Open License.

century. Many of these travelers took a route south from the ports of the Black Sea, passing through the Caucasus on their way to Persia. We have illustrations from the 1670s by both Chardin and Tavernier of Yerevan and surrounding sites. Both of these early modern accounts are remarkable for their acute awareness that Armenia is the land of an ancient Christianity: they are much more interested in the religious significance of the Ararat plain than they are in the people currently living there. Both visit the holy see at Ejmiatsin, and Tavernier travels to the semi-subterranean monastery at Kickart (Gełard, built in the tenth century), where he was shown various relics including a lancehead understood to be that of Longinus, the Roman soldier who pierced the side of Christ. Taviernier included an engraving of the spear (which object is still on display today along with other relics at Ejmiatsin) to reiterate the verity of his eyewitness account. An effect of the writings of these early modern travelers is the construction of Armenia as a collapsed spacetime: there is a simultaneity to biblical events and the lives of people living in the Ararat plain. This simultaneity is effectively demonstrated by Chardin's engraving of Yerevan, as viewed perhaps from a vantage point on the western slopes of the Gegham mountains (see fig. 2). Chardin's illustrator presents us with the buildings and gardens of Yerevan and surrounding mountains—and includes Noah's ark perched atop Ararat, peeking above the clouds on the horizon.

Tavernier notes that Yerevan "lies in a most plentiful country of all things necessary for human life, but especially abounding in good wine. It is one of the best provinces of Persia, and yields the King (Shah Abbas I) a very large revenue, as well as by reason of the goodness of the soil, as for being the great thoroughfare of the caravans."[59] Indeed, Tavernier's experience of Armenia was no doubt enriched by the fact that he was traveling in a band of Armenian merchants, who were agentive in perpetuating networks of travel even while operating under Safavid hegemony.[60] It was almost certainly these anonymous Armenians who told Tavernier the names of active medieval monasteries like Gełard, as well the names of places like Ani and Artashat, the then-ruined capitals of medieval and classical Armenia.

Imperial Imaginaries

During the eighteenth century, the southward expansion of the Russian Empire resulted in a boom in scholarly and literary imaginaries of the Caucasus and its peoples. In this period production of knowledge about the Caucasus was transformed into an explicitly imperial project, situating Russian power as both authoritative and inevitable within the history of the region. The labors of explorers, scientists, and travelers constructed the Caucasus in this period as an object of imperial interest and control, specifically through the writings of a series of research expeditions in the second half of the eighteenth and the early years of the nineteenth century. These expeditions were ordered by Catherine the Great in the service of better imperial understanding of peoples living beyond the pale of Russian civilization. According to historian Charles King, the mission statements of some of these fact-finding expeditions, such as the 1807 mission of Julius Klaproth, took a distinctly literary tone: "The academy was highly specific about the kinds of things on which Klaproth was expected to report. Are there traditions respecting the existence of Amazons? Who are the likely descendants of the Scythians, the ancient steppe dwellers described by Herodotus?"[61] The Russian expeditions which would produce authoritative accounts about the Caucasus and Caucasians thus set out with expectations for what (and whom) they would find in that landscape extracted from wondrous classical and medieval spacetimes. I can imagine the members of Klaproth's party enquiring about Amazons in Tbilisi with the same earnest tone in which William of Rubruck asked priests at the court of Möngke Khan about the nearby existence of monsters such as blemmyes and cynocephali described in the writings of Isidore of Seville.[62]

Over the course of the next century, the landscapes of the Caucasus would be further explored and explicitly rewritten, transformed into literary landscapes for the habitation of imperial Russian imagination and yearning. The early nineteenth-century entrance of Russian imperial troops, scientists, and explorers into the Caucasus coincided with the blooming of Russian (and European and American) Romanticism and its component Orientalism.[63] The Russian literary obsession with the Caucasus is an enormous topic; for the purposes of this book it is interesting to note Susan Layton's critical point that poets and novelists such as Tolstoy, Pushkin, and Lermontov did not *discover* the Caucasus—they *produced* it.[64] So compelling was the literary world created by these writers that their accounts of mountains and mountaineers emerged as authoritative information on the "real" mountain landscape. For instance, Pushkin's self-described "true, if barely etched, representation of the Caucasus" was consumed by readers looking for factual information about the region.[65] The significance of the dominance of such a literary landscape in the imagination of travelers, administrators, and later generations of writers and filmmakers is that it was a Romantic spacetime. Within such a spacetime the Caucasus were not just mountains but a sublime and transcendental landscape, and its inhabitants were not modern nineteenth-century people but medieval heroes, villains, and tragic maidens. As a result, the various populations of the Caucasus were captured in a Romantic time-out-of-time, contained like Gog and Magog behind mountain walls of literary imagination.

The Treaty of Turkmenchay in 1828 facilitated European travel into Armenia in many ways, and the following decades of weakening Persian power saw a number of Europeans crossing through the Caucasus in the name of science, diplomacy, or (in the case of the novelist Alexandre Dumas) Romantic curiosity.[66] What emerges from the writings of Frederich Parrot (who crossed from Russia to scale Ararat), or Sir Robert Ker Porter and Sir Austen Henry Layard (both British antiquarians and diplomats) is an Orientalist tension between a fierce appreciation of Armenia as the land of Ararat, a heroically historic landscape, and a resolute emphasis that the dignity and heroism of that landscape be in fact situated in the past.[67] What is particular about nineteenth-century natural history and antiquarianism is the way that encounters with ruins were used to produce total histories that were then linked to political and specifically imperial projects, and also the way that these moments of encounter generated ideas about the self. Specifically, the transcendental experience of standing in landscape, looking at ruins, and reflecting on the passage of time and of the mortality of human endeavors is tightly bound to modern ideas of what makes a cosmopolitan subject. Of course, this process of regard and reflection works exceptionally well if ruins of past societies are visually or narratively juxtaposed with the humble lives of contemporary ones, yielding an allegory of savage decadence held up as a mirror to modern Enlightenment.[68]

This period is also of critical importance for the territory of the modern Republic of Armenia, which gets drawn into historical and imperial geographies which claim stakes not only on the past but on modernity. The narrative of the Silk Road itself—remember that the term was coined in the latter half of the nineteenth century—was part of a historical project of understanding the role of Eurasian landscapes in the construction of trade economies and flourishing city-states; the travelers' tales of the medieval period acquired new currency, new "reality," as early accounts of territories where modern nations sought to build their empires. The translations and new editions I used in the writing of this chapter were themselves produced in many cases by the Hakluyt Society, a group of scientists and military officers based in Great Britain. Many of the Hakluyt Society, having served in the West Indies and under Crown rule in India, shared the conviction that historical primary sources were crucial for nineteenth century British geopolitical knowledge of and control over the Eurasian world.[69]

The reliance of imperial travelers on medieval and ancient accounts didn't merely consist of translation and research of those older sources. Part of the praxis of a learned traveler was to carry books for on-the-spot consultation; this practice had the secondary effect of submerging travelers and those they encountered into a timeless imagined landscape that, as we have traced, was inherited from the classical and medieval periods.[70] Reading their accounts, it is hard not to imagine that travelers like Robert Ker Porter and Sir Austen Henry Layard rode through the Caucasus with one finger marking the page in a worn copy of the *Anabasis*. Passing from Erzerum to Mosul, Layard remarked on the subterranean houses of the Armenians merely that "the villages are still such as they were when Xenophon traversed Armenia."[71] In a similar mode, upon entering the Caucasus from Georgia, Ker Porter allows himself a moment of pure romance: "With the advance of night succeeded a severe but brilliant frost; and the romantic scenery, with which we were surrounded, only became more animated by the change. Numerous fires appeared at various distances, under the shelter of trees, or beneath hanging shelters of rock. Around these, were seen groups of Cossacks, mingled with Georgians and Mountaineers, whose rude athletic figures, marked countenances and savage military garbs, formed pictures of the wildest character."[72] This scene clearly evokes Xenophon's description of the Ten Thousand's entry into the Caucasus, and casts Ker Porter himself in the role of the courageous soldier on a mountain campaign. Note how he describes the mountain natives: rude, athletic, savage, military. By thus evoking a dark and stony land of noble savages living in a state of wild nature, Ker Porter reveals himself to be traveling through the literary adventure-scape not only of Xenophon, but also of Herodotus, Alexander, Mandeville, and of course, of imperial Russian Romanticism.

Nearly a century after Layard's journey, the novelist and historian Vassily Grossman wrote his own account of entering Armenia from the north, though this time by train. The trip itself was a liminal journey: Grossman had recently been designated a "nonperson" due to Soviet rejection of his writings, and he was in failing health that would lead to his death a few years later. Though Grossman is a richly unreliable, resolutely postmodern narrator, his description of his first glimpse of Armenian landscapes is clearly situated in literary landscapes with a long pedigree: "A mountain had died, its skeleton had been scattered on the ground. . . . The houses seem not to have been built by human hands. Sometimes a gray stone comes to life and begins to move. A sheep. The sheep too must have been born from stone; probably they eat powdered stone and drink the dust of stone. . . . the men are like the stones they live among."[73] This description is striking, both in its effective conveyance of the alienation and discomfort of the traveler, as well in its reducing the Armenians to part of a timeless, antagonistic, stony natural landscape. Yet Grossman's account of Armenia does not rest here, in the space of (mis)adventure; the core of the novel sits in moments where the alien Grossman is welcomed and fed by his Armenian hosts. Ultimately, his exile has eliminated the potential of return, on which cosmopolitan transcendence supposedly depends. The author himself is the stranger dependent on tolerant locals who let him into their world.

I end this chapter with these descriptions from early modern and modern travelers to make a point, not about the chauvinism of Europeans or Soviet Russian intellectuals traveling in Armenia, but about the power of literary landscapes and chronotopes to continue to shape our perceptions of place, and of people in places. Even the brief review of more than a thousand years of writing about travel in Armenia that I have just provided shows a breadth of reasons for traveling (missionary work, pleasure, mercantile gain, military conquest), as well as different subject positions vis-à-vis the people these travelers encountered on the road. In pulling apart these differences and similarities, my goal is not to reveal the "real" Armenia that was accurately or inaccurately described by progressively more scientific travelers. If anything, the persisting literary romance that still runs through the descriptions of Ker Porter and Layard effectively demonstrates that modern "scientific" travelers were just as inclined to wonder and allegory as the medieval travelers they followed. But I *do* want to call attention to the evocation of Armenians as, at best, noble primitives, and at worst, subhuman stone-people, in these travel accounts that are, almost exclusively, adventure stories with male protagonists.

The persistence of the literary landscape of male adventure and transcendent encounter with strange local Others within these texts, over time, is as significant as the wealth of information that each of these accounts provided about the world at their time of writing. But we must foreground the literariness of each of these sources, and their indebtedness to old and often medieval ideas about what the East is and who and what is found there. This foregrounding reveals a bias in writing about the Silk Road that is part of the Orientalist tradition of "the West's imagination of the East," but which also extends beyond the prejudices of any single traveler or writer. The persistence of the Silk Road as a written world demonstrates the hold of medieval imagined worlds upon the present, to the extent that they shape our perceptions of the past and the people who lived there. Exceptions to this casting of medieval Armenians as nameless roadside hosts are the princes like Šahnšah and Zacharias who have names, and who make it into the histories of western travelers like Het'um and William of Rubruck. These named Armenians are yet more indelible because of the texts they themselves produced. In the next chapter, I shall scale down and look at Armenia on its own terms through the spaces produced by these texts—though I explore them in resolutely material ways.

3

Techniques of World-Making in Medieval Armenia

In the last chapter I explored the Silk Road and Armenia as stories told, in the Middle Ages and in modern imaginations. Now I will "zoom in" on Armenia, one of the worlds that made up the wider universe of the Silk Road cultural ecumene. As I discussed in the introduction, I do not want to say that the medieval world was just a scaled-up version of daily life in Armenia, or conversely that daily life in the medieval South Caucasus was a scaled-down iteration of broad cultural phenomena happening "everywhere at once." Both of these presume a sameness about the global medieval that I want to turn over and look beneath, in order not just to understand the large-scale cultures of what we now call the Silk Road, but also to understand how people living in relatively remote places related to their world through practices which reached across scales. Plural scales of distance and difference and their embodied, emplaced experience are important for the imagi-nation of worlds and thus for cosmopolitanisms, for either medieval or modern people. So, I will look at the ways whereby the world was "told" in Armenia as a bundle of threads tangled up in the broader shared imaginary of Silk Road culture that many of us still live within.

IMAGINING MEDIEVAL ARMENIA: HISTORICAL AND ARCHAEOLOGICAL CONSTRUCTIONS OF A SPACETIME

If the Silk Road is a place first imagined in literary narratives, then, through the work of historians and archaeologists, medieval Armenia has likewise been cre-ated. I used the lens of travelers' accounts in the last chapter to show how Armenia appeared as a place inhabited by certain kinds of people—or as a landscape of uninhabited, stony ruins. In this chapter I will continue that thread and look in particular at the textual and material ways that high medieval Armenia has been made and imagined, both in the recent past and in the medieval period.[1] This discussion draws from a combination of texts, including medieval manuscript texts as well as epigraphic texts or inscriptions, and from data produced by archaeological excavations over the last century and a half.

The explicit imagination of high medieval Armenia by historians began in the medieval period of course. This period in Armenia begins just after the contraction of the Seljuk sultanate out of the highlands, and hinges in many ways on the Mongol invasions of the 1230s and the subsequent Ilkhanid period, when Armenia was a province of the Mongol Ilkhanate centered in Tabriz. During this period the Armenian highlands were ruled by a class of princes known in historical documents as *mec išxan, tanuter, paronac' paron*—that is, as princes, lords, and "lords among lords."[2] Though deliberately self-referenced with a similar nomenclature, the princes of the high medieval period were not of the same landed *naxarar* dynasties that had been favored by the Sasanian Persians, crowned by caliphs and emperors, and dispersed before the Byzantine and Seljuk armies.[3] According to Robert Bedrosian, this emergent princely echelon was comprised of, on the one hand, "men of ambition and military talents" who were rewarded with titles and lands by the victorious Zak'arids for their service; and on the other, by the so-called *mecatun* class: merchants who had prospered from expanding highway trade and who accumulated assets and estates through purchase, often in cash.[4] Ongoing research suggests that the Seljuk impact on the structure of the *naxararut'yun* had more to do with the redistributive effects of the *iqta* patronage system on estates already consolidated under the Bagratids than with a violent, physical dispersal of the aristocracy.[5] Regardless, in the post-Seljuk period a number of new princely lineages were founded "by sword or by gold," and by the thirteenth century there were one hundred such families recorded, including the Vač'utyans, Orbelyans, and the neophyte houses of Tigran Honenc', Umek, and Samadin.[6] One thing these new dynasties had in common with their early medieval antecedents was a strong interest in the writing of history, and of their own history in particular. Our knowledge of this period comes from the pens of historians who were supported by princely houses, or who were in fact members of those houses. A primary legacy of medieval Armenian society—beyond the spaces it built and the cultures it participated in—was an account of medieval events written by Kirakos Ganjakec'i, Step'anos Orbelyan, Vardan Arewelc'i, and numerous others. Unsurprisingly perhaps, the protagonists of these medieval sources were the same princes and princely actors under whose patronage the histories were written. Within these texts, the Caucasus landscape is frequently reduced to the backdrop of battles, treaties, patriotic miracles, and other princely exploits.

After residing in monastic scriptoria for several centuries, this medieval corpus (including historical texts from the previous centuries of the Middle Ages) was revived, transcribed, and printed for a mass readership in the eighteenth century

–not in Armenia, but in centers of the renaissance of Armenian language and scholarship such as Venice and Vienna. There, members of the Mekhitarist order of Armenian Benedictine monks produced medieval imaginaries of *naxarars* and pastoral Christian kingdoms carrying on an ancient and autochthonous way of life.[7] The Mekhitarist historical tradition is a classic example of what Benedict Anderson called "imagined community" or what Eric Hobsbawn and Terrence Ranger termed "the invention of tradition."[8] These are disparate historical paradigms that call attention to the effervescent production of shared imaginaries of national and individual selfhood, in relation to (though not necessarily located within) a common homeland. Anderson made the critical point, relevant in the case of the Mekhitarists, that the modern imagination of national communities takes place across borders and at global scales, mediated by circulating print cultures. As Razmik Panossian has argued, "aware of and in conjunction with the intellectual currents of European thought, [the Mekhitarist writers] were very consciously and systematically carrying out an enlightenment project on behalf of the nation."[9] They achieved this project, printing and distributing primary historical sources and synthetic histories of Armenia and her peoples from presses on the island of San Lazzaro in Venice.

The work of the Mekhitarists as historiographers was as significant or more so than their achieved revival of Armenian language. In both new and widely distributed reprints of the original texts, as well as in authoritative synthetic works,[10] they produced medieval Armenia as a landscape that readers could imagine. Their version of Armenia was particular and nationalistic: proud mountain dynasties, ancient traditional Christianity, remote monastic centers, and heroes taken from the dynastic histories. This imagined medieval world is rooted in the built world of medieval monuments that survived in the nineteenth century, and which sparked the imagination of historians like Łevond Ališan. A member of the Mekhitarist congregation in Venice in the first half of the nineteenth century, Ališan produced historical geographies of regions of Armenia including Ararat, Shirak, and Sisakan (Syunik). These geographies contain records of Urartian and Persian as well as Armenian inscriptions, and engravings of Armenian villagers living among medieval ruins in the mountainous landscapes of the South Caucasus.

This medieval landscape has played a central role in the imagined Armenia which has united diasporic communities, and in the political knitting-together of the modern Armenian nation-state. Medieval spaces are the location of major acts which produced the Armenian nation as it self-identifies, such as the state conversion to Christianity (memorialized on a seventh-century stela at Talin) or the fifth-century referenda against diophysite tenets of Chalcedonian Christianity at the city of Dvin. Increasingly important in the twentieth century as Armenian nationalism was oriented in relation to the Soviet Union, the medieval past presented a bucolic rural Armenia as an opposition view to Soviet modernism.[11] Armenian tradition (like that of many of the minorities within the USSR) was discursively situated as the past to the future of Soviet state citizenship. Medieval churches and monastic sites—among them Gełard and Ejmiatsin—are a reference point for diaspora identity, influencing the shape both of Armenian churches and also of community centers in other countries.[12] The medieval landscape has long been the dwelling place of Armenian national nostalgia for an idealized past, prior to the stresses of both genocidal dispersal and modern global marginalization. This is well illustrated by Sergei Parajanov's 1969 film *Color of Pomegranates* (*Sayat Nova*), one of the most famous and highly regarded expressionist films of the Soviet period. In portraying the life of eighteenth-century poet Sayat Nova through the lens of surrealism, the film provided variations on the theme of an eternal medieval Armenia, filmed in a series of ruined *gavit* (narthex) spaces and on the roofs of high medieval churches.[13] Key scenes in the film were produced at the sites of Hałpat, Sanahin, Sałmosavank', and Ałtala, tenth- to- fourteenth-century monasteries restored in the Soviet period. Parajanov combined Safavid and Qajar imagery (of Sayat Nova's own time) with medieval spaces, to create a sense of a timeless, attenuated, and medieval premodernity. The vision of medieval Armenia that dominates artistic narratives is often that of a place to go in the mind to *escape* modernity, with all of the complexity, interconnectivity, and change that modernity entails for many people. This wishful imaginary has in many ways discouraged the scholarly development of an image of a complicated medieval Armenia, even though—as I will explore in the next sections—life in medieval Armenia was dynamic and profoundly engaged with multiple worlds, be it the produced worlds of Armenian politics or the Silk Road world(s) beyond the mountain horizons.

Nodes and Networks: The History of High Medieval Armenia
as a History of Trade

If popular imaginations of medieval Armenia focus on pastoral and monastic scenes, the gaze of historians and archaeologists has long been focused elsewhere, on the "trade cities" of the medieval highlands. In long-standing historical conceptualizations of the medieval period the later centuries of the Middle Ages are important because it is at that point that somehow the conditions are established for various forms of emergent modernity. In mid-twentieth-century models of economic and political history written in both the West and the Soviet Union, this meant that agrarian societies needed to form urban centers, places where people would be crowded together, and where identities like artisans, craft specialists, and a middle class could form.[14] Furthermore, the social mobility in medieval cities enabled medieval people (according to these same models) to break free from "local" ties to land, and to become worldly, enlightened cosmopolitans. If towns were considered important as central concentrations of complex social life, they were also understood as nodes in networks of movement and exchange. Histories of high medieval trade frequently emphasize cities and towns,[15] in stark contrast to the desert dunes and romantic, isolated oases at the center of historical imaginaries of the Silk Road. Histories of the medieval social landscape of Armenia are caught up in the old idea that active trade and dynamic urban life depend on each other—and that cosmopolitanism is a capacity exclusively of cities. For our purposes, these models are important because they are the "story" about the Middle Ages that was used to tell other stories in places like Armenia, and which guided the questions asked of archaeological and historical records. They also provide the cast of potential protagonists of those stories: cosmopolite urban mercantile elites, making their fortunes from the wide world rather than the narrow breadth of a plowed furrow and the tight cycle of the seasons. To rephrase an old German phrase loved by historians of the medieval economy, "city air makes us cosmopolitan."

The fundamental historical source for discussions of the Armenian highlands' role in regional trade, and the relationship between trade movement and urbanism, is Hakob Manandyan's *Trade and Cities of Armenia in Relation to Ancient World Trade*.[16] Manandyan traces the rise and fall of urban places in the highlands based on the mention of cities in medieval texts, and from this narrates the ebb and flow of trade which nourished, and was supported by, those cities—though he does not use the term *Silk Road*. Reconstructing itineraries from late classical and Arab sources, Manandyan tethers the highlands into connections of movement and trade with the worlds to either side. For the period between the late twelfth and fourteenth centuries, this means drawing maps of networks in flux. Manandyan draws special attention to the crystalization of routes and markets made possible by the Venetian and Genoese colonies on the Black Sea coast, in particular the Venetian port at Trebizond. According to Manandyan, these waystations for the European quest for eastern goods galvanized travel, and in turn trade cities, on the routes through the Caucasus.[17]

For Manandyan, the Mongol invasions of the mid-thirteenth century present a quandary of evidence: on the one hand, historical sources attest to the destruction of cities and general depopulation; on the other, he argues that the shrewdness of the Armenian nobility spared the highlands from the destruction meted out elsewhere, such that social life was restored in Armenia by the latter part of the century. Manandyan argues that trade was not only restored but in fact flourished, supported by Mongol grants of safe passage for caravans and attested in epigraphy.[18] Manandyan draws on the description written by the Florentine agent Balducci Pegolotti of the transit fees required for transporting merchandise overland from Ayas to Tabriz under the Ilkhanids. Writing in the fourteenth century, Pegolotti had divided the total fees into categories, which are also categories of place: the taxes paid by load ("whether of camels or of other beasts") at the entrances to cities, upon leaving cities, and at bridges and caravanserais.[19] The landscape of Manandyan's imaginary medieval highlands draws on the landscape as evoked in such itineraries, a network of cities strung like beads on a string made of infrastructure, tautened at either end in accordance with the desires of distant urbanites in Venice and Guangzhou.[20]

The narrative of Armenia's role in a wider medieval world is elaborated by Babken Arak'elyan, who served as the director of the Institute of Archaeology and Ethnography from 1959 to 1990. In his two-volume synthesis of historical and archaeological evidence, Arak'elyan argues that the ninth to the thirteenth centuries witnessed the transformation of Armenia's feudal society through the development of a division of labor in urban artisanal production, and a proliferation of trade organizations centered in the highland cities.[21] Arak'elyan cites the chronicles of medieval historians, who remarked on trade in the cities of Dvin, Ani, Xlat, and Kars, as well as Nprkert, Arzn, and Baleš; he also extrapolates from the midcentury excavations at Garni to argue for the widespread development of commodity production and market activity in towns.[22]

According to Arak'elyan, despite the nugatory effects of the Seljuk invasion and rule of the Caucasus, "in the second half of the twelfth century, and lasting until the Mongol invasions, the cities experienced a rise, and as in the rest of the Near East, in Transcaucasia craft production and trade reached its medieval apex."[23] This corresponds to what archaeologists and historians after Arak'elyan have referred to as the later "developed" (*zargacac*') medieval period (late twelfth through mid-fourteenth century); a phase of rapid transformation, as the division of labor and class differentiation in cities pulled the highlands towards capitalist modernity.[24] A phrase that Arak'elyan used constantly through his analysis was "the uncoupling of the cities from village agrarian subsistence," casting Weberian emphasis on the funneling of human labor and creativity out of the static relationships of subsistence agriculture into the dynamic proto-capitalism of merchant cities. Drawing on the work of the Russian historian Yakubovski, Arak'elyan even went further to assert that social life in Near Eastern cities (among which those of Armenia are numbered) surpassed Europe in its "richness and culture."[25] This process only deepened in the latter centuries of the high Middle Ages. Arak'elyan argued that over the course of the late twelfth to early thirteenth centuries trade and craft production expanded despite the slowing effects of Seljuk rule, accompanied by a greater contrast between city and village, and a deepening of class differences within the urban population—including the emergence of an elite upper class.[26]

But I want to draw attention to another argument of Arak'elyan, which has been overlooked in the emphasis on transit trade and the "rise" of cities. Critically, Arak'elyan switched the emphasis from external, transit trade to internal trade as a prime mover for the economy of tenth- through thirteenth-century Armenia. Arak'elyan drew on the epigraphic evidence from the city of Ani to argue for a rising importance of urban shops and markets in this period, as a source of social as well as actual capital.[27] Though carried out, as he argued, in urban markets, this trade economy followed seasonal cycles, and was punctuated by festivals.[28] Likewise, through an examination of the implications for the geography of trade of the laws contained in Mxitar Goš's *Lawcode*, Arakʿelyan argued that trade in the twelfth through thirteenth centuries took place "not just in cities, but in settlements as well, and in the provinces trade may have been contained within particular places, such as the nodal points of roads, in convenient places and during festival markets."[29] Likewise, this regional trade "embraced as well the products of agriculture and pastoralism and their processed materials (wine, oil, wax etc.) and raw materials (leather, cotton, silk, vegetable fibers etc)."[30] It is important that Arakʿelyan drew attention to regional economies in Armenia, and in particular, to the landscapes and cyclical, ritual practices within which such economies were rooted. Arakʿelyan's point confirms and encourages my own impulse to look, not just at world-cities, but also at local landscapes for the construction and support of trade cultures and of cosmopolitanism.

Soviet historians of the latter twentieth century referred to the twelfth and thirteenth centuries in the highlands as the "Zakʿarid period," after the Armenian Zakʿaryan noble house which led the Georgian Bagratid armies in driving out the Seljuks from the highlands, and who ruled much of central and northern Armenia in the name of the Georgian crown.[31] Within the arc of high medieval transformations, the Zakʿarid period is presented by historians as a window of progress—though a brief one. According to Arakʿelyan, the Armenian cities experienced a rebirth once freed from the "yoke" of Seljuk rule.[32] Barely a generation separated the end of the Seljuk era and the Mongol invasions of the Caucasus; as we saw in the last chapter, these changes occurred within the living memory of people like Šahnšah (Rubruck's Sahensa) Zakʿaryan. The Zakʿaryans were praised by the thirteenth-century chronicler Kirakos Ganjakecʿi, in terms that demonstrate that the impact of these administrators and their Georgian rulers manifested in concrete ways in the architecture and landscape of this period: "They restored many monasteries which for a long time—since the invasions of the Ishmaelites—had been in ruins. They restored the churches once again and the clerical orders shone forth. They also built new churches and monasteries, which from antiquity had not been monasteries."[33] This excerpt from Ganjakecʿi demonstrates for the medieval period a fact that geographers have repeatedly asserted for modern globality: that trade dynamisms and integrated economies depend on built space.[34] Manandyan argues that the evidence for monumental and urban construction under the Zakʿarids was further evidence for the role played by mercantile elites in international trade.[35] Arakʿelyan stresses the necessary links between expanding medieval trade economy and built infrastructure: "the developments of trade depended on the improvement of trade highways, on the construction of bridges and caravanserais on the highways and in mountain passes, and on the creation of *pandok-ijevanatnner* (inns), shops, hostelries, and other facilities in the cities."[36] Such assertions push against the nodal understanding of trade and cosmopolitanism as moving fluidly between cities; the resulting broad geography of trade infrastructure and culture also raises questions for a medieval archaeology decentered from urban sites. Arakʿelyan's assertion also centers the importance of cultures of construction, endowment, and maintenance—what he called an "issue of care in Armenia"[37]—for the creation and perpetuation of a cosmopolitan world linked through the highlands.

Modern Encounters with Medieval Landscapes

The narratives devised by Armenian historians for the high Middle Ages were co-constructed with the study of standing ruins and excavated physical landscapes of that period. Active interest in the physical remains of the medieval past began, of course, in the Middle Ages. As I will discuss in the following chapters, we know that people in the high Middle Ages both actively reconstructed ruined buildings, such as churches, and recorded partially effaced inscriptions. As mentioned earlier, interest in this ruined past was revived by antiquarians and travelers in the nineteenth century. Compiling histories of the Armenian provinces, Łevond Ališan and his contemporary Yovhannes Šahxatunyan created records which remain some of the only descriptions of buildings and inscriptions which were extant in the nineteenth century and have since collapsed or been destroyed.[38] Multiple European travelers in the early modern period remarked on medieval sites in Armenia. Jean Chardin, en route to Isfahan in 1672, visited Ejmiatsin and the neighboring monasteries of Sb. Hripsime and Sb. Gayane.[39] By the nineteenth century, a major attraction for antiquarian travelers was the ruined medieval city of Ani. Located on the Akhurean River west of Mount Aragats, Ani was the capital of the Bagratid kingdom in the tenth century and was a bustling city until the fourteenth century. Due to shifts in trade routes, a series of seismic disasters, and the vicissitudes of geopolitics, the core of Ani was empty by the beginning of the nineteenth century. In 1817, Robert Ker Porter passed by the ruins of "Anni" and fitted them into a larger reflection (which dominates his travel account) on the decline of great eastern civilizations and the rise of the West:

> On entering the city, I found the whole surface of the ground covered with hewn stones, broken capitals, columns, shattered, but highly ornamented friezes, and other remains of ancient magnificence. Several churches, still existing in different parts of the place retain something more than ruins of their former dignity; but they are as solitary as all the other structures, on which time and devastation have left more heavy strokes. . . .
>
> . . . As I passed by [the ruined houses], and over the almost formless masses of yet more extensive ruins, I could not but think of the interesting stores of antiquity which might be lying hid beneath those mighty fragments of columns, walls, and heaps of stones. Even a few days gathering on the surface would furnish a traveler (could it be attempted with any degree of security) with very fine specimens of the most beautiful ornaments of architecture.[40]

As is clear from these brief excerpts, Ker Porter was typical of the "antiquarian moment" in the history of archaeology as a science, when archaeological sites (picturesque ruins) were useful primarily for the furnishing of romantic reflections

FIGURE 3. A Romantic nineteenth-century view of the walls of Ani, by Charles Texier, from his 1842 *Description de la Armenia, la Perse, et la Mesopotamie*. Note the figures in the foreground which both provide scale and a dynamic contrast between Christian past and Oriental present. Public Domain from archive.org.

and beautiful ornaments to the sentimental gentleman traveler. Nearly a century later, as archaeologists took advantage of the potential Ker Porter observed beneath his feet, the ruins at Ani furnished evidence for similar arguments for medieval Armenia's relationship to medieval and modern worlds (see fig. 3).

The excavations undertaken at Ani by Nikolai Marr were the first such scientific excavations carried out in Armenia.[41] The first director of the Russian Academy for the History of Material Culture, Marr has been described as "a linguist with archaeological interests," and was primarily invested in constituting a unilinear, singular, and transhistorical Armenian culture tied to the Armenian language.[42] Marr initiated systematic excavations at prehistoric sites as well as at the great medieval cities of Armenia, Ani and Dvin. Marr's excavations at Ani in 1892, 1905, and 1907–13 exposed enormous areas of the site and produced a wealth of architectural data and material artifacts. Marr's landmark publication primarily focused on the historical context of the city of Ani, and left much of the task of analyzing this material corpus in the hands of his successors.[43] The first generation of Marr's students in Armenia, working after the First World War, expanded the remit of archaeology to include investigations at multiple urban centers as well as the fortified citadels and monasteries built by the medieval nobility. Critical during this period was the work of T'oros T'oramanyan, an architect who is best known for his reconstruction of Zvartnoc' Cathedral. T'oramanyan undertook and published regional surveys throughout Armenia, which left as a legacy a landscape-scale dataset of medieval churches, fortresses, caravanserais, cemeteries, and village sites from multiple historic periods (see chapter 4).[44]

As geopolitical realities forestalled research at Ani, archaeologists within the newly formed Armenian Soviet Socialist Republic turned their attention to major urban sites within the country, specifically the site of Dvin, the capital of Sasanian and Arab Armenia (fifth to tenth centuries) and a major urban center into the High Middle Ages. Marr had begun test digs at the site in the early part of the century; systematic excavations were resumed at Dvin in 1937 under the direction of historian Smbat Ter-Avetisyan and archaeologist Karo Ghafadaryan. Excavations at Dvin would continue nearly uninterrupted until the collapse of the USSR in 1991, to be reopened again in recent years by Ghafadaryan's students; excavations were directed from the 1970s onward by Aram Kalantaryan, who worked at Dvin with a team of medieval archaeologists until the year of his death, in 2009.[45] The synthetic publications, monographs, and dissertations generated from the Dvin excavations have supplied a broad and rich conceptualization of social life at that capital city during its span of medieval occupation, from the seventh through thirteenth centuries. The extensive and rigorous work done at Dvin over the last century provided the basis for comparative analysis and stratigraphic dating for contemporary sites from the high medieval period, including the medieval levels at Garni, the Bagratid fortress at Anberd, and the Zak'arid-era castles at Vardenut and Daštadem.[46] The extensive corpus of artifacts from the citadel, lower town, and central quarter of Dvin also generated a body of data for ongoing, detailed research on the production, use, and circulation of late medieval material culture, including ceramics, glass, and metal work.[47]

Life beyond the Cities

For most of the twentieth century, the archaeological focus on Ani and Dvin shored up the historical model of high medieval society as being city-centered. In recent years, however, motivated in part by the need to rescue or rebuild sites across Armenia, excavations have been carried out at a greater diversity of sites. The majority of these sites are monasteries, many of which now consist of only a few standing church buildings, as their refectories, outbuildings, and adjoining settlements are built over by modern villages. In rural and mountainous parts of Armenia, this tendency to reduce extraurban medieval settlement to a church and a cemetery was exacerbated by agricultural amelioration in the Soviet period. Though recognizable church buildings might be assiduously avoided, outbuildings and entire ruined villages were bulldozed into canyons or collected into heaps of rubble to make room for industrial farm collectives and upland fields.[48]

Many of the monastic sites excavated were chosen because they had ties to historically significant princely houses, such as the Bagratunis, Orbelyans, or Vač'utyans. Excavation at these sites thus served a dual purpose of augmenting the textual record by producing new inscriptions—and indeed, many of these

FIGURE 4. An engraving showing the fortress of Daštadem (Nor Talin), from Łevond Ališan's 1890 *Ayrarat*. Note the contemporary Armenians added for scale and romance, as well as the medieval and later fortifications. Public Domain, Bonn University Digital Armenian Archive.

excavations were led by historians rather than archaeologists.[49] These include the twelfth-thirteenth century site of Tełenyacʻ Vankʻ, located in the foothills of the Tsaghkunyats in the juncture of the Kasakh and Hrazdan River valleys, or the monastic site of Marmašen, nestled in the Akhurean canyon, north of Ani.[50] In other cases, excavations were undertaken for rescue or reconstruction purposes; a prime example is the fifth-through seventeenth-century site of Uši Vankʻ, located on the southeast shoulder of Mount Aragats.[51] Extensive sections of this monastery dating to the developed medieval period were excavated in order to reconstruct a small chapel at the complex's center.[52] These monastic excavations are complemented by recent work at fortified and monumental sites associated with the medieval elite, including excavations at the sites of Bjni, Tsałatskar, and Yełegis.[53] For almost a decade, archaeologists from the Institute of Archaeology in collaboration with a series of international teams have excavated the fortress at Daštadem, located on the southwestern shoulder of Mount Aragats, south of the city of Talin (see fig. 4). These excavations have uncovered fortifications dating to the Sheddadid, Zakʻarid, and Safavid periods, and have also provided extensive material data on daily life in a highway town in the twelfth to fourteenth centuries.[54]

Shifting Perceptions of the Landscape of High Medieval Armenia

For more than a century, excavations into Armenia's medieval past have generated a material narrative which has been interpreted through, but which also sometimes challenges, the models constructed by historians. Of primary interest to me, and to this book's project, is the reconfiguring view of the Armenian social landscape that is emerging from accumulated archaeological evidence, and from changing archaeological questions. This is happening due to a number of factors, many of which have to do with the reconfiguring sources of institutional support for archaeology and increased international collaboration. But also, our imagination of the medieval Armenian landscape is reconfiguring as medieval archaeology more generally moves from what were long thought to be the centers of medieval life—the castle, the church, and the city—and engages with a broader social landscape.[55] It is also, slowly, reconfiguring away from a traditional focus on the lives and doings of a small number of royal figures. Patricia Blessing and Rachel Goshgarian, writing on the social production of space in medieval (twelfth to sixteenth centuries) Anatolia, phrase this shift nicely: instead of asking "who was in power," the collective focus of their study is "where, in what places, was power?" in this period.[56] Medieval archaeology in Armenia is therefore following a trend already established elsewhere,[57] though one which has not fully transformed the narratives of medieval social complexity everywhere.

This expanding landscape of excavation and research is the context for my own projects in Armenia. Moving from an urban-centered to a landscape-scale imaginary of medieval sociality in Armenia is crucial for rethinking that world, and what it meant to people living in it. Put another way, if we expand our imagination of medieval Armenia to include small towns, village houses, and roadside places, then those too become locales for the situating of cosmopolitan subjects, people who imagined the Silk Road into being. To begin, I will examine how this landscape—of cities, towns, and churches, but also fields, villages, roads, bridges, and inns—was imagined by political actors in the thirteenth through fifteenth centuries. By looking at how places were tied to one another through the practice of inscription (engraving in stones), we can get a sense of how the world was linked together for and by medieval people both living in Armenia and passing through it. This step in my multiscalar archaeology of Armenia's place in the Silk Road world is important, especially for helping to show that that world was situated not just in skeins of connected, nodal cities, but also in landscapes integrated and meshed with other mobilities, concerns, and rhythms of life.

MAKING WORLDS FOR OTHERS TO LIVE IN: EPIGRAPHIC AND ARCHITECTURAL SPACETIME IN MEDIEVAL ARMENIA

In medieval Armenia, shaping the landscape—whether in written representation or physical fabrics—was understood as a practice that was inherently political, and inherent to politics. According to the late twelfth-century *Lawcode* of Mxitar Goš, constructing monumental buildings was a right reserved for princes, and part of the princely obligation to maintain societal infrastructure. As he wrote: "If a king builds a city or a keep, if he keeps a census, and if he stamps or mints dahekans or drams, let him have authority according to the legal code. But it is not legal for princes to mint dahekans or drams; if he should mint them, it should be with the permission of the king. Likewise in building cities and castles. To build bridges over great rivers is the prerogative of kings; and as for hostelries and inns (*pandok, ijawanac'tun*), for these let it be with their permission."[58] In the context of the mechanics of power in medieval Armenia, the "prerogative of kings" here demonstrates that the construction of a bridge or caravan inn was cause to cite the power and grace of the king to whom a prince owed their fealty, just as in the case of monastic donations.[59] It makes functional sense for several reasons that to build castles, bridges, or caravanserai would be a right set aside for princely rulers. On the one hand, building these sorts of monumental public structures was expensive, and required the kind of resources that only the very wealthy could command. In another sense, however, Goš's stipulation about the princely right to build touches on the power invested in making spaces. Structures like churches, palaces, and caravan inns were (and are) spaces imbued with cosmological connotations; they were small worlds that situated and shaped the worldviews of people who moved within and around them.[60] To have one's name attached to such a building was therefore to stake a claim as a builder of worlds. This link between power and infrastructure was not particular to medieval Armenia; rather, it was part of the shared culture which made travel, trade, and encounter possible in the medieval Eurasian world. The excerpt from Goš cited above is strikingly familiar to a piece of political advice given a century earlier, by Nizam al-Mulk, then vizier to the Seljuk Sultan Malik Shah I: "Further he will bring to pass that which concerns the advance of civilization, such as constructing underground channels, digging main canals, building bridges across great waters, rehabilitating villages and farms, raising fortifications, building new towns, and erecting lofty buildings and magnificent dwellings; he will have inns built on the highways and schools for those who seek knowledge; for which things he will be renowned forever."[61] The similarity between these two philosophies of power suggests two things: first, that the practice of hospitality In Armenia was always-already cosmopolitan, participant within a rich world of Central Asian, Persian, and classical ideas. Second, these texts also reiterate the perceived unity between princely or royal power in or over a world, and the built spaces—including infrastructural landscapes—which were evoked as smaller worlds constructed in the name of that power.

Inscriptions, or texts carved into the stones of public buildings, served a parallel function. In addition to conveying literal information about what date churches were built and through whose donations, architectural inscriptions rooted themselves in the built landscape, constituting a distributed topography of mutually implicated structures, spaces, and texts that shaped the movement and imaginations of medieval people in Armenia and the broader Silk Road world. Within the more intimate space of the building itself, inscriptions could function as mnemonics for ritual and devotional acts in similar ways to imagery, enabling the iterative production of communities of practice.[62] For the rest of this chapter, I explore how the nested practices of inscription (engraving text into stone) and circumscription (the interpellation of landscapes and everyday lives within such engraved textual projects) were ways by which Armenian men and women with aspirations to princely power built political worlds for themselves and their subjects. Central to this exploration is thinking about the ways that inscribed spaces produce subjectivity, or how the cosmological properties of architecture shape "people" as always-already "publics." The aim in these discussions is to frame architectural spacetimes built in medieval places like Armenia as microcosms of the world spanned by medieval Silk Road culture, and to inquire how they mediated the scalar transforms between embodied princely selves and plural worlds of medieval dwelling.

The medieval Armenian placement of donation inscriptions on the walls of churches was a practice rooted in long tradition, whereby the beneficence of the princely donor ensured a reiterative practice in that space by the *katołikos* (patriarch), monks, and congregants; these repeated Masses and prayers were engendered by the reading of the inscription, and guaranteed the salvation of the donor's soul. Mxitar Goš's prescriptive argument within the law code, that kings and princes must build monasteries "not for the sake of any corporeal hope but rather for a spiritual one," speaks to the clerical awareness that such endowments were a significant source of worldly influence as embodiments of princely piety.[63] The practices undertaken by the medieval princes who were Goš's audience and patrons had long roots in highland tradition. Based on a collected corpus of Armenian inscriptions from the early medieval period (fifth through eighth centuries), Timothy Greenwood has demonstrated the coherence of the lexicon of epigraphic performances of power in the highlands.[64] The builders of churches and donators of outbuildings, bell towers, libraries, and martyria were concerned with defining themselves both in terms of worldly networks—that is, in relation to kin, kings, and bishops—as well as assuring their place within a vertical order of Christian piety. The inscriptions displayed the donor's concern that their gifts ensure the salvation of their soul, to be remembered in prayer by the worshippers who congregated and circulated in the spaces they had constructed, endowed, decorated, or renovated.

Building on Greenwood's analysis, Christina Maranci argues that the inscribed exteriors of churches and other buildings in the medieval Armenian highlands were not meant to be merely tacit markers of ownership or attribution, but were intended to be read and reread in repeated rituals that involved movement and the evocation of shared ecumenical landscapes.[65] This observation lends itself to the frequent medieval inscriptions which encircle churches in bands of writing, intended perhaps to be read during a liturgical circumambulation of the building, and also suggesting links to a broader medieval culture of decorating buildings, as well as human and nonhuman bodies, with bands of apotropaic text.[66] Medieval Armenian inscriptions thus indicate a community of practice, for which the concept of inscribing social power through the reading of carved stone and the movement of bodies through space was epistemologically not only sensible but sensuously pious. That is, the practice of reading political cosmography from inscribed and endowed places was part of embodied practice for medieval Armenian people in places like the Kasakh Valley, who conceived of themselves as situated within legible worlds of holy and human power which were nested reflections of one another.[67] The way these practitioners understood them, churches were machines built from words, stone, moving bodies, voices, scents, and objects, which worked to perpetuate the form of the social and spiritual cosmos.

I have discussed at length the idea of the Silk Road as a spacetime that has been written into being as much as lived, encountered, or constructed. At the local scale, Armenians in the Middle Ages also produced inscribed landscapes, both in historical texts and in a complex material-literary mode of writing about place *in places*. The inscribed landscape we can reconstruct from distributed, overlapping, and differentially legible inscriptions is a story told by medieval Armenians about themselves in stones and in the spaces between them. These are not the same as the stories contained in documentary histories (which have their own material and spatial properties). Think about the texts located in mountain valleys, above busy market squares, above the plastered halls of churches that bloomed with incense smoke and glowed with candles, ringing with the sounds of Mass. Other inscriptions were traced by the fingers of travelers as they passed through the low doors of caravanserais, having paid their fee to get out of the snow or heat and into a shelter for themselves and their pack animals.

The architectural inscriptions of princes in post-Seljuk Armenia demonstrate the efforts of people to situate themselves as political actors within worlds of their own making—and worlds which included not only the intimate details of everyday life in the valleys of Aragatsotn, Shirak, Ararat, Lori, and Vayots Dzor, but also a world of influence, taste, and power that stretched as far as quasi-mythical places like Venice or the Mongol court. These worlds of power contained not only the usual suspects of medieval history—priests, kings, and princes—but also a whole cast of characters, spaces, and material things, all of which were assembled together and circumscribed as a world on the wall of a building. The quintessential, and most studied, Armenian example of this practice of epigraphic world making is the case of the merchant prince Tigran Honenc', who endowed buildings and left his mark in inscriptions around the medieval capital of Ani. Tigran Honenc' is exemplary of the *mecatun išxanner*, the group of princes (or men and women who aspired to princeliness) in the thirteenth through fifteenth centuries who staked the claim of their political power in worlds that they set in motion, and commemorated in text and stone.[68] Nikolai Marr, who uncovered many of the prince's inscriptions on fallen blocks and walls at Ani, called Honenc' one of the most brilliant representatives of his medieval world of trade.[69] In the year 1215, Honenc' dedicated the church and monastery of St. Gregory the Illuminator (Sourb Grigor Lusavorich), overlooking the Akhurean River. The entire south wall of the church is covered with an inscription framed by blind arcades, and carved flowers and birds. As you read the inscription, translated here, notice the variety of human and nonhuman agents drawn into Honenc''s inscribed world:

> In the year 664 (1215) by the grace and mercy of God,[70] at the time of the rule in the city of Ani of the *amir-spasalar* and *mandaturtuxuces* Zak'aria and his son Šahnšah, I Tigran, servant of God, son of Suleyma Smbatawrenc', of the family of Honenc', for the long life of my lords and their sons built the monastery of St. Gregory, which was formerly called "Mother of God of the Chapel," on a rocky spot with precipices and covered with thorns, bought by me from the owners with honestly acquired means to its hereditary owners and with great labor and cost I surrounded it with a rampart. I constructed this church in the name of saint Gregory the Illuminator and I decorated it with all kinds of ornament, with Signs of the Savior and with holy crosses of gold and silver and decorative images, ornamented with gold, silver, precious stones and pearls, as well as with gold and silver lamps and with relics of the saintly apostles, with a fragment of the divine and lord-receiving cross, and all kinds of precious vessels of gold and silver and various ornament. I built all sorts of apartments for the monks and princes and I placed there priests who offer the body and the blood of Christ such that the mass is offered without fail in order to prolong the life of my lord Šahnšah and of his son and for the forgiveness of my sins. And I have given in gift to the monastery of St. Gregory the hayrenik,[71] which I have bought in cash paid to their owners and so thus assembled: half the village of Gawrohonik, 5 dangs of K'arhat,[72] half of the village of Mšakunik, half of the village of Kałatk, the whole of the village of Šamaksov, the village of Xuzac-Mahmund in the land of Kars, two dangs of the village of Šund, fields and the pandok [inn or caravanserai] of Xač'orik. Of properties in the city the baths and the public fountain, the local hotel with its shops and the vaulted-roof pandok, the barn behind the baths, the stables of Ter Sargis and the barn which I bought, the threshing floor and the income from two oil-pressing mills, the stables and barns of the monastery, the garden which is in front of the gates of the monastery and the slopes from the Glijor Gate until the river, as well as the riverbanks, the garden that I bought at the Dvin Gate, half of a milling from the mill, all of [the revenue from] a fish trap, and two days a week [the revenue from] another fish trap, from the Glijor mill two days a week [the revenue] from a fish trap, between Besk'enakap until the bridge I bought a half of the river; four dangs of the hostelry of Papenc' and the shop which is at its door, all of the houses on the Street of Hatec'ik, all of the fields bought at the gates to the city, a vinery in Yerevan and one in Ošakan, a garden in Koš and one in Aruč, in a place called Mazot, one garden in Mren, in Tsmak, that called "the field of the katołikos." All the goods which I have bought, as well as the many others which are in mortgage which I have not inscribed here, I have given them to the monastery and their owners may reclaim them, as I have written in another will, if they pay in gold to the monastery.[73]

The inscription juxtaposes scales in fascinating ways. As he enumerates the properties and objects that he has endowed to the monastery, either as gifts or as sources of income, Honencʻ moves from the sacred (the vestments of priests, bodies of saints, and the body and blood of Christ offered as sacrament during Mass) to the apparently prosaic (fish traps, oil presses). Honencʻ's "matters of care" include single objects which are themselves spatiotemporally complex,[74] such as relics or fragments of holy bodies, and a piece of the true cross, which is directly indexical to the body and power of Christ, as well as to the place of crucifixion in the Holy Land. While inscriptions tend to be regarded as evental or temporally flat (the date of their commemoration), the temporality of this inscription is expansive and complex. The timespans with which Tigran Honencʻ concerns himself, which he collects within the assemblage of his influence, include the daily routines of monastics as well as of farmers and shopkeepers, innkeepers, and hostlers. He bestows two days in the flow of a river through fishtraps, the growing seasons of vines, fruit, and other crops, and the everyday activities as well as the life-courses of villagers.[75] Honencʻ donates not just from wealth, but from his care for cyclical times—of seasons, of masses, of festivals and daily prayers—as well as slices of transient time: nights spent by travelers in the pandok of Xačʻorik. These diverse timelines are bracketed by the lifespans of Honencʻ's Zakʻaryan benefactors (Šahnšah and his son), as well as by the afterlife of Honencʻ's own immortal soul, the beneficiary of prayers, Masses, and monastic commemoration. This example demonstrates that the practice of epigraphic donation overall complicates oppositions between the spacetimes of local and global, and between the cyclical everyday, the eternal, and the historical.

Buildings/Bodies/Worlds

Honencʻ's inscription works as a world in miniature: he seems to think of, to care for, everything necessary for the perpetual life of the monastery he endowed. But there is more going on here as well, tied up in medieval Armenian ideas about cosmology and architecture. Within medieval Armenian (and broader Anatolian) religious cosmologies, the nature of reality was symbolic, and nested. The human soul was believed to be eternal and yet contained within the body; likewise, the body was a cosmological monad, a microcosm or miniature version of an enclosed, finite, and perfect world.[76] Buildings like churches were also thought to be microcosmic, oriented in the path of the sun so as to stand in for the world in miniature, and enclosing the congregants assembled inside as a symbolic representation of a complete ecumene. The microcosmic symbolism of bodies and buildings could thus slip between each other, such that the self is thought of as a house for the soul, and buildings as extensions of selves. In other words, the metaphorical concept of "my body is a temple" was more than a figure of speech in medieval Armenia. This is vividly illustrated in the deployment in Armenian (and broader Caucasian) architecture of a Byzantine technique of donor portraiture.[77] On church walls across Armenia, from the late twelfth into the fourteenth centuries, donors were physically represented as carved stone miniatures, holding in their hands a miniature model of the church they had donated (and upon which they were depicted). These architectural *mises-en-abyme* enable a fascinating visual and corporal nesting of metaphorical scales, between the church model, the modeled self, and the church—which, by suggested analogy, the viewer is invited to imagine resting in the cosmologically scaled grasp of embodied princely piety and power.

This slippage between selves, bodies, and built spaces is especially relevant to the case of Tigran Honenc''s church at Ani. Mattia Guidetti has pointed out the linkages between the decorative motifs on the exterior and interior of St. Gregory's church and the broader material world of early thirteenth-century eastern Anatolia and the Caucasus. In addition to ties between the relief decoration and styles found on ceramics in the same period, Guidetti observed that the interior of the church is decorated in motifs drawn from Persian textiles.[78] In particular, I am drawn to the encircled *senmurvs*, winged creatures with canine heads, above the southern pastaphorion entrance. As has been explored by Hakobyan and Mikayelyan, such creatures were a popular motif in Sasanian and Islamic textiles, as well as being common in Armenian art, both illuminations of princely garments and architectural sculpture adorning the "fabric" of churches (see figs. 5 and 6).[79]

The art historian Eva Hoffman has demonstrated the mobile cultures which influenced medieval craftspeople, discussing the way that images and decorative motifs spread across portable things like ceramics, metal wares, and wooden objects, architectural decoration, and bodily adornments like textiles.[80] Silk textiles were not only one of the most portable of medieval luxuries, they were also tied closely to royal or noble bodily identity. This medieval idea of a recognizable and desirable powerful body is part of the shared lexicon of ideas about the world, and of the action of humans within it, which tied together diverse communities and cultures within a Silk Road world. As Thomas Allsen has explored in detail, clothing and cloth were critical technologies in the making of powerful people, and of worlds of power within and overlapping with the Mongol sphere.[81] The medieval Eurasian political economy of clothing—and in particular, of silken gowns and robes—was central in solidifying relationships between Mongols and their subjects; however, it was not as such invented by the Mongols. Lynn Jones has reviewed in detail the role played by textiles in fashioning common political worlds at the Caucasus frontier earlier in the medieval period, specifically in the constitution of Armenian Bagratuni authority.[82] In particular, the ceremonial bestowing of robes wrought with gold (literal investiture) functioned to situate Armenian kings as vassals of the Abbasid caliphate.[83] Jones notes that the crowning of Gagik Artsruni as a king of Armenia was accompanied by a gift of embroidered robes from al-Muqtadir, the caliph of Baghdad. It is thus no coincidence that Gagik is in turn represented wearing elaborate robes figured with roundels on the walls of his renowned reconstructed church at Aghtamar.[84] In this depiction

FIGURE 5. A panel of marvelous animal designs enclosed in crimson roundels above the entrance to the southern pastophorion of the church of St. Gregory at Ani. Photo credit: Ioanna Rapti, Crossing Frontiers Project at the Courtauld Institute of Art.

(one of multiple portraits), Gagik stands draped in silk, holding a model of the church; this portrait is part of a larger bas-relief decorative program which in turn clothes the church at Aghtamar in vegetal and figural designs. Jones further noted that the use of robes to transform a man into a king was adopted by the Bagratuni for their own ceremonies, thus constructing a local world of power in parallel; significantly, this second investiture took place within a church.[85]

Returning to the thirteenth century, the fact that Tigran Honencʻs cathedral is "dressed" in the same way that he himself would have dressed (or aspired to be dressed) is an intimate allegorical link between the microcosmic space of the church and the spacetime of Honencʻs powerful body.[86] These cosmological links between souls, bodies, and worlds are important when we look more closely at the process of epigraphic inscription and architecture as world-making. Epigraphic inscriptions demonstrate the ability of medieval actors to draw spaces, people,

FIGURE 6. A Cilician Armenian medieval illumination from 1260 (Jerusalem MS 2660), showing King Levon and Queen Keran in silk robes with designs of lions and sirens. Note especially the roundels and rampant lions on the king's robe. WikiCommons Open License.

animals, objects, and landscapes into the spatial performance of their embodied efficacy. The version of a prince like Tigran Honenc' that we encounter on the wall of St. Gregory's (which we must read, our back to the rushing Akhurean, our neck craning to make out the words) is a sum total of the assemblage of things he had under his control. The fact that these things included the very prosaic (fish traps, stables), the exotic (wealth from long distance trade, the future embodied actions of priests) and the mystical (the body and blood of the Savior) is a testament to the encompassing nature of Honenc's political world and the detailed, even loving attention of his princely care. Because this encompassing political world is assembled upon the building endowed (materialized or given body) by Honenc', the assemblage along with the building itself takes on a unity with the embodied self of the merchant prince. Tigran Honenc' *is* his endowment, *is* his assembled and donated world. The St. Gregory monastery of Tigran Honenc' at Ani is therefore a compound body, which is further compounded by the palimpsest of inscriptions layered upon it, that extend and permutate the embodied power of the original builder. A 1251 inscription on Tigran Honenc's church was commissioned by a couple who described how "in the time of the Tatars" (after the Mongol invasion, under the Ilkhanid administration) they donated their familial storefront (*kułpak*), in the street of the shoemakers adjacent to the church.[87] On the same church a similar inscription describes the bestowal of a stall in the street of the smiths (*i darbno p'ołoc'in*). As hopeful people continued to carve their gifts into the walls of Honenc''s church, they appended their embodied selves, and the fabric of the city, to his corporeal power. Considered this way, politics in medieval Armenia is a strange but also fascinating cyborg of humans, animals, spaces, times, objects, labors, and words grafted onto each other through construction, endowment, and daily practice.

Over the course of this chapter, I have moved from the place of medieval Armenia as literarily and materially constructed by travelers, historians, and archaeologists, to the nested worlds constructed from words and stone (as well as assembled spaces, peoples, and things) by high medieval Armenian princes. One thing this span of discussion has suggested is the importance of scale for thinking about the question of how to make worlds, and how to live in them. This question in turn has implications for how we think about cosmopolitanism, the situation of self in relation to a world. Over the twentieth century, Armenia was written and materially reconstructed as a series of spacetimes with particular properties. It was evoked as a timeless land of national tradition, an engine of social transformation centered in medieval cities, a heroic landscape of princely exploits. By looking more closely at this last spacetime, I reflected on how princely power in medieval Armenian was intensely invested in the making of worlds for others to live in. Unlike the worlds reconstructed by Marxist historians, these inscribed, architectural worlds were complex and themselves multiscalar in time and space, framed by the span of a human body and spanning a whole cultural universe. This capacity of made worlds to collapse and expand, to enclose and reorient time and space will be further developed in the next chapter, situated in the Kasakh Valley.

4

<hr>

Making and Remaking the World
of the Kasakh Valley

Two or three days' travel on horseback eastward from the medieval site of Ani, the Kasakh River Valley runs north to south, following the curve of the eastern flank of the broad volcanic cone of Mount Aragats. The eastern margin of the valley is defined by the sweep of the granitic Tsaghkunyats range, punctuated at its southern end by the smaller volcanic peak of Arai Ler (Mount Ara). Just south of the mountain shoulder occupied by the medieval sites of Uši, Hovhannavank', and Sałmosavank', the highland drops off sharply into the broad plain of the Araxes River: near the edge of the plateau the Kasakh River becomes deeply incised in a precipitous canyon, just north of Arai Ler. Its steady change in elevation from south to north makes the Kasakh Valley a climatic transition zone, with the lower reaches currently covered by dense fruit orchards and the northern extent transitioning to fodder and grain farming, as well as pasture, toward the town of Aparan. The flanks of Mount Aragats and the Tsaghkunyats are marked by remains of seasonal pastoralist campsites, from villagers and groups of Yezidi Kurds moving their flocks, herds, and horses (as well as trucks and campers) between the lower and upper slopes (see fig. 7).

In this chapter I will think at the scale of the Kasakh Valley, at the small world of fields, roads, rivers, and towns framed by mountain passes and peaks. This framing is somewhat arbitrary. During the twelfth to fourteenth centuries, the Kasakh was part of a much larger administrative territory, which incorporated towns and villages in Shirak to the west as well as Lori to the north. As the materials and texts discussed in this book repeatedly demonstrate, people in the valleys of Armenia also participated (with greater or lesser degrees of agency and awareness) in global cultures and worlds of desire and distinction. My decision to situate the "local" scales of this discussion in the span of a single river valley is, however, also rooted within longer, twentieth-century habits of categorization, of thinking about this

FIGURE 7. A view of the Kasakh Valley from among the ruins of the Arai-Bazarǰuł caravanserai. Photo by the author.

place as a geographic unit, as a landscape. I want to think about the Kasakh Valley as a place constructed by the rhythms of medieval lives, and also by a century of geographical and archaeological practice in Soviet and modern Armenia. I will explore how the place that we call the Kasakh Valley was made with apparatuses of scientific knowledge, through storytelling, through writing of various kinds. One aim is to think about the intersections of landscape archaeology, cartography, and epigraphy as a way of bringing a medieval landscape into being. Another is to materialize the Kasakh Valley as a landscape constructed in the modern as well as medieval periods, as a participant in overlapping world-makings rather than as the setting or backdrop within or against which human beings carried out their projects. As discussed in chapter 1, cosmopolitanism as a universalizing Enlightenment virtue struggles to make space for difference, or to account for the ways that more ordinary people experience difference in their daily lives. My ultimate aim is to materialize the Kasakh as something more than the "local" to the Silk Road's "global," to think about the landscape that frames everyday lives, and the complex scales of memory, mobility, and imagination, as well as situated "views of the transcendent."[1] This requires thinking about the Kasakh as a landscape in the way it has been envisioned and mattered as a scale of cultural imagining—

as Barbara Bender's "time materializing,"[2] or Kathleen Stewart's "proliferation of signs written tentatively or persistently."[3] Methodologically, it requires framing the Kasakh Valley as a place made through intersecting projects of dwelling in the medieval period, and various techniques of research in the recent past and present.

Survey is the primary methodology associated with landscape archaeology, a branch of the discipline which engages past human practices at the scale of *landscape*—an amorphous category that voraciously incorporates *environment, nature, space, architecture, infrastructure, ecology,* and other frameworks for thinking about human physical and imaginary *senses of place.*[4] My own orientation focuses on landscape archaeology's strengths with spacetime, for thinking about human life at complex and multiple spatiotemporal scales. Explicitly making scale a problem is important for attempting to think beyond the patterns of visible monumentality and architectural "authorship." Likewise, thinking in terms of nested and overlapping landscapes conceptually links all the places within this book: moving human and nonhuman bodies, monumental buildings, villages, imagined places, tangible and/or tasty materialities. On a practical level, survey encourages thinking about the past while literally in motion, driving and walking across changing topographies; though not all landscape archaeologists would admit it, published accounts of surveys record the artifacts of bodily experiences of landscape.

To write the Kasakh Valley as a landscape means not just to tell the history of this place, but to reflect on the ways that such a place has been rebuilt, renamed, razed, and reinhabited in material fact and in scientific knowledge—and how all of these versions of place are layered within any earnest history of the valley and the people dwelling in and with it. In the medieval period the Kasakh was part of a broader region referred to as the province of Nig, with the same name being applied to the town now called Aparan. The name of the town changed multiple times over the early modern period, until the 1930s when it was changed again from Kasał to Aparan. In a similar manner, the villages of the Kasakh valley (and indeed all Armenia) were renamed multiple times in the course of their history, usually with the last renaming occurring in the period after the dissolution of the Soviet Union.[5] The landscape of Nig-Aparan was researched in terms of its archaeological and architectural features in the early part of the twentieth century by a team led by the architect and archaeologist T'oros T'oramanyan, while individual buildings were studied by multiple archaeologists and historians, and continued to make major contributions to the study of Armenian history and prehistory.[6]

The archaeological surveys led by T'oramanyan provided the foundation for a generation of publications and further research, not least by generating an archive of photographs of inscriptions, buildings and sites.[7] T'oramanyan's *Materials for Armenian Architectural History* is a two-volume compendium; the first volume presents a general history of Armenian architecture, with a central focus on Ani and early medieval churches. For the present discussion I will focus on the second volume, which includes a brief but significant essay on the origins and development

FIGURE 8. The *gavit* of Astvacnkal, facing the door into the main church. Note the muqarnas vaulting of the *gavit*. T'oromanyan archive: figure used with the permission of the Service for the Protection of Historical Environment and Cultural Museum-Reservations SNCO.

of Armenian architecture including the church form,[8] in addition to a case-by-case discussion of Armenian monuments. The main part of this latter section takes the form of a survey of the country, divided into "travel notebooks" (*čambordakan c'ogatetr*). The fourth of these covers the trip "from Ejmiatsin toward the slopes of Aragats,"[9] containing a technical account of the standing medieval remains from village to village up this road, recorded in terms of their degree of preservation, with sketch plans of their architecture, and exemplary photographs (see fig. 8).

These images are themselves evocative records of the survey as part of a broader history of regime consolidation and the construction of a cultural past. The majority of the images are remarkable to a modern archaeological gaze, in that people are visible (archaeologists tend to crop people out of "scientific" images), standing in front of and upon the medieval buildings. A whole troupe of schoolchildren sits cross-legged and grinning within a ruined *gavit* at Marmašen;[10] village men in cloaks and fleece hats perch atop the remains of the fifth-century basilica church in Aparan (called Kasał at that time). An image of the church at Tełer, endowed in 1232 by Mamaxatun Vač'utyan, shows two shadowy figures seated within the decorated doorway; one of them holds a sketchbook open on their lap. The T'oramanyan photos preserve a way of living with the medieval architectural past which is increasingly hard to find in Armenia, as a result of Soviet projects of renovation and monumentalization which transformed ruins into landmarks—as well as the revival of Christian practice in the last thirty years which has further brought medieval churches out of the ruined past and into contemporary use. In a broad shot of the church of Astvacnkal we see the ruined church and *gavit* (now collapsed) in the background, surrounded by a wall of fieldstones; in the foreground, greenery covers ruined walls. To the left of these, a woman peers away from us and waves around the corner of a house, her head in shadow; behind her, a small child is blurred by movement. Above the lintel of the house we can barely make out the trace of carved decoration, suggesting that the house (like many in Armenia) is constructed from medieval spolia. This house no longer exists: the population of Astvacnkal was removed to Yerevan in the 1950s, founding a neighborhood on the northern edge of the city called Kasax.[11] Despite active projects of reconstruction, the T'oramanyan survey recorded traces of buildings which no longer stand, and which are especially visible in the clear original photo prints. One of these shows a man sitting on the steps leading from the *gavit* into the church at Astvacnkal (fig. 8); above him arches the original thirteenth century ceiling, now collapsed. But we can see in this photograph that the ceiling was configured in delicate muqarnas, or carved stone canopies formed from complex, interlocking geometrical shapes.[12] T'oramanyan's text, like most archaeological survey reports, is a bound spacetime, containing spaces, landscapes, and ways of dwelling, frozen in the time of writing. The details T'oramanyan recorded are precious—for instance, T'oramanyan records a now lost inscription from the caravanserai south of Arai village, dating that building to the year 1213. Throughout my analysis I rely on this date provided by T'oramanyan, and I am aware that my own archaeological and historical world-making builds on this trace-within-a-trace, a landmark in a written world that is lost from the "real" landscape.

In 1988 V.M. Petrosyanc' took up the task of compiling a total history of the ancient and medieval monuments in Nig-Aparan, for the first time "systematically organizing the history of Nig-Aparan on the basis of textual and epigraphic evidence."[13] The introduction to Petrosyanc''s work effectively demonstrates the issues of authorship, visibility, and historical agency that I discussed earlier. Successive rulers and political figures were assessed based on their ability to contribute to the "text" that Petrosyanc' was himself editing: the legible historical-architectural (*patmačartarapetakan*) landscape of the broader Kasakh region. Petrosyanc' began his history, predictably, with the first named subjects of history in the Kasakh: the Gntuni princely dynasty, which administered the territory from the first century till the tenth century, when they were noted among the vassal princes of the Bagratuni. From the mid-tenth through the late twelfth centuries Nig-Aparan was under the control of a succession of Turkic groups; first the Sheddadids and Delmiks (a group from what is now Iran), followed by the eleventh-century Seljuk conquest. Interestingly, Petrosyanc' dismisses this period, saying of the Pahlavuni and their followers: "unlike the Gntuni, during the near century of their reign[s], they did not undertake a single architectural construction."[14] From the perspective of Petrosyanc''s late-twentieth-century archaeology, the presence of these groups in the Kasakh Valley was disciplinarily invisible. This pattern was, of course, completely reversed after the Zak'arid conquest of the valley in the late twelfth century, and the installation of the Vač'utyans in the early years of the thirteenth.

The Vač'utyans were among the largest and most influential of the Armenian feudal houses subject to the Zak'aryans. The founder of the house was Vač'e (pronounced *vah-che*), son of Sargis Vač'utyan; Vač'e was described by the historian Levon Babayan as one of the "pillars" of Zak'arid rule.[15] Like Tigran Honenc', Vač'e Vač'utyan appeared as a princely historical figure in the early part of the thirteenth century, as the landscape of power shifted in the highlands. In return for valiant service in the wars of the Zak'aryans against the Seljuks, Vač'e was rewarded with the governance of territories and also with the title "prince of princes" (*išxanac' išxan*). Vač'e and his successors liberally deployed this honorific in dedicatory inscriptions on their building projects, including renovations and new constructions from the canyons of Alaverdi in the north to the southern Kasakh Valley. While Vač'e's most famous reconstruction projects are the monasteries of Hałpat and Sanahin (now registered as UNESCO World Heritage Sites), I am most interested in his—and his wife and childrens'—campaigns in the Kasakh Valley. The works of the Vač'utyans in Aragatsotn include the rebuilding of early Christian (ca. fifth century) churches and the expansion of monastic endowments, including the sites of Astvacnkal, Tełer, Uši, Sałmosavank', and Hovhannavank'. Also probably included in this group is the church complex at Mravyan (Yełipatruš), located at the far eastern extent of the valley in the Tsaghkunyats foothills. Petrosyanc' dated the later church (about a hundred meters west of the fifth-century chapel) to the early thirteenth century based on its formal similarity to Tełer.[16] The reconstructive strategies of the Vač'utyans entailed making their mark on architectural monuments built by others, perhaps most famously illustrated at Sanahin and Hałpat; however, this strategy is also visible at the edge of the Kasakh Valley at the site of Tełenyac', where Vač'e and Mamaxatun recorded donations to the church endowed a few years earlier by another vassal of the Zak'arids, Vahram Č'avuš.[17] This array of sites line the slopes of Aragats and the Tsaghkunyats and the canyon rim and floor of the Kasakh River, between the medieval towns of Ashtarak and Aparan (see maps 3 and 4).

The monumental constructions and epigraphic traces of the Vač'utyans were dutifully recorded by Petrosyanc', producing a built geography of the broader district of the Kasakh Valley (Nig Aparan in Petrosyanc''s pamphlet also includes the Tsaghkahovit Plain to the north of Mount Aragats).[18] Petrosyanc''s monumental geography is divided according to nearest village, a technique used by both Soviet and modern Armenian administrators to organize records of archaeological sites. In fact, Petrosyanc''s pamphlet reads as an expanded version of the Monuments List maintained by the Ministry of Culture since the Soviet period.[19] For each of the villages located along the rim and across the valley floor, he listed prehistoric (fortresses and "tombfields") and medieval sites. Remains of the medieval period are predominated by forts and churches, each of which is given a sketch plan along with their attached buildings: *gavits* (narthexes), side chapels, bell towers. These monumental structures stand out, the hard bones of medieval built landscape poking through the soil, marking the location of larger medieval places destroyed over time or buried beneath.

The lauded architectural exploits of the Vač'utyans only end in the fourteenth century, once the territories of Armenia were reconfigured under Mongol, Persian, and Turkoman rule and the Vač'utyans and their fellow dynasts "were removed from the stage of history."[20] This idea, that landscape is built in the same register as history is written, has shaped archaeological approaches to the Middle Ages in Armenia, and has shaped what has been thought possible to say about what happened during this period. The idea also reinforces the elite authorship-focused understanding of practices that I framed as epigraphic world-building in the last chapter. Let me further complicate this relationship between authorship and the making of landscape, specifically in the context of my own construction of the Kasakh Valley through archaeological surveys.

RECONSTRUCTING THE MEDIEVAL KASAKH THROUGH ARCHAEOLOGICAL SURVEY

In 2009 and 2010 I carried out exploratory survey in the southern upland section of the Kasakh Valley, between the modern villages of Kuchak and Apnagyugh.[21] This work consisted of a combination of survey techniques, both "nonsystematic" exploration of villages and a series of systematic fieldwalking surveys across selected sections of the landscape. Nonsystematic or nodal survey is infrequently discussed by archaeologists, perhaps because it represents a point in research when we are least certain, and most dependent on the help and hospitality of local people. In other words, it is when archaeologists least feel like they are "discovering" something. This practice of survey requires driving or walking into a village and trying to locate buildings, complexes, or sometimes single stones through triangulations of management documents, publications, and the (usually) helpful advice of local passersby.

Fieldwalking survey is a particular archaeological technique, designed to pull patterns of past human activity out of the fields, forests, and hill slopes between highly visible archaeological sites like castles, churches, fortresses, or other standing architecture. In addition to being crucial for detecting features beyond the site (roads, terraces, check-dams, corrals), survey can be especially useful for locating small settlements, which through combinations of time, natural processes, and human practices become masked to easy view. In landscapes subject to erosion— whether from rain, runoff, or human activities like road building or plowing—

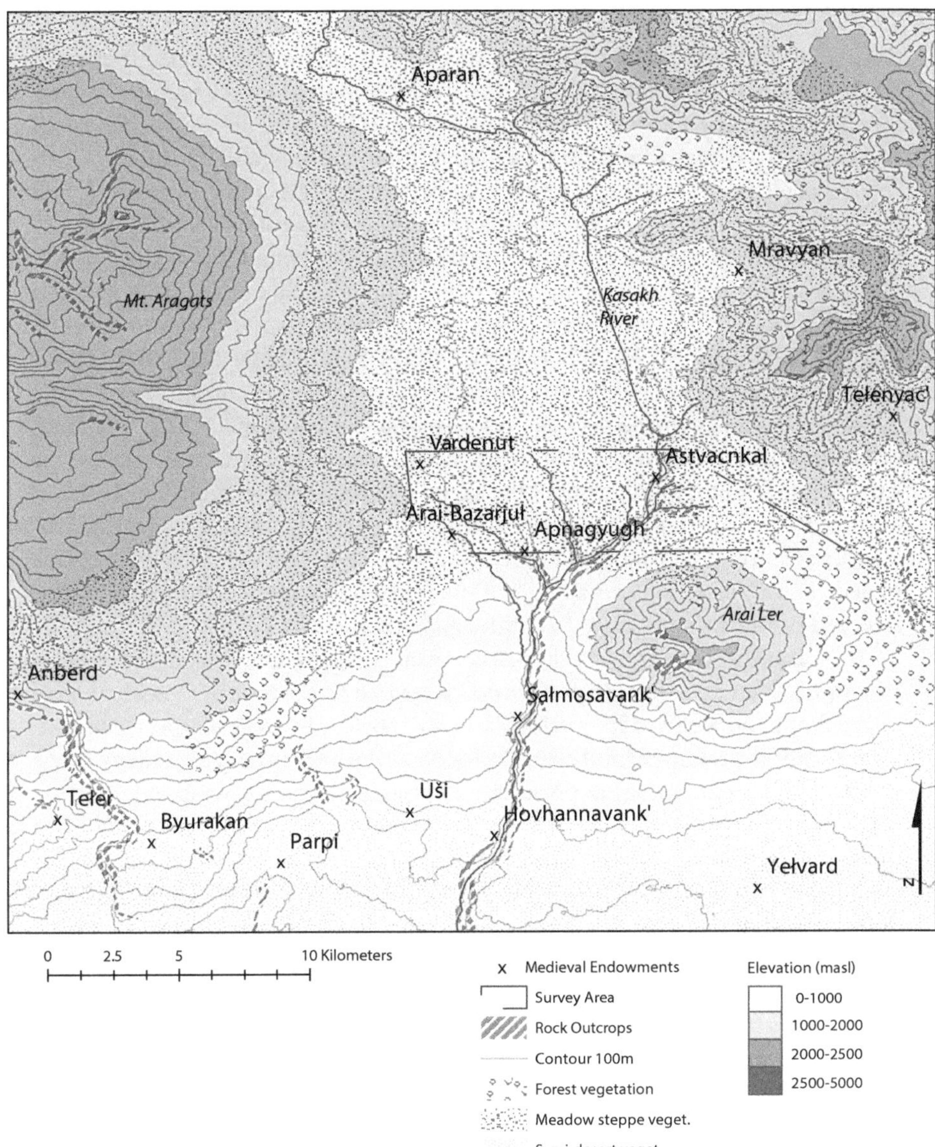

MAP 3. Contour map of the southern Kasakh Valley, with medieval places noted. Map created by the author.

archaeological artifacts, especially ceramic potsherds, can emerge and linger on the surface. A core task of archaeological survey is detecting patterns in the distribution of these artifacts, and in particular observing the higher densities which, in combination with other features, could indicate the presence of settlements or other sites beneath the soil.

These two interrelated forms of survey produce different kinds of overlapping data, and different spatial understandings of a medieval landscape. The world created through archaeological survey and represented in survey reports is therefore always already a palimpsest of multiple worlds based on these evidences, each of which is a balance of collaborative memories, inferences, and intuitions.

Archaeological survey is carried out in the hope that these detected and interpreted distributions will provide a counterpoint to patterns of visible monumentality or place names extracted from history or epigraphy—that they will ultimately help to tell a different or at least complementary story about life, and time, in a place. The central goal of my own systematic surveys was to generate material data about the Kasakh as a place in the high Middle Ages, to fill in the blanks between the sites that were known to archaeologists and listed in official documentation like the Soviet passport system or the Monuments List. The focus of our fieldwalking survey was therefore not discovery of "new" sites so much as a deliberate attempt to understand the social and temporal relationships between occupied places in a mountain landscape. The 2010 season of the Kasakh Valley survey covered ten square kilometers of the valley, recorded coordinate data, images, and observations for a range of site types, and collected more than twelve hundred ceramic sherds as well as lithics and other artifacts.

The ceramics collected on the survey were divided into two broad categories; those that had complete profiles and were of a size sufficient to analyze were selected out and assessed for attributes: color, fabric, production aspects, decoration. Part of the intent behind ceramic systematization was to date as many of the sherds found on the survey as possible, and thereby to provide temporal information for the human activity indicated by ruined settlements, cemeteries, and so on that we recorded in the sector. Using ceramic artifacts as a chronological indicator means that past human activity is perceived through the lens of ceramic production, use and deposition; this in turn means that the activities dated and spatially assessed by the following analysis are related to the use and reuse of certain kinds of storage, transport, cooking and eating vessels, and this suite of ceramic-based activities is used as an analytic stand-in for medieval daily life in general.

Ceramic materials were identified as falling within one of six chronological ranges,[22] based on synthesized information about medieval ceramic chronology in Armenia. A few key ware types were determined to be diagnostic of certain periods: for instance, fine, high-fired white-slipped white ware and white-slipped red ware were indicative of Medieval I, while red-slipped red ware cooking pots and table wares were diagnostic of High Medieval I. A few glazed examples fell into the High Medieval I category, primarily green-on-white monochrome sgraffito wares; the transition to the High Medieval II period is marked by decorated forms such as piecrust-applique decorated red ware bowls as well as glazed fritwares. A critical analytical issue is related both to the ceramic sample size from the survey and to the state of knowledge of medieval plainware (unglazed ceramics) chronology in Armenia, in that many formal plainware categories seem to cut across established chronological divisions (which have traditionally been built from typologies of exclusively decorated fineware forms).

Mapping the distribution and relative density of these ceramic finds shows that the recovery of ceramic materials within the survey area was not random, but significantly ($p < .05$) clustered around particular locales. Specifically, instances of clustering occurred around the high medieval Vardenut castle, in the canyon bottom at Apnagyugh, and on the edge of the valley south of Arai village at Ambroyi. I spatially plotted the results of the chronological ceramics analysis in an ArcMap GIS, yielding a series of map outputs which demonstrate both concentrations of ceramic deposit suggestive of occupation, as well as shifts in landscape occupation through time by people making and using pottery. These maps showed that settlement and activity was not randomly distributed, and that densities of activity shifted to different areas over time. In the High Medieval period, sites tend to cluster in a few location types. Rather than a consistent distribution of remains across the valley, materials were concentrated in two primary areas. The first of these areas consisted of the wide riverbanks where the Kasakh River and its primary tributary cut deeper into canyons. The second area of denser occupation is the low shoulder of Mount Aragats, in the undulations carved by streams running off the mountain between basaltic outcrops. We also recorded an area of high sherd density (dated later, into the Early Modern period) on the eastern rim of the Kasakh canyon, on the slopes of Arai Ler north of a modern *dacha* village. Settlement during the medieval period was not (according to the ceramic data) located in the middle of the exposed Kasakh Valley, but rather demonstrated a regard for relatively sheltered, well-watered sites. Many contemporary villages persist on or near the sites of medieval settlements, though the patterns of abandonment and occupation also indicate shifts in land use and social relationships since the medieval period—specifically, into regional administrative centers like Kuchak and Aparan, nearer to the modern highway connecting Yerevan with the north.

Patterns in ceramic distribution assessed over time suggest that sites which were occupied earlier in the medieval period continued in use in the High Medieval period. Furthermore, diachronic shifts in ceramic distributions and quantities indicate an increase in activity during the High Medieval period, concentrated on in the central and western sectors of the survey quadrant. The chronologically differentiated distributions demonstrate that Early Medieval and Medieval I material was more sparsely and widely distributed over eastern and western areas of the survey sector. The High Medieval period into the Early Modern period shows, in contrast, a strong concentration of material in the western sector, around Vardenut and Ambroyi settlements, as well as near the site of Apnagyugh. This distribution suggests a link between the settlement of villagers in the western section of the valley and the construction projects of the Vačʻutyan princes in the thirteenth century—many of which were supported by personnel and materials from those villages. The patterns of the data also suggest that currently isolated clusters of contemporary material such as Vardenut, Ambroyi and Apnagyugh

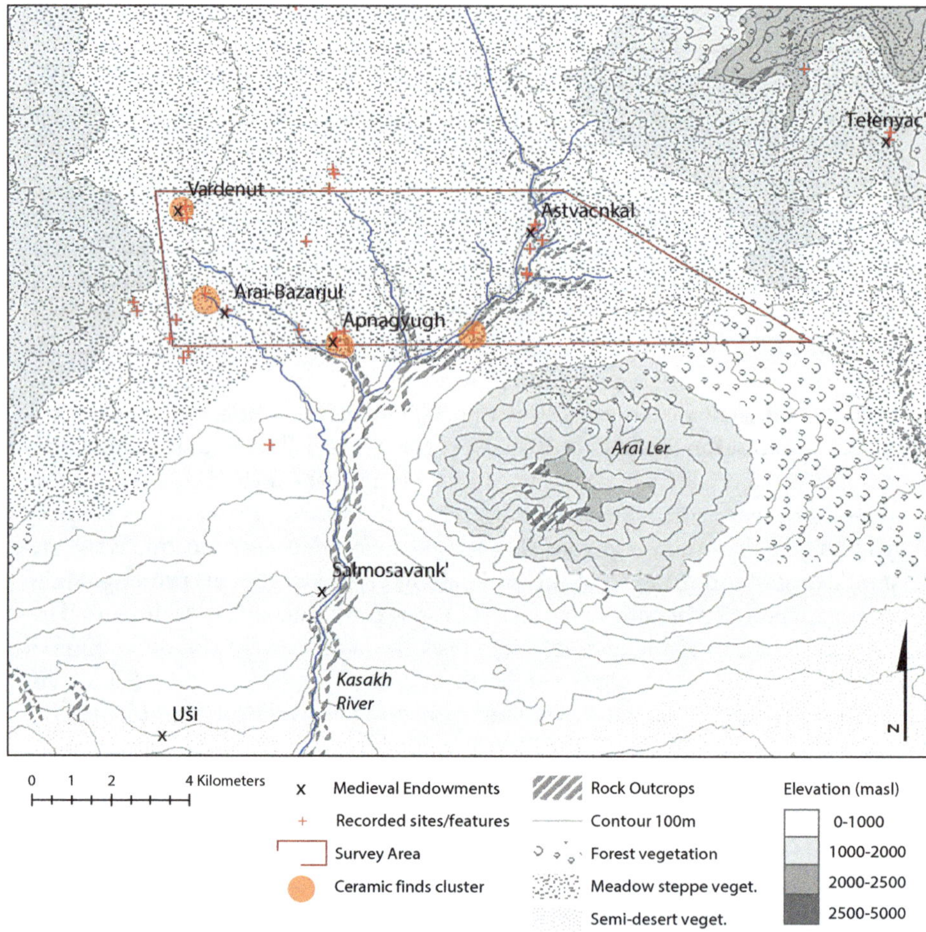

MAP 4. A closer view of the survey area, showing high-high sherd cluster points (orange). These indicate points of high density within the collection of ceramic materials within the surveyed area. Map created by the author.

were during the medieval period a more continuous area of settlement, cultivation, husbandry, church, cemetery, and caravanserai. This is a critical thing to remember: that inhabitants of the Kasakh and travelers through it, like their modern counterparts, lived in a knit-together landscape in which ruined forts, fields of mounds, villages, bridges, and churches were all legible parts of a cohesive world. And ceramic scatters in themselves do not show us straightforward evidence for a whole range of medieval daily life, including herding, hunting, and, of course, travel. In fact, recent continuing research in the Kasakh by my friends and colleagues has recorded medieval and early modern (thirteenth through nineteenth centuries) settlements high on the slopes of Mount Aragats;[23] future material and spatial analysis may further expand the medieval world in these valleys.

The relationship between patches of sherd density and the more widely ranging practices of medieval life raises an issue of archaeological evidence, and of the processes by which patterns on the ground are "read" as patterns of life in the past. This legibility of landscape is summed up in the frequently invoked archaeological metaphor of the *palimpsest:* landscapes which have been inhabited and reinhabited through time are thought of as medieval vellum manuscript pages that have been written on, scraped, and rewritten, resulting in a layering of texts, traces, and erasures.[24] To imagine archaeological landscapes as palimpsests requires us to think about practices of reuse that alter or destroy previous patterns even as they produce new ones. This is especially relevant to the material patterns recovered in the Kasakh Valley which, like many agrarian zones of the South Caucasus, were aggressively transformed during the Soviet era in a process called *meliorizatsiya* or landscape amelioration. The drastic results of amelioration, combined with the heavy alluviation of such damaged mountain surfaces, frustrates techniques of archaeological survey developed in the plowed fields of the Mediterranean.[25] We encountered the effects of amelioration in the Kasakh as strange patterns of ceramic distribution and stark sculpted contours of hillsides and fields. As we recorded fields which had been scraped bare, leaving a curving berm of rubble and medieval artifacts like an arched eyebrow on the edge, we learned firsthand how to interpret the history of a violently altered landscape. My survey record of the medieval Kasakh thus includes "ghost sites," such as a village of unknown size that would have been located south of Hartavan near the edge of the river gorge. Luckily, the high medieval village of Ambroyi–Hin Bazarǰuł, located south of the modern village of Arai-Bazarǰuł, was only partially erased by ameliorations. A section of preserved, buried rooms remains from an original village which would have probably extended as far as the medieval road and the *karavanatun* or caravan inn.

From Surface Assemblage to Assembled Medieval World

This review of archaeological survey provides a complementary narrative to the images of the Kasakh Valley presented in textual sources like those written by T'oramanyan and Petrosyancʻ. The village sites and concentrations of material culture demonstrate the world of activity and daily life which was the necessary context for practices of architectural and epigraphic world building undertaken by powerful Armenians during the high Middle Ages. In the medieval period, the southern Kasakh Valley was located two- or three-days' journey east and north from Ani and participated in the shared worlds of imagined space and monumental spacetime laid out in the last chapter. As discussed in that chapter, Tigran Honencʻ of Ani was only one of a broad network of princes, princesses, emirs, and other officials in the Caucasus, Anatolia, and the eastern Mediterranean connected by imaginaries of power and social prowess, and by the shared cultural spacetimes of the Silk Road world. For the rest of this chapter I am going to focus on one dynastic house or family of these Armenian princely men and women, the Vačʻutyans. As discussed above, the Vačʻutyans loom large in the architectural and historical

FIGURE 9. The remaining bastion of the Vačʻutyan castle of Vardenik (now called Vardenut), photographed from atop the wall. Note the later medieval gravestones, and Arai Ler in the righthand background. Photo by the author.

memory of Aragatsotn, due to their prolific (re)construction projects and to the number of their dedicatory inscriptions. Traveling up the road from Ashtarak, the pass to the highlands is effectively overseen by the Vačʻutyan endowments of Hovhannavankʻ and Saɫmosavankʻ, both perched on the rim of the at-that-point dramatically encanyoned Kasakh River. The Vačʻutyans' construction projects were concerned with the gaze of travelers approaching the Kasakh Valley; their standing buildings are notable for their exceptional views over mountains and plains as much as for their commanding presence.[26] During the medieval period, the drum-shaped domes of the Vačʻutyan endowments would have punctuated the horizon as travelers passed up the valley, mirroring the grandeur of the peaks of Ararat and Arai Ler. Notably, as discussed above, these buildings frequently incorporated renovations of earlier structures which were multiple centuries old and perhaps ruined, but still culturally meaningful, at the opening of the thirteenth century. The Vačʻutyans' buildings therefore gazed across time as well as space, and were complex, compound spacetimes in themselves (see fig. 9).

One of Vačʻe Vačʻutyan's first known renovation projects in the Kasahh Valley was the reconstruction of a chapel and an endowment to the monastery of Uši, located on the southeastern shoulder of Mount Aragats. Uši is a shrine as well as a monastery, centered on the fourth-century relics of St. Sarkis (known as Sourb Sargis Zoravar or St. Sarkis the General), contained within a small chapel to the north of the main church. A martyr to Sasanian persecution, the presence of Sarkis's saintly bones situates Uši within the heroic spacetime of early Christianity. In his 1203 renovation inscription on the Uši chapel, Vač'e Vač'utyan described his pious donation to the monastery: "I Vač'e Vač'utyan, Prince of Princes, Son of Sargis, Governor of this land, by the edict of Ivane and Zak'are, adorned this church with the pyx (for) holy communion of silver and donated much other property,[27] including the garden of Dapaghent in Yerevan bought for my money (*dramagin*) and established a mass to be served regularly on Palm Sunday in all the churches to the glory of God and for the salvation of my soul. Dated 652 (1203)."[28] Note how, like Tigran Honenc' did in the last chapter, Vač'e begins his inscription by naming himself (and his father Sargis) and situating himself in relations of worldly power with his lords, Ivane and Zak'are Zak'aryan. Even though this is a much shorter inscription than that of Honenc', Vač'e still undertakes the same strategy of assembling, as he brings together places and practices (gardens, masses) as well as objects. Again like Honenc', Vač'e makes explicit the fact that he has purchased his donations with cash; in other words, he is grafting his prowess as a merchant onto his performance as a donor. This tactic works to circumscribe the world of trade relationships into the heroic spacetime of the Uši martyrion.

This practice of place-making is further exemplified by the Vač'utyans' donation invocations at the monastery complexes they renovated throughout their purchased province of Nig. In 1211 Vač'e built "at great cost" a *gavit* for the eleventh-century monastery of Sanahin, which is located on a rim of the Lori canyon to the northeast of the Kasakh Valley.[29] In two inscriptions on the walls of the *gavit*, Vač'e describes in this increasingly familiar language how he donated not only his "oath-space" (*uxt*: generally *covenant* but in this case the *gavit* or assembly hall) itself, but also the instruments (gold-bound gospels) for liturgy to be said every Saturday and Sunday in the name of himself and his wife, Mamaxatun.[30] The inscriptions denote Vač'e as the servant of the Zak'arids, and also invoke his father Sargis as well as his privileged relationship with the elders of the church, designated to intercede on behalf of his soul.

The epigraphic landscape of the Uši and Sanahin inscriptions overlaps with the world circumscribed in the inscription commemorating the Vač'utyan's renovations at the monasteries of Saɬmosavank' and Hovhannavank', situated on the rim of the Kasakh River gorge. According to tradition, the basilica church at Hovhannavank' was built in the fourth century by Gregory the Illuminator to house the relics of John the Baptist; the single-naved structure on the site is generally dated to the fifth century.[31] In 1217 Vač'e and Mamaxatun endowed a cruciform church attached to the earlier basilica, which they had rebuilt. Both churches were decorated with relief carvings of birds and intricate panels of geometric decoration; the bema of the main church especially is faced with a beautiful tracery of interlaced five-pointed stars (a similar pattern adorns the tympanum of the *gavit* at Sałmosavankʻ). Vačʻeʻs donation inscription on the north wall of the main church reads:

> 666 (1217). Created by the grace of God, in the established region, enlightened by the church, of Ayrarat in the hands of the two kin brothers Zakʻaria and Ivane, and by the just-born heirs of those same Šahnšah and Avag, I Vačʻe prince of princes, son of Sargis Vačʻutyan, beloved of him, with great honor and for my faithful service am I enabled as warden of the district. In union I am coupled together with my Mamaxatun for the holy [*uxt*/oath] of our St. Hovhannes, in laying a foundation with gifts and offerings and have built an illustrious new-built purgatorium. And may the leaders within the holy [oath] be sure in every month to say a Mass to Christ in my name, for the festival of Lazarus in every church, new and old. And for the pious Mamaxatun Mass shall be said to Christ in the old and new churches, until the coming of the Son of God. And he who shall not do so, let Christ judge him, Amen.[32]

The choice of words in these inscriptions is not incidental, but rather consciously refers to the pious *naxarar* traditions that the Vačʻutyans were attempting to renovate and reinhabit, even as they renovated buildings from earlier periods in Armeniaʻs Christian history and built them into new topographies of power. Christina Maranci has shown that the tradition of referring to an endowed church as an "oath" dates back to the seventh century in Armenia.[33] Maranciʻs approach to medieval church building is thus oriented around this idea of the church as an oath or covenant-in-stone, a way of tying the spatial down with the power of the textual. In referring back to the traditional concept of church-as-covenant, the Vačʻutyans were clearly staking a claim to the power embodied in the built heritage of the pre-Seljuk Armenian landscape. The idea of a building as an oath directly evokes the spacetime compressions proposed by Munn as inherent in hospitality or gift giving. The inscribed church extends the promise of good governance made by the donor forward in time, rooted in built space. But I am also interested in how the Vačʻutyans—and their contemporaries—incorporated this text into a political assemblage along with human bodies (their own and their subjectsʻ, the relic body parts of saints), and scales of space and time ranging from everyday life, to season liturgical ritual, to the large scale of long-distance trade relationships. Even though they made extensive use of inscriptions, their technique of circumscribing the local in the large-scale extended beyond the mode of textuality. These inscriptions serve as a narrative practice of world-making that was undertaken in spacetime and material culture as well as in words carved into church walls.

Like Tigran Honencʻ, the Vačʻutyans performed a world-assembling in their donation inscriptions, which was mirrored in their purchase and dedication of places, goods, and practices within the Kasakh Valley. For instance, in 1244 Vačʻeʻs son Kʻurd and his wife, Xorišah, dedicated a *kathołical* church abutting the recently restored fifth-century basilica at Astvacnkal (discussed above), located on the floor of the Kasakh River gorge. The spaces endowed at Astvacnkal are noteworthy in their design. As shown in figure 10, the vaulted ceiling of the *gavit* (now collapsed) was wrought in geometrical *muqarnas*, making Astvacnkal a primary example of a pan-Anatolian style of architecture which united Islamic and Christian spaces in the thirteenth century.[34] K'urd and Xorišah's dedicatory inscription is located above a doorway to the south side of the bema, the same location as the textile-style decoration in St. Gregory's cathedral that I discussed in the previous chapter (indeed, T'oros T'oramanyan described Astvacnkal as modeled on the example of St Gregory's church). In this inscription, K'urd describes the couple's gifts to Ast-vacnkal: "I K'urd, prince of princes, son of the great Vač'e, and my wife Xorišah, daughter of Marzpan, built this our Holy Katołike in memory of our souls. We have decorated it with every ornament and gave as well the garden bought by us in Parpi, one plot of uncultivated land in Ošakan, one garden in Karbi,[35] a com-moner servant [*šinakan*], and three hostels [*voljatun*], and to the chamber of the Episcopos a cross and book, in the year 693 (1244)."[36]

Written a few decades later, K'urd's dedication calls back to Tigran Honenc''s inscription on the other side of Mount Aragats, as well as the epigraphic practices of his parents. The Astvacnkal inscription weaves together a plurality of space-times in the service of K'urd and Xorišah's memory: the produce of gardens and the tilling of new land, as well as the labor of servants and specific costly objects to be used in ritual practices. Among the assemblage would also possibly have been potent human remains; T'oramanyan hypothesized (drawing on Šahxatunyan) that the original church renovated by the Vač'utyans was built as a shrine to St. Hakop and contained his relics.[37] Recall back to the nested, embodied space-times built into the architecture of medieval churches in Armenia discussed in the last chapter. By exhuming these relics and reburying them within the new church, K'urd and Xorišah incorporated the powerful body of the saint into their own "body," joining the world of their pious memory, and that of their lineage, with the *fame* of St. Hakob. The church would continue to embody the assembled realms of K'urd and Xorišah's power—even as the floor of the *gavit* is lined with the accu-mulated buried bodies of their medieval kin and subjects.

A decade later K'urd and Xorišah recorded their renovations and donations of new facilities (a belltower and a scriptorium, respectively) to the monasteries of Sałmosavank' and Hovhannavank', adding their names to the walls inscribed by K'urd's parents.[38] Their matching inscriptions—dated 1250 at Hovhannavank' and 1255 at Sałmosavank'—further orient their embodied spacetime within even broader 'scapes of Silk Road history and temporality. In particular, these texts give us a glimpse at the ways the Vač'utyans worked to house the world of the Kasakh Valley within a world that had been knocked about its axis by the Mongol inva-sions. In their preambles, the inscriptions relate how, having proved themselves worthy to their new rulers, K'urd and Xorišah set about rebuilding sections of the churches built by Vač'e and Mamaxatun that had been ruined during the conquest. Interestingly, the inscriptions invoke these new rulers not by name or as Mongols, but as "the world-conquering army of Archers" (*ašxarhakal zavracn netołac*).[39]

This phrase calls us back the epistemological spacetimes, or worlds, within which Christian people in Armenia and Europe made sense of the Mongol invasions. As Zaroui Pogossian has argued, for more than a decade into the Mongol conquest of the Caucasus, earlier, apocalyptic narratives of a "Nation of Archers" locked behind mountains by Alexander mediated people's experience of the invasion.[40] I am fascinated by K'urd and Xorišah's choice of words in their inscriptions, even as I hesitate to read *too* much into them. Their endowment inscription at Saɫmosavank' commemorated the new space to their sons and daughter,[41] and extended the fame of their built world into the future that those children embodied. This shows the practical, narrative work of mending political cosmologies so as to stretch beyond the invasion that their contemporary historian Kirakos Ganjakec'i understood as the "end of time."

Through their epigraphic evocation of a genealogical future, the Vač'utyans tied down a stable axis for their own world even as the wider world shifted. These inscription practices show the wide variety of spaces—villages, gardens, inns, stables, as well as sacral and monastic spaces—which were participant in that world, and in political life in the medieval Kasakh Valley. The breadth of this landscape argues against a narrow historical or archaeological focus on text as the exclusive domain of power, or on "elite spaces" (cities, forts, monasteries) as the exclusive loci of social (re)production. Quite the opposite: medieval Armenian princes were concerned with the extraurban landscapes of the highlands, as well as the wider world of Silk Road travel and trade. The scope of their political care was also expansive in temporal terms. Vač'e and Mamaxatun, K'urd and Xorišah, and their successors not only built new monuments to their piety and political power, but also worked the historical landscape within a spatiotemporal assemblage of built, perceived, and lived places to situate themselves in a world of traditional values—the conjoined "new and old" of their inscribed texts. These values themselves were legible within the bounds of medieval Armenian institutions: sovereignty, religious authority, personal piety, and hospitality.

The world inscribed—or circumscribed—within the epigraphic space created by the Vač'utyans on the walls of buildings combines in interesting ways with the understanding of landscape constructed through my survey. The reconstruction of churches and the layering of inscriptions and reiteration of donations constructed a palimpsest of a different scale than that of village houses and distributions of pottery sherds—and different again from the scale of the landscape as written by T'oramanyan and Petrosyanc'. But these scales overlap and intersect. The span of space invoked, for instance, by the Astvacnkal inscription encloses fields and gardens on the southern shoulder of Mount Aragats, between Astvacnkal and the monastery of Teɫer where Mamaxatun and Vač'e were buried; some of these sites are visible on map 3. The inscriptions also only sketchily refer to the lives of other inhabitants of the valley, or their everyday lives. The Hovhannavank' inscription calls upon the labor of the monastic clergy, whose liturgical calendar is augmented with prayers and masses in the Vačʻutyans' memory. The Astvacnkal inscription invokes a servant as well as the maintenance work contained in (and sustaining) three hostels. Turning from the epigraphy to the surveyed landscape, I can only speculate on which village the servant lived in, or where the hostels were located. The 2010 survey recorded ceramics and architectural remains in the canyon south of the monastery, in addition to the remains of the village that actually surrounded the church described above. Perhaps the canyon settlements included resting places for travelers and visitors to the monastery to stay close by, similar to the guest house at Noravankʻ (discussed in the next chapter). Working back and forth across these datasets I frequently reflect on the intersecting processes of erasure—whether epigraphic elision (and erosion) or large-scale landscape "amelioration"—which impede our perceptions of the active, busy landscapes of which the Armenian churches were but a part.

At the same time, the evidence we *do* have lets us think in multiscalar ways about those busy, dwelled-in landscapes, by considering the material practices that made and sustained those worlds. The survey data and inscriptions reiterate that many of the construction projects undertaken in the Kasakh Valley by the Vačutyans were actually reconstruction projects, emphasizing the interpretive and contingent aspect of landscape production stressed by John Barrett: "the construction of monuments is always an interpretation of a pre-existing world."[42] The people who lived in the Kasakh Valley in villages like Apnagyugh, Vardenut, and Ambroyi dwelled in a landscape that was not only in-process from their own agropastoral activities, but was also already full of the remains of past human actions. The practice of survey challenges archaeologists to simultaneously parse landscape into "signatures" and to reflect on how that landscape was dwelt within by people in the past. For instance, future excavations of the Bronze Age fortresses above Arai-Bazarǰuł and Vardenut might demonstrate the occupation and use of those sites by people in the Middle Ages, as was the case at the Bronze and Iron Age site of Tsaghkahovit to the north.[43] The traces of recent pastoral camps along the slopes of Aragats and the Tsaghkunyats provoke me to reflect on how these upland zones would have been utilized by medieval people in ways that left few enduring traces, even as they supported dairying and textile production in the valley villages and monastic centers. Rather than a static "local" landscape, the Kasakh itself would have been tied together by seasonal, habitual, and everyday mobilities. Some of these are attested to in the inscriptions described above: for instance, the donations of gardens and fields in Ošakan, Karbi, and Parpi to Astvacnkal suggest the movement of produce and paid rent revenues from the southeastern slope of Aragats to the monastery in the canyon. The donatory inscription at Uši indicates that the monastery did not merely physically overlook the Ararat plain; rather, it drew rents up from the gardens around Yerevan. Our ceramic datasets collected on survey suggest the movement of pottery within the valley, from village to village, as well as from larger production sites outside the valley (see chapters 5 and 6 for more discussion of this). Overlapping these skeins of data at various scales, stretched in different directions, I imagine the Kasakh Valley as more than a feudal holding or a place passed by the traffic of a minor capillary of the Silk Road. Combining material, spatial, and epigraphic data in place evokes the business of everyday medieval life, and also the multiplicity of projects, of little and not-so-little worlds. The realities of donated spaces constructed through epigraphic practice, and the world of political alliance, patronage, and aspirational power, were co-constructed with (and thus dependent on) the overlapping worlds of farm work, seasonal rents, holidays, and Masses, as well as with the mobilities of travelers and trade through the valley. The trek up the valley made by Het'um and described in the introduction was a short section of a longer journey for him, but also a brief window into a dynamic local world that carried on after he had passed over the horizon.

The next chapters will explore how the imagining of Armenia's place within a broader Silk Road world was undertaken everyday by people in their material lives, as they moved within the spaces endowed by princes like Vač'e Vač'utyan but also as they sat and ate, and shared food, goods, and stories with passersby on the mountain highways. In order to do this, I will spend some time in a space where the broader world of the medieval Silk Road and the everyday, "local" worlds of the Kasakh encounter one another. According to the inscription recorded by T'oramanyan but now lost, in the year 1213 Vač'e Vač'utyan (perhaps in partnership with Mamaxatun) endowed a *karavanatun* in the Kasakh Valley. This caravan house or highway inn was strategically located near both the highway north through the highlands from Yerevan toward Tbilisi, and the Vač'utyan castle at Vardenik (Vardenut). The ruins of the *karavanatun* still stand on a raised hill in the middle of a field, south of a modern village which is named Arai on signs and maps, but whose inhabitants know it as *Bazarǰuł*, the marketplace.

5

Traveling through Armenia

Caravan Inns and the Material Experience
of the Silk Road

The world is an inn, and you are, as it were, a caravan: how many days
does the caravan stop at the inn? This is a caravanserai, a place of earnings:
whatever you gain here, consign it there. Send ahead the baggage train, for
you will soon resume the journey.

—YUSUF KHĀṢṢ ḤĀJIB BALASAĞUNI, ADVISING HIS PRINCE, ELEVENTH
CENTURY (ḤĀJIB 1983)

The world is a caravanserai, and we are the caravan. Do not raise a
caravanserai within a caravanserai.

—INSCRIPTION BY THE SAFAVID SHAH ABBAS I ABOVE THE DOORWAY
OF THE SEVENTEENTH-CENTURY CARAVANSERAI AT KASHAN
(CHARDIN 1811)

On a swelteringly hot summer evening in 2011 I arrived back at the project house
in Aparan, crusted in sweat and dirt from another day's excavation at the caravan inn near Arai-Bazarjuł. I sat on a low garden wall taking off my boots and
scritching one of the passing neighborhood cats, and watched Dr. Roman Hovsepyan, the team's archaeobotanist, washing soil samples in a custom-made flota-
tion setup made from a blue oil drum and a garden hose. I asked him how the day's
work had gone.

"Not bad, Kate *jan*. I washed some of your samples today, you know."

"Oh, the ones from the floors? Great! Find anything interesting?"

"Oh yes." He practically gushed. "Kate, they were full of *dung*."

I was surprised, and excited: dung is good news for archaeologists, especially archaeobotanists, since it can be full of plant material, and is evidence for
past lifeways.

"Animal or human?" I asked. I wanted to know who had been . . . living on those floors. Roman grinned at the question.

"Both," he said, gleefully.

This conversation in the garden, surrounded by raspberry plants and roses and rows of washed potsherds laid out to dry, illustrates the kinds of small observations that go into archaeological reconstructions of social life in medieval (and other) pasts. The fact that humans and animals—specifically, equids—had been sharing a caravan inn was not surprising. Already, we had found pieces of harness and medieval iron horseshoes along with the broken dishes and fallen architecture. Plus, common consensus on medieval caravan inns in Armenia was that they held humans and beasts of burden together. The well-known fourteenth-century caravanserais at Selim and Harjis preserve the masonry mangers built in the spaces between their arches. But to have data at this small scale confirming that idea not only enriches our imagination of what it would be like to eat and sleep in a stone building which also housed a number of horses and donkeys, it also underscores the particular kind of monumental structure that is a caravanserai. As I will explore in this chapter, a caravanserai (called *pandok, karavanatun* or *ijevanactun,* caravan or dismounting house in Armenia) were constructed with the same techniques and care as other medieval monumental places like churches and were linked to some of the same performative practices of endowment and epigraphic donation. But the "congregation" enclosed within a caravan inn was a community of transitory strangers: travelers, foreigners, perhaps even slaves. This is not to say that the power associated with caravanserai was secular or rational—they were not "churches of commerce." Instead, I understand the medieval caravanserai in Armenia and neighboring regions as a space produced by and for a culture of mobile sociality and commensurability which overlapped with that world of enticing differences and desires that we now think of as the Silk Road. As buildings constructed through local cosmological, multiscalar logics, caravanserais were made as containers for both global cultures and local stakes (thus dissolving that apparent opposition), and were thus themselves "world-buildings," spaces housing and sustaining cosmopolitical aspirations and projects as well as everyday doings (see fig. 10).

Just as in the previous chapters we considered the spatial production tied up in history, architecture, and epigraphy as doing particular kinds of work in the social world, we will now look at what it means to build a place, like a caravanserai, that mediates the perception and experience of overlapping and nested worlds. What kind of power does that accumulate to a person—and what kind of transformative power is activated at that site? In other words, if the caravanserai is a world, what kind of world is it? As we will see, caravanserais worked in medieval Armenia in a mode similar to the written worlds of inscriptions: as *world-buildings* they marked out the limits of a social order, containing that order inside and barring a door against an unruly or dangerous outside. But as a constructed cosmology, a

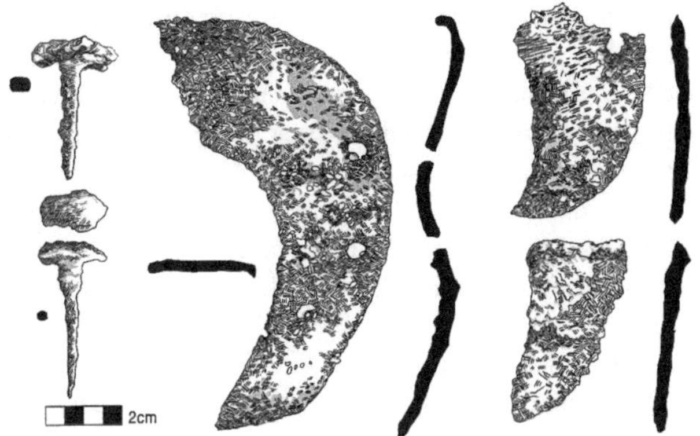

FIGURE 10. Iron nails and fragments of horseshoes from the Arai-Bazarǰuł caravanserai excavations. Drawn by the author.

world-building is more than the imposition of self-other (insider vs. outsider, guest vs. host, friend vs. stranger) distinctions; world-buildings mediated the experience of difference in more positive ways than the merely binary. The enclosing of fellow travelers within a shared space produces leveling effects and emergent out of this leveling is a politics, as the inhabitants of a caravanserai are also made equivalent as subjects—even if just for the night—under the hospitality of the caravanserai patron prince.[1] Caravan inns are therefore slippery in the ways they situate people, bring them into new relations and configurations. This slipperiness is reminiscent of the polysemy that Michel Foucault attributed to places that challenge simple scales of time and space. Considering museums, theaters, cemeteries, and ships, he called these "heterotopias," or places "capable of juxtaposing in a single real place several spaces, several sites that are in themselves incompatible."[2]

Foucauldian heterotopias, as he defined them, were exceptional: places that, like a hotel or a cemetery, referenced the everyday world but stood outside it. This, for me, marks a limit of the utility of heterotopia for thinking both about travel and about cosmopolitanism as a situated imagination of multiple scalar relationships. There are so many places where people open themselves to wider worlds, places that do not have to be outside or other to the everyday or even to the "mundane." Think about the places where you find yourself, in various ways, imagining a world that is bigger than you, that contains people far from you living lives different from yours. This could happen in a movie theater, a restaurant— even your own kitchen. Perhaps, like me, you like to flip over the bottle of wine or the tin of paprika or the palette of eyeshadow you are about to open and read where it was made. Do you, standing in your bare feet in your kitchen or bathroom, find yourself also simultaneously with one foot in a place that you imagine to be Argentina, or Spain, or Korea? One of the far-reaching aims of this book is to expand our definition of the spaces where we live the global in the everyday, where we situate ourselves in relations of distance and difference, where we "do cosmopolitanism." So, this chapter will explore the caravanserai as a technology of cosmopolitan imagination in the medieval period. At the same time, I am under no illusions as to the ordinariness of time people spent in one of these buildings. This is the point. The long-term significance of hospitable infrastructures like caravanserais to politics in Eurasia indicates that part of what made up "the medieval Silk Road" was a commitment to the importance of these everyday spaces, and of the everyday activities (eating, drinking, feeding animals, storytelling, elimination, sleeping, sex) that happened within them. At the same time, this commitment also entails a central interest on the part of potentially violent politics in the coming and going of strangers.

A caravanserai encloses a broader world within it and frames the time scales of the journey within the respite of an evening, a meal, a night's sleep. Because of this framing power of the caravan inn, people in the medieval and early modern period thought of these buildings as microcosms, or miniature versions of the human world. This is evidenced in numerous references to caravanserais in political writings from the period, including this chapter's epigraphs, from the eleventh and seventeenth centuries. The first text comes from a "mirror for princes" written by the vizier Yusuf Khāṣṣ Ḥājib Balasaǧuni for the Karakhanid prince of Kashgar, located in modern Xinjiang; the second is from the lintel of a caravan inn built by Shah Abbas I in the heart of the Safavid Persian Empire. Both of them express a sentiment about politics, human life, and travel that was shared across the Silk Road ecumene: life is a transient thread that continues beyond the bounds of the mortal body and of the world, just as a journey continues beyond the enclosing walls of a caravan inn.[3] Shah Abbas echoes the advice given by Balasaǧuni to his prince: don't waste time piling rocks in a moving river (to mix metaphors); your concern should be in your destination. Hence, "don't build a caravanserai within a caravanserai," an ironic thing to proclaim on the wall of the caravan inn that he has in fact built. But with this declaration, Abbas signals his own awareness of transience: the caravanserai is an endowment made by a prince concerned simultaneously with this world and the next. In their capacity to function as a microcosm, these institutions bring the medieval sovereign care for the world(s) into the realm of the everyday lives of travelers, and of the local people whose lives were occupied in the mundane tasks of hospitality.

THE CARAVAN INN IN THE MEDIEVAL PERIOD

What were these places, these world-buildings? In this chapter I look at the caravanserai as both a space and as a tethering point, not just for donkeys, but also for social institutions and cultural ideas about travel and power. After a discussion at the regional scale of what caravanserais meant and did through the high medieval period generally, we will move to a more intimate scale, and consider the experience of traveling to and staying inside a particular caravan inn, the *karavatun* built by Vačʻe Vačʻutyan at Arai-Bazarǰuł.

A caravan inn is, like all institutions, an entanglement of physical structure, localized practices, and extensive infrastructural relationships. The physical form of medieval caravan inns varied across the many regions where they were built. All are sturdy buildings for the housing of mobile people, pack animals, and valuable trade goods. Caravan inns across the Silk Road world were built from a variety of materials (mudbrick, stone, brick, wood) and to a variety of plans, but tend to have a few things in common: strong walls, a large interior space (either covered or open), and a large, frequently sole, entrance.[4] Most caravanserais allowed for a measure of privacy: their interior spaces were divided into cellular bays, or their columned internal arcades provided opportunities for a curtain to be raised—though this risked blocking the precious flow of air. The practices and activities associated with a caravan inn also varied across regions and through the long history of overland travel. Much of our knowledge of activities within caravanserais in Iran and South Asia, for example, comes from the accounts of early modern (fifteenth through eighteenth centuries) European mercantile agents traveling through the Safavid and Mughal Empires, or of courtly travelers from that same era. These early modern travelers described the breadth of services available in caravanserais by that period—from food and drink for humans and animals, to mail, to horse and camel rental, as well as farriers, tailors, bazaars, and sex workers. Evliya Çelebi, traveling in the sixteenth century, provided in his travel account a phrasebook for Ottoman courtly travelers moving through Armenian lands. His phrasebook essentially coaches the traveler through the solicitation of an Armenian youth from fetching fodder for the horses, to wine drinking, to sex.[5] According to his chronicler Aflaki, the thirteenth-century Sufi poet Rumi had a famous encounter with a prostitute in a caravanserai in Konya.[6] Finally, the individual caravanserai was part of a system, both in the sense of a broad cultural understanding of patronage, hospitality, and politics, and in the physical sense of a (usually) reliable network of equivalent places spaced along the roads from Damascus to Delhi, and beyond.

As an architectural form and an institution, the medieval road inn combined remnants of Roman fortified infrastructure (especially in the Levant) with Central Asian traditions of benevolent rule, and particularly with practices of pious charity within Muslim and Armenian Christian practice, which were historically entangled with that Central Asian tradition. Recorded as early as Ibn Hawqal's compiled tenth-century descriptions,[7] and extending to the end of the nineteenth century, road inns and urban hostels functioned as direct or indirect charity performances on the part of their royal or noble patrons. Inns would provide free lodging to those who could not pay for it; or the profit in fees, taxes, or rents from the caravanserai would be designated in perpetuity as a charitable donation to a madrasa, mosque, or (in the Armenian case) church.[8] Within Islamic juridical tradition, this practice was known as *waqf*; generally, this legal practice covered all acts which rendered movable, alienable property inalienable and isolated for the use of designated persons, with a specific aspect of *waqf* covering endowments to mosques and other institutions.[9] As La Porta has pointed out, high medieval Armenian donations to Christian institutions were also understood as and sometimes referred to as *waqf*, attested at Sanahin as early as 1173.[10] Medieval piety therefore had the transformative ability to transubstantiate alienable property into inalienable property under the law. While this may seem like an arcane point, it has been of almost exclusive interest to medieval historians discussing the Zakʻarid period: this transformation enabled merchants like Tigran Honencʻ or Vačʻe Vačʻutyan to metamorphose into dynasts of property. Under the conditions of the *waqf*, this power of conversion required that a portion of the profits or rents from the designated property go toward pious acts. Caravanserais were part of the technology through which the world of trade and travel was implicated within projects of authority—and conversely, through which the world of a prince's (or princess's) power was made to contain the "whole wide world" of the Silk Road. Thus, if we refer back to the quotations at the beginning of this chapter, when a donor like Shah Abbas I referred to "this world," he really intended the reader of his inscription to understand that he meant also "*my* world."

This intersection of politics and mundane activities housed in caravanserais—eating, hygiene, sleep—brings into relief the power relation that is inherent to hospitality, the function of infrastructures as mechanics of subjection. As Marcel Mauss originally argued, the political obligation to give hospitality is paired with an equally binding obligation to accept; "a gift is received with a burden attached."[11] To stay in a caravanserai was thus to step inside the proprietary world of the donor, to participate and embody the cosmology of their power. Jacques Derrida discussed the paradox of hospitality further, positing that in the act of receiving hospitality the stranger/foreigner (*l'étranger*) is made un-strange, as he must ask for and receive hospitality "in a language which by definition is not his own, the one imposed on him by the master of the house, the host, the king, the lord, the authorities, the nation, the State, the father, etc."[12] As with the cosmopolitanism defined as hospitality, the spacetime of the caravanserai was therefore politically ambivalent, an infrastructure within which the political duality of care relationships emerged, where the "citizens of the road" were transformed into subjects of a cosmologically ambitious sovereignty.

Hospitality tied the cities and towns of medieval Eurasia together as surely as did the cobbles of roads, the masonry of bridges, and the fortitude of humans, horses, camels, and donkeys. The ambivalence of hospitable spacetime, of roadside cosmopolitanism, speaks to the symbolic fecundity of hospitable places within a broader medieval politics—a politics that could be violent as well as refined, bigoted as well as tolerant. At a fundamental level, the gifts which linked pious sovereignty and sovereign hospitality included unfree labor, and enslaved people.[13] Moreover, and to contradict a beloved Silk Road canard, "free trade" does not in itself a harmonious cosmo-polity make. One of Manandyan's core arguments about the medieval period was that highway regions between areas of state control were as crowded with brigands, highwaymen, outlaws, and robbers as they were with merchants and pilgrims.[14] Such an impression is corroborated by thirteenth-century Armenian laws which provide for the proper disposal of "legitimate booty," as well as for the punishment of brigands and expiation of the sin of illegitimate plunder on the part of Armenian warlord-nobles.[15] This image of dangerous roads applies to the medieval world beyond Armenia as well. The roads and routes of the Silk Road cut across political boundaries which shifted through this dynamic period, and power played out, not only in the protection of trade, but also in the disruption and interception of it. Consider this example of the crusader company led by Richard the Lionheart, which in the late twelfth century overtook and seized the caravan of some Turkish merchants. An account of the contents of the caravan was related by the chronicler Geoffrey de Vinsauf:

> The caravan, with all its riches, became the spoil of the victors. . . . They led the yoked horses and camels by the halter, and offered them to our men, and they brought mules loaded with spices of different kinds, and of great value; gold and silver, cloaks of silk, purple and scarlet robes, and variously-ornamented apparel, besides arms and weapons of divers forms; coats of mail, commonly called *gasiganz*; costly cushions, pavilions, tents, biscuit, bread, barley, grain, meal, and a large quantity of conserves and medicines; basins, bladders, chess-boards; silver dishes and candlesticks; pepper, cinnamon, sugar, and wax; and other valuables of choice and various kinds; an immense sum of money, and an incalculable quantity of goods, such as had never before (as we have said) been taken at one and the same time, in any former battle.[16]

Immediately remarkable in this description is the sheer variety of things contained in the caravan. These merchants were carrying many of the core commodities of Silk Road trade: silken textiles including robes, cushions, and tents; forest products (spices) and sugar from the Indian Ocean route; wax potentially from the northern, Volga route. Beyond the misery of these unlucky merchants, note Geoffrey's comment that, as far as booty was concerned, highway robbery was much more profitable than warfare! Similarly, Ibn Battuta, traveling a century and a half later relates being set upon by armed bandits on his way to Delhi.[17] In his fourteenth-century handbook, Francesco Pegolotti reassured travelers that the road between Tana and Cathay was during this period (the height of Mongol administrative integration) quite safe,[18] except in regions where one ruler is in the process of replacing another. In such cases of uncertain sovereignty, Pegolotti warned, "there have sometimes been irregularities practiced on the Franks, and other foreigners."[19] Traveler safety was dependent on the presence of a secure, and supervisory, authority overseeing life in in-between places.

As institutions established for the safety and comfort of traveling others, caravanserais served a real function within a broad medieval society reliant on various forms of mobility. Travelers relied on the "space of the road" being securely enclosed within the walls of towns or caravanserais when the sun went down. Traveling in the medieval period had a necessary rhythm and spatiality: stages were measured in lengths covered by a day's travel not only because humans and animals needed rest, but because they needed to be someplace safe and warm at night, especially while traveling through open desert plains, or through mountainous (and sometimes snow-covered) regions like the Caucasus. Throughout the medieval period road inns as an institution not only traversed geopolitical boundaries, but also blurred two categories frequently used by archaeologists to talk about architecture: the infrastructural and the monumental.

Infrastructural and monumental constructions might appear, at first glance, to be opposites of each other. Monumental architecture, as the name implies, is built to last, on a grand and public scale, and clearly proclaims its ties to the power, benevolence, wealth, fame, and memory of an individual or group. In the archaeological context, this means temples, stelae, churches, palaces, agoras, mausoleums—anywhere you might expect to find inscriptions, murals, or statues. Infrastructure, on the other hand, is supposed to be invisible to us: if the sewer system is working properly, we don't think about it, and politicians or other public figures usually become associated by name with the sewage system or power grid only when those infrastructures break down.[20] Monumental infrastructures like caravanserais signal a weird hybrid,[21] and a desire on the part of their patron builders to have, not only their memory associated with the space of road rest and care, but also a sense of monumental awe. As sturdy, standardized, and reliably situated buildings, caravanserais made up an infrastructural network, a material-spatial-social system that made travel and trade possible the same way that electrical wires, power stations, repair technicians, and grid operators make electrical power possible. A better modern comparison might be the system of highways, bridges, hotels, park structures, airports, and toll booths constructed under American President Franklin Delano Roosevelt's Works Project Administration, as part of his New Deal program. Some of the projects funded by Roosevelt's WPA are highly visible and clearly monumental, such as airports or the murals painted by artists like Diego Rivera or Carlos Lopez in major public buildings such as the Detroit Institute of Art. Other WPA projects are harder to see, including hundreds of bridges of varying scale across the United States, and murals painted in post offices to inspire people waiting in line. I remember driving between small towns in Indiana one spring, and passing over an otherwise forgettable, vine-covered river bridge that was marked with only a small inscription identifying it as a WPA construction. Likewise, I have spent a good amount of time staring up at Harry Sternberg's 1937 mural at the Lakeview post office on the north side of Chicago.[22] Sternberg's painting depicts the city of Chicago as a pulsing hub of life, industry, and destiny, and invests the humble citizen waiting to post a letter (or perhaps, a parcel of archaeological samples) with the sense that their everyday errands are part of the historical narrative of American progress.[23] Caravanserais along the high medieval Silk Road, built in places like Karakhanid Central Asia, Seljuk Anatolia, the Levant, or Armenia, worked in a similar way to bring everyday life into the monumental. They knit the mundane activities of travel within the monumental scope of political performance. Just as importantly, they demonstrate the concern of medieval Armenian politics with the everyday needs and comforts of travelers.

*Housing Travelers in Anatolia: The Inn as a Tradition
and Technique of Politics*

In 1960 the archaeologist and historian Varazdat Harut'yunyan published a unique book on the road infrastructure of medieval Armenia.[24] *Karavanatn'ner yev kamurjner mijnadaryan Hayastanum* (Caravanserais and bridges in medieval Armenia) recorded plans and inscriptions and provided invaluable photographic evidence for a corpus of roughly contemporary medieval caravan inns. Taking a look at the map in the front pages of the book, however, a question immediately arises: the caravanserais noted by Harut'yunyan are spaced along routes passing along the rivers and mountain passes, tracing lines which are then arbitrarily cut by the modern borders of the Republic of Armenia.[25] What about the caravan inns and routes on the other side of the border? How do we understand an architectural phenomenon that does not neatly correspond in spacetime to a single modern nation or ethnic group? (See fig. 11.)

The tradition of caravanserai building in high medieval Armenia was entangled with cultures of patronage and piety which were practiced throughout the central Caucasus and Anatolia under the Seljuk Empire (eleventh through twelfth centuries) and, after the mid-twelfth century in western Anatolia, by the Rum Seljuk sultanate. According to analysts of the Seljuk period, the main impetus of Rum Seljuk construction efforts was on public buildings such as hospitals and caravanserais—called *hans* in the Seljuk context.[26] These buildings were constructed in Anatolia by the Rum Seljuk sultans, active patrons from the reign of Kiliç Arslan II (1156–92) up to the Mongol invasion in 1236.[27] During this latter period the social influence of the state was superseded in many ways by that of local emirs, whose wealth and property continued to increase under the Mongols: many of these emirs also endowed buildings.[28] Ahmet Ertug has argued that the Rum Seljuk sultans erected state-controlled *hans* along the Konya-Kayseri-Sivas route in order to develop Sivas as a trading center, making it more attractive to Genoese trading factors.[29] According to Semra Ogel, the Seljuk caravanserai system embodied a "definite economic policy" at a regional scale, a policy in which the Seljuk sultans and emirs took into account the time depth of the Anatolian trade routes as well as the efficacy of road inns as a way of "set[ting] their seal on the land."[30] The *han* in Anatolia represented a conscientious intervention of state-level engineering in the issue of traveler accommodation on mountain roads, and the *han* buildings themselves embodied aristocratic concern for the relatively mundane needs of

FIGURE 11. Interior of the thirteenth-century caravanserai at Harjis, photographed from the west, opposite the entrance (visible in the center gallery). Photo by the author.

traveling humans as well as their animals and goods. If the medieval caravanserai as an institution was a world-building, embodying political cosmology in miniature, then the cosmology of Rum Seljuk *han* projects was centered on the well-being of the highway traveler.

The distance between Rum Seljuk-endowed caravanserais was one *manzil*, which in the medieval period could indicate not only the length of one day's journey but also the stop at the end.[31] Seljuk *han*s consist of long galleries roofed in vaulted arches and sometimes topped with a dome, usually with single decorated entrances.[32] A prototypical example of the Seljuk *han* building is the Alay Han, which is thought to have been endowed in the late twelfth century on the Nevşehir-Aksaray road. This caravan inn consists of a long rectangular hall, divided into five arcades by broad square pillars: the galleries themselves are divided by transverse arches. In the center of the central arcade is a windowed dome, releasing heat and smoke and letting in light. The *han* is augmented by a large enclosed courtyard, now ruined. When it was newly built, the courtyard would have been surrounded by rooms or alcoves for cooking and eating, bathing, or storage.[33] The *han*, and perhaps also the courtyard originally, is reached through a single gate; this gate is crowned by a breathtaking muqarnas canopy surrounded by stellate and geometric stonework.

In their proportions, technologies of construction, and decorative motifs, *hans* in Anatolia formed part of a broader corpus of Seljuk architecture, one that also contained madrasas, mosques, baths, tombs, and other structures.[34] These architectural forms in their turn had a long tradition, linking back to mud-brick buildings from early medieval Central Asia.[35] Semra Ogel has characterized the Seljuk road inns as a rural, roadside extension of the architectural developments underway in Seljuk cities in Anatolia.[36] Cengiz Bektaş meanwhile has argued that what distinguished the Seljuk inns from predecessor transit structures like Levantine *ribatat* was that they were not intended to fulfill a frontier-holding or military function, but were built explicitly to provide services to the traveling public, as well as to the traders in textiles, soap, thoroughbred horses, and slaves that passed through the sultanate.[37] Seljuk *hans* were therefore constructed explicitly to knit together an orderly society, rather than simply to stake out a frontier or as "outposts." They were considered necessary plumbing for the functioning of a balanced, even beautiful, world—and this is indicated in the attention paid to their architecture, to their form as microcosmic buildings. The directionality of entrances and layouts of these buildings (usually cardinal) was a cosmographic statement deliberately made by their endowers, and was mirrored in the muqarnas vaulting and geometric designs—often of fields of stars—which decorated their monumental portals.[38] The exteriors of Seljuk *hans* were also frequently decorated with animal figures: for instance, the Alay Han mentioned above depicts a fantastical lion with a single head and two bodies, staring down at entrants through the muqarnas portal.[39] The *han* buildings were complete architectural cosmologies, knitting together heraldic symbolism and cosmographic design around the people assembled inside.

In the social and economic climate of thirteenth-century Rum Seljuk Anatolia, sultans and emirs were not only political authorities but also patrons, making the sultanate in this way similar in its political particulars to post-Seljuk (or perhaps Seljuk-adjacent) Bagratid-ruled Armenia.[40] The Rum Seljuk sultans from 1155 to 1237 took measures to generate and protect trade through Anatolia,[41] granting travelers insurance from robbery and assault along the highways connecting the Mediterranean and Black Sea. During the reign of Sultan Kaykaus I, the Rum Seljuk state granted freedom of movement and tax reductions to Venetian merchants and traders from the Lusignan kingdom of Cyprus, in order to drive trade to their ports and routes.[42] As safe stopping points on potentially dangerous roads, places where letters of passage from friendly governments would be read and accepted, Seljuk *hans* had considerable social meaning as spaces where the boundaries between subject and foreigner could be underscored or suspended. A possibility of everyday cosmopolitanism is that politics hinges in this way on the distinction between welcome guests and unwelcome enemies (whether outlaw bandits or actual combatants in war), but also that politics across apparent boundaries perform a similar culture of hospitality through mutually intelligible practices. We shall see that this is demonstrated by the way that caravan inns in both

Seljuk and Armenian Anatolia were built according to a shared plan, orienting the traveler in ways that would have been familiar to them. This similarity also appears in the shared ways that caravan inns factored into the construction of princely or lordly selves in both the Seljuk and the Armenian context.

In a mode that will by this point be familiar to us, the inscription panels of Seljuk caravanserais generally reference the name or identity of the donor, the year of the building's construction, and the name of the regnant sultan.[43] Building a *han* thus situated a prince in relation not only to a traveling public, but also within the hierarchical ranks of competitive aristocracy. This aspirational cosmography is nicely illustrated by the trilingual endowment inscription from Hekim Han on the Kayseri road. Hekim Han is unique, as it is currently the only Seljuk-era caravanserai in modern Turkey not apparently built by a member of the Seljuk elite, having been endowed by an Armenian Syriac Christian.[44] The inscription is currently located above the entrance to the courtyard, on a block of stone inset above the arch.[45] The center of the block is taken up by an Arabic version of the inscription; to the left and right sides are Armenian and Syriac translations. For our purposes, let's compare the Arabic and Armenian texts. The Arabic inscription (translated by Anthony Eastmond) reads:

> In the days of the reign of the victorious, exalted Sultan, the most powerful Shahanshah, possessor of the necks of nations, master of the sultans of the world, Mu'sharrāf al-Dīn al-Aziz [?], Lord over land and sea, strength of the world and religion, triumph of Islam and of Muslims, crown of kings and sultans, honor of the house of Seljuk, Abu i-Fath Kai Kā'us ibn Kay-Khosrāw ibn Kiliç Arslan, proof of the ruler of the faithful—God give strength to his victory—ordered the building of this blessed Han of this poor servant in need of the Mercy of the God by the exalted Abu Sālim ibn Abu l-Hasan, the deacon and doctor from Melitene, at the date of the month of the year six hundred and fifteen.[46]

The Armenian inscription reads:

> In the year 667 (1218) in the reckoning of the Armenians I had this hostel built as an act of welfare. [Greatly] blessed are you who enters here and rests. This you must say without forgetting: the god of the Heaven and the Earth, may you be merciful to Po-Selem, the senior doctor, the son of the great Pulhasan, the doctor, of the Syrians from Melitene.[47]

Note the difference in emphasis between the inscription that would be read by Arabic-literate Seljuks, and that which would be read by Armenian-literate travelers. Abu Selim/Po-Selem takes care to clearly delimit, in the Arabic inscription, his place within a worldly hierarchy surmounted by the Seljuk sultan Kaykaus. Scott Redford observed that Abu Selim in praising his sultan is careful to cite certain Seljuk epigraphic tropes and avoid others, specifically those that would cast his patron prince as a persecutor of infidels rather than a welcomer of guests.[48] The content and location of this inscription as well as the fact of its trilinguality demonstrate that medieval actors like Abu Selim constructed and endowed *hans* in part to situate themselves within a world which they imagined at intersecting scales of local and global. It also indicates a social actor sensitive to his place between worlds. Though its original entrance has been lost, the inn was constructed with the standard vaulted arcades and divided bays (though interestingly, it is divided into thirds rather than fifths).[49] As a world-building Hekim Han made sense to medieval travelers moving between regions, languages, and political universes, including that of medieval Armenia. It is interesting that Abu Selim addresses himself directly to the readers of the Armenian inscription and enjoins their blessing; while in Arabic he is a subject, in Armenian he is a host.

The Caravanserai as an Institution in Medieval Armenia

In the previous chapter I discussed the building of caravanserais as appearing in the list of royal obligations stated by the Armenian cleric Mxitar Goš in the early thirteenth century. Mxitar's *Lawcode* also included a stipulation that travelers who could afford their own lodging ("nobles and mounted riders") stay at facilities available in villages along the road, leaving the accommodations at monasteries for the poor and members of the clergy, and sparing the monastic inhabitants the horror of "minstrels and singing girls" and other ribaldries of highway travel.[50] These references to *karavanatn'ner* and travel in the *Lawcode* imply not only that road inns were a project associated with princely or kingly authority in high medieval Armenia, but also that such inns could be one of the points where fees were collected on trade routes from those travelers who possessed means to pay them. In addition to sources such as Pegolotti's handbook that list the fees paid at Armenian caravanserais, this implication is corroborated by epigraphic evidence from the same period, in which caravanserais were assembled as parts of projects of pious charity by merchant princes. Recall the dedicatory inscriptions of Tigran Honenc' and K'urd Vač'utyan in the last chapter; these princes both mention inns or hostels as sources of revenue for their endowed churches and their inhabitants. This is well illustrated by an inscription from a *hyuratun* (guest house) at the high medieval monastery of Noravank' in the region of Vayots Dzor. According to a long inscription, which is all that currently remains of the structure, the guest house was constructed by the Bishop Sarkis under command of Tarsayič' Orbelyan, an Armenian prince who ruled in Vayots Dzor as subject of the Mongol Ilkhans.[51] The editors of the *Corpus of Armenian Inscriptions* date this inscription, and the donation of the guest house, to the period between 1273 and 1290. In the text, Sarkis describes not only the donation of the caravanserai, but also the villages and mill revenues that he donated to maintain it. He concludes by asking the guests, strangers and needy (*hyurer, otarner*—literally "others"—and *karot'yalner*) housed in the inn to remember him and his colleagues. In so doing, Sarkis enfolds these people of the inn within the spacetime of hospitality, which contains a multivalent cosmopolitanism of both travelers and hosts. While they may only be his guests for the space of the night, the text of the inscription projects this reciprocal relationship forward in time, carried by the embodied memory of the traveler. The caravanserai itself plays a significant role, literally housing this relationship of mutual obligation at the moment of its creation.

The collaboration between the built space of the road inn and the construction of reciprocal relationships between guests and hosts is further illustrated by a caravanserai built a generation later, and more than a thousand meters above Noravankʿ in the pass connecting the canyons of Vayots Dzor to the plains around Lake Sevan. Tucked below the head of the pass, with a commanding view southward is a three-nave caravanserai built of tuff blocks. The entrance to the inn is oriented at a right angle to the galleries; the doorway is decorated with a remarkable combination of a muqarnas canopy above the door, and zoomorphic reliefs to either side—a winged quadruped to the left, a bull to the right. At the time that Łevond Ališan was compiling *Sisakan*, his 1883 geography of historic southern Armenia, the road inn was known as the Selim Caravanserai (the pass is known as the Selim pass).[52]

The Selim caravanserai has two inscriptions. One was carved into the tympanum above the door, beneath the muqarnas canopy. This inscription is in Persian and was heavily and deliberately damaged in the last century; however, the text of the inscription was recorded in fragments by Ališan.[53] A translation of the Persian inscription (as Ališan's proxy noted it) is as follows:

> Abu Saʿid Bahadur Khan,[54] In the days of the sovereignty of the Sultan of the World, the King of the Descendants of Adam, the Ruler of the Arab and the Ajam, the Holder of the Reins of Days, may God make his reign everlasting and his sovereignty eternal. The owner of benefactions, Čʿesar son of Lebarid [Liparit] son of Ivani [and] Xursha daughter of Vartan son of Ivani [and] Tup on the date of Seven Hundred and Twenty Seven
>
> (*In Turkish mixed with Persian*): May there be compassion in front of the Most High. May the status of this lowly Mahmoud be elevated. Goodwill to the owners.[55]

The Armenian inscription is located on the right-hand side as one enters the caravanserai, on the wall of the vestibule. This inscription reads:

> In the name of the all-capable and powerful God, in the year 761 (1332), of the world-rule (*ašxarakalutʿiwn*) of Busaid Khan, I Čʿesar son of the Prince of Princes Liparit,[56] and of my mother Ana, the grandson of Ivane and of my brothers, strong like lions, the princes Burteł and Smbat and Elikum, of the family Orbelyan, and of my wife Xorišah the daughter of Vardan and Rupen of the house of Senikarams, out of our well-gotten proceeds (*i halal ardeancʿ*)we constructed this spirit-house (*hogetun*) for the salvation of our souls and those of our ancestors and brothers reposing in Christ.[57] And of my living [brothers] and sons Sargis and Hovhannes the priest, Kʿurd and valiant Vardan. We implore passersby (*patahogh*) to remember us in Christ. Begun under the high-priesthood of Esai and completed through his prayers in the year 761 (1332).[58]

FIGURE 12. The entrance to the Selim caravanserai, Vayots Dzor. The Persian inscription discussed above is on the semicircular lintel above the door. Photo by the author.

These bilingual inscriptions from the Selim caravanserai raise many intriguing questions. One of the things that you might notice first is the similarity to the Hekim Han case discussed above, in the difference in tone between the Persian inscription and the Armenian one. The Persian text spends much more space expounding upon the power and importance of Abu Saiʿd Khan, who at that time (and until his death by plague in 1335) was ruler of the Ilkhanate. Note as well that the Armenian inscription surmounts the worldly authority (literally "world-rule") of Abu Saʿid with the more total, cosmic authority of their Christian deity. Much less space is given in the Persian text to the builder of the inn or to a description of that endowment (though again, we are dealing with a fragmentary inscription). Also like the Hekim Han case, the Armenian inscription is differentiated by its explicit claim upon the memory of travelers who pass by the inn. This sense of transience and serendipity is intriguing; Čʿesar Orbelyan (through his epigrapher) makes a specific contrast between the transitory nature of the encounter with his guests, and the longer relationship of guest and host—or subject and sovereign— that is engendered within the space of the inn. As in the case of the guest house at Noravankʿ, the spacetime of the Selim Caravanserai "houses" multiple scales—the temporality of passing travelers, the ritual, iterative spacetime of prayer, the complex spacetime of memory, the embodied continuity of lineage (see fig. 12).

These inscriptions demonstrate the close relationship between the institution of the *hyuratun/karavanatun* and a politics of pious charity in Armenia. This in turn shows the commonality in cultures of political hospitality and charity between medieval (Christian) Armenia and Seljuk (Muslim) Anatolia, and on the part of Christian Armenians within the Muslim Ilkhanate. As Sergio La Porta has argued, such overlaps in tradition demonstrate a practical cosmopolitanism, which could cut across antagonisms between Seljuk Muslims and Armenian Christians attested in literary accounts.[59] This doesn't mean that those antagonisms didn't exist; rather, it points back to the concept of an everyday cosmopolitanism at the material scale of doings. Such similarities of practice are carried over into similarities in the architectural spaces of the inns as well.

True to form as infrastructural buildings, the majority of Armenian caravanserais are of a standardized plan, what Harut'yunyan called the "single hall, three-naved type." These inns are long, rectangular buildings divided into three galleries by lines of arches supported on even numbers of plinths or low columns. These three-galleried halls would have been profoundly similar in their interiors and entrances to the inns endowed by sultans and emirs in the Rum Seljuk sultanate.[60] The arches running parallel to the long side of the structure divide the *karavanatun* into low transverse arcades, which run across the three long barrel-vaulted galleries. At each end, the lines of arches abut the walls; arches and roof vaults are constructed of tuff ashlar blocks on a core of rubble and mortar fill. Beyond the ornament at Selim discussed above, extant architectural decoration on Armenian *karavanatn'ner* is limited to skylights and entrances, which are sometimes ornate. The three preserved Armenian *karavanatun* entrances are that at Selim,[61] a similar entrance with semicircular inscription at Harjis, and that at the Zor caravanserai in modern-day eastern Turkey. This caravanserai has an ornately geometric inset entrance decorated in stars and lacework, which was photographed during the Marr expedition at the end of the nineteenth century and so forms part of Harut'yunyan's dataset.[62] Significantly, the style of decoration at Zor is strongly evocative of the geometric star-and-flower designs on the reconstructed Ani *xanaparh*, as well as that found on the bemas (altar platforms) and entrances of early and mid-thirteenth-century churches in Aragatsotn built by the Vač'utyans (for example Tełer, Hovhannavank', and possibly Mravyan as well). And of course, both the *karavanatun* and church *gavit* entrances are formally and decoratively similar to the entrances to Seljuk buildings.

This discussion has so far demonstrated how much we can learn about caravan inns and their role in medieval society from their architectural form, and from the words carved into their stones. Observing their forms, we see the links in building traditions, and think about the craftspeople, masons, and architects who built palaces, monasteries, churches, and road inns as well as other buildings across the South Caucasus and Anatolia in the twelfth and thirteenth centuries.[63] These built spaces represent a combined project on the part of local princely patrons and workers, from the stonecutters to the skilled masons who carved the inscriptions, to the bakers and water carriers who made sure the whole team was fed, all in the interest of furthering trade and making a resting place for Silk Road travelers. But what were these buildings like inside? What was it like to stay in one? Investigating these questions requires a combination of multiple forms of archaeological data in tandem with the history, architecture, and other information we have been compiling. But until recently there have been very few systematically excavated medieval caravanserais. Though medieval and early modern road inns in Central Asia and Iran are popular places to visit now that the Silk Road has been designated an object of UNESCO world heritage and a source of tourist revenue, for a long time there was a shortage of interest in these places as archaeological sites, or even necessarily in the activities that may have occurred within them.[64] I still remember a time when I was presenting my research in graduate school, and a professor said "But, you're making caravan travel sound fascinating and romantic. I've been in caravanserais. They *smell*." In the spirit of that remark, let's explore a high medieval caravanserai from the gutters upward. This means returning to the Kasakh Valley in the time of the Vač‘utyans, and in particular to a point on the slope of Mount Aragats where the medieval road brought travelers a day's journey up into the mountain air from the plain below: the site of the Arai-Bazarǰuł caravan inn.[65]

CARAVAN HALLS AND VILLAGE HEARTHS: HOTEL AND HOME IN THE KASAKH VALLEY

Before we started to excavate it, the Arai-Bazarǰuł caravanserai consisted of a mound in the middle of the fields topped with a picturesque ruin: a ragged wall of stones and concrete rising five meters above the ground surface and oriented roughly cardinally. If you climb the rise and walk among the rubble, you can see that this standing ruin would have been the north wall of a rectangular building, the other walls of which have fallen to the south and west in large chunks. The wall's original ashlar facing stones, shaped from Aragats's volcanic tuff, have been almost entirely stripped, leaving the concrete-and-rubble core of the wall exposed. The roof of the caravanserai was constructed of stone rubble and concrete as well, a technique that evokes both high medieval Seljuk and Armenian construction techniques.[66] This roof had collapsed outward, leaving large ruins to the exterior of the building but a fortuitous lack of debris within the caravanserai's interior, where we laid out excavations.

According to a now lost inscription, the Arai-Bazarǰuł caravanserai was constructed in 1213.[67] Its role in local life of the Kasakh Valley must be reconstructed from this date, from the material remains of the site itself, and from the contextual information we have about caravanserais in medieval Armenia and nearby places. The inscription date would place the caravanserai within the span of Vač‘e Vač‘utyan's construction projects in the Kasakh Valley—only a few years after his endowments at Uši and a decade or so before his wife Mamaxatun's reconstruction of Tełer monastery, both sites to the southwest on the shoulder of Aragats. So far, I have not been able to find this caravanserai mentioned by name or location in any of the Vačʻutyans' inscriptions, so we don't know if, for example, the Arai-Bazarǰuł caravanserai was donated as a revenue source to a nearby monastery like Astvacnkal or Hovhannavankʻ. We also don't know from written documents if, like the fourteenth-century inn at Noravankʻ, the caravanserai at Arai-Bazarǰuł was supported by incomes or produce from a particular village or villages. However, the caravanserai is located on the edge of a medieval village currently known as Ambroyi or Hin (Old) Bazarǰuł. This field of ruins was almost entirely obliterated by Soviet-era agricultural amelioration, but was inhabited at the same time as the caravanserai was in use.[68] As I will explore in the next chapter, the overlap between material assemblages from the caravanserai and village suggest entanglements between local and large-scale as part of the routine experience of the Silk Road on the part of both travelers and local Armenians.

Extant data on the Arai-Bazarǰuł site is contained within the general architectural survey of Tʻoramanyan and in Harutʻyunyan's summary of Armenian *karavanatun* architecture.[69] These texts compiled information which is also represented by the corpus of standing caravanserais from the Middle Ages at sites like Aruč, Selim, Harǰis, and Jrapi, sites that are available for consultation by archaeologists who are interested in what to expect from the general layout of a caravan inn. Among the many questions driving our dig was finding the caravanserai door. I was interested in finding decorative ties to other buildings and material links to any entrance activities; my colleagues at the institute wanted me to relocate Vačʻe Vačʻutyan's dedication inscription, and perhaps find a few more precious inscribed ashlars. Within Harutʻyunyan's account of the *karavanatun* ruins, he contradicted the earlier observation by Tʻoromanyan of a door in the northern side with a *still* earlier ethnohistorical account by Šahxatunyan, who visited the site in the early nineteenth century and recorded the 662 (1213) date inscription and door in the south.[70] Although the external ashlar face of the northern wall was removed and reused, my examinations of the wall core structure revealed the outline of the *karavanatun*'s three-arched gallery design, as well as the locations on the wall where the transverse arches connected. These connection points are visible as thickenings in the rubble masonry. Thus I could identify the Bazarǰuł caravanserai as belonging to Harutʻyunyan's "three-nave type," and link it formally to the Seljuk tradition as well (remember that the Hekim han, dedicated in 1214, also had three galleries). This also meant that I could rely on the entrance being axially located, on the opposite (south) side from the standing wall. My team and I opened four excavation units (AC1–4) in order to explore this possible gallery scheme for the Bazarǰuł *karavanatun*, and to investigate the cultural deposits in different sections of the building (see fig. 13).

Over eight weeks of excavation we dug multiple meters down into soil and rubble,[71] and uncovered the history of this fascinating building a layer at a time—

FIGURE 13. A view (looking north) of the excavated floor (lower left) and gutter (center, dark area) of the Arai-Bazarǰuł caravanserai (Unit AC2). Note the "drape" of fallen ashlars in the lefthand part of the trench, and the two square plinths from off of which the arch collapsed. Photo by the author.

from the period when it was inhabited by travelers in the Middle Ages, to the later years when a badger dug tunnels through the upper levels of the rubble, finally dying in its own hole. Archaeological excavations tend to reveal the story of a place in reverse (if you're lucky) or in a disordered series of events that the archaeologist or team of specialists reorganize into a narrative that make sense. What remains is the challenge of integrating bits of data that reflect sometimes jarringly different time frames, from the length of a meal to the life of an animal or person, to the length of time a building stands before collapsing. In weaving the story of the Bazarǰuł caravanserai, I hope what emerges is that the materiality of this site gets tangled up with other scales of thought and imagination that we have been exploring up to now: the scale of the route, of the caravan network, of people's everyday lives, of a day's walk through the highlands, of the spans crossed by traded goods.

The first thing we learned about the caravanserai was how it fell down. Once we had removed the topsoil from the site, we encountered thick deposits of rubble and the sandy remains of decaying concrete from the rubble walls and roof. As I mentioned, we were lucky: when it collapsed, possibly due to an earthquake, the caravanserai had cracked open, dumping chunks of roof to the outside. The exception to this was in the southern end of the building, where the vaulted roof of the *karavanatun* fell directly downward on top of the floors, to be recovered as a quilt of tightly nestled stones. These ashlar blocks or *voussoirs* were carved on a curve, a bit like a squared-off slice of melon. When mortared side-by-side and locked in place by the downward weight of the thick rubble roof of the caravanserai, they formed a long barrel-vaulted ceiling. As soon as the rubble roof and the outer walls began to buckle, the whole barrel of the vault collapsed. In an excavation unit (AC2) in the central-western part of the caravanserai we discovered how other sections of the building had fallen outward. In this excavated area, we found the toppled remains of one arch of the caravanserai's north-south arcade, fallen westward off of its low piers. The piers themselves were still in place, large square plinths covered with the remains of stone and mortar from where the arches had been uprooted.

Inhabitants of the village of Arai remember that the remains of the eastern wall fell down in the winter of 1964 during a heavy snowstorm. The date of collapse of the southern wall fragments testified by Šahxatunyan in 1842 is unknown, but must have occurred before T'oramanyan's surveys in the 1930s and 1940s. Based on the sequence of soil and artifact deposits, I could determine that the caravanserai initially collapsed fairly soon after it stopped being used, if not while it was in use. Across the excavation units, levels of architectural collapse were separated from the floors of the building by thin layers of fill, which contained organic material, animal bones, and fragments of thirteenth- to fourteenth century ceramics. Archaeologists can infer the relationship between objects and surfaces by paying attention to the orientation of things like sherds, bones, and bits of charcoal in the three-dimensional space of the excavation: as you approach a floor, you find more objects lying flat upon that floor's surface rather than "floating" in the matrix of collapsed pebbles, sand, and grit above. In the southern section of the caravanserai where the ceiling fell in place, we found right below it the smashed remains of medieval cooking jars, smeared along the dented clay floor. This was an interesting fact about the Bazarǰuł *karavanatun*: unlike the more famous, later-dating road inns at Selim pass and Harǰis which have floors made of stone flags, the floor of

FIGURE 14. A view (looking north) of the flagstone-lined lateral gallery of the caravanserai (Unit AC1). You can see the stone manger on the lefthand side, and the remains of an arch plinth emerging from the unexcavated baulk. Photo by the author.

the inn at Bazarǰuł was a hard, red clay, beaten in place between kerbs of basalt or tufa. We found sections of this floor in all four of the excavation units: it appears to have run as an elevated platform up the central gallery of the inn, between and under the two lines of plinths that supported the caravanserai's arcades (see figs. 13 and 14). Clay floors are very common in medieval living and working spaces, and most of them are not as fine, level, and easily cleaned as this one; though the floor was damp and slightly soft under the trowel when we first uncovered it from under layers of rubble, a day in the air and summer sun rendered it as hard as the stones it was set in. This clay floor would have served as well as any stone as support for bales of goods and sleeping travelers. Furthermore, as we found, it absorbed the heat from small fires built on top of it, burning the red clay to gold, gray, and black. In a few places we uncovered, the clay floor was cut by gutters or channels that sloped out toward drains in the building's walls: these were edged with stone kerbs and lined with broad flagstones (see fig. 13).[72]

But not everyone spent the night in the caravanserai on a tamped clay floor. Digging in the eastern- and westernmost extremities of the building, the excavations kept going down, finally hitting the kinds of regular floors paved in tuff flagstones that are familiar in Armenian monumental buildings. These paved floors sloped down perceptibly from the center of the caravanserai outward. Where the flagstone floors met the clay platform in the caravanserai's middle, we found that the height differential (fifty centimeters) was used to create one side of a long running trough built from thick slabs of volcanic tufa. Clearly, the lateral galleries of the caravanserai were intended for caravan animals—we even found one of the telltale holes pecked in the trough rim, used to tether an animal's head to their place. These troughs (or mangers, really, since they would not have been waterproof) ran the length of two five-meter excavation units before disappearing into the rubble baulk. Based on the comparanda at Selim and Harjis, these mangers probably continued most of the length of the building, along the outside of the column bases. Looking comparatively at these three caravanserais, you can see the development of the idea of incorporating stable areas into the architecture of a galleried building. Arai-Bazarjuł appears as a sort of "prototype" before someone had the idea of inserting the mangers *between* the individual arch bases, thus freeing up more of the inn's space for human and animal guests (see fig. 14).

Let's return to Bazarjuł. How do these details of architectural spaces and materials help us to imagine what it was like to stay in this particular caravanserai in medieval Armenia? Artifacts and other classes of archaeological data intersect with architectural reconstruction and textual history to provide us glimpses of what that experience would have been like. A major indicator is the distribution of different kinds of material traces across the spaces of the building. The hard clay floors of the *karavanatun* did not contain many artifacts; it seems that during the life of the building the majority of trash and refuse which was not swept out of the *karavanatun* collected in the channels cut into the clay floors. These gutters were filled with successive lenses of darkly stained, pooled deposits, which contained ceramic sherds, bone fragments, and a number of small metal artifacts—and of course, human and animal waste. In one operation (AC2) especially, the waste channel contained a number of personal objects that, perhaps, had fallen into the muck and been lost. These included a knife, several large needles, and two arrowheads, among other items that will be discussed below (see fig. 15). Significantly,

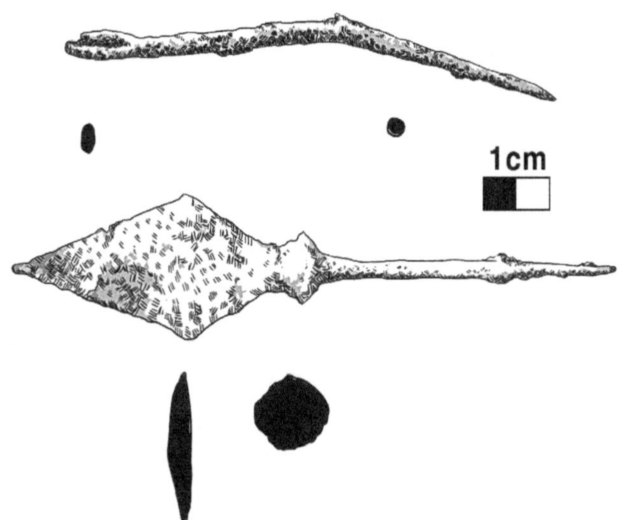

FIGURE 15. Iron objects from the caravanserai gutter: a needle and a Mongol-style arrowhead. Drawing by the author.

the layers of organic deposit were lying directly underneath the collapsed ashlar masonry, suggesting that the deposits in the channels were directly capped by the collapse of the building. These channel features also contained a large amount of broken thirteenth- to fourteenth-century ceramics.

I will discuss the forms and types of ceramic objects found in the caravanserai in the next chapter; for the moment, I want to speak more generally about human and animal life in the road inn. The architectural space of the caravanserai indicates a shared, though divided, space for human and nonhuman travelers to comfortably eat and sleep; in this, the Arai-Bazarǰuł caravanserai differs significantly from contemporary or earlier Seljuk buildings discussed above, where animals were presumably kept outside in the attached courtyard. When the southern door at Arai-Bazarǰuł closed at night, the world within the inn was a multispecies community of mutually dependent caravan travelers. And not just them; we also recovered a number of small, light bones from the fill above the stable floors. I was later informed that these were probably bones of starlings, common in medieval Armenia as they are today.[73] You can thus begin to imagine the interior of the caravanserai at night; it would have been smoky and close from the breath and sweat of humans as well as from the horses and donkeys whose heads lined the troughs, forming a sort of equine rogues gallery for the travelers in the center. The caravanserai almost certainly had at least one skylight or high window for smoke; the rising smoke from lamps and small fires would have been pierced by the swooping passes of starlings flying between the arches, and roosting in the late evening—perhaps after plucking fallen grains and crumbs out of the tramped earth at the edge of banked fires.

The artifacts found in the caravanserai gutters confirm that the road inn was a site for the care and maintenance of animals as well as for human rest. The most numerous category of metal artifact was flat-headed iron nails, of which we found a handful in our limited exposures. We also found a number of fragments of thin iron shoes, for horses or donkeys.[74] The majority of iron artifacts were found in the gutter features of the central excavations; this suggests the use of the central part of the *karavanatun* for various habitual tasks linked to the routine "maintenance activities" of trade, such as repairing the trappings of the caravan as well as meal preparation and animal care.

Among the metal artifacts was a complete arrowhead, made from well-forged iron. Through initial comparison with arrowheads found in the highlands and eastern Europe, I have characterized this arrowhead as "Mongol," raising further questions regarding the role of the *karavanatun* within negotiations of regime in the highlands after the thirteenth-century Mongol invasions.[75] Arrowheads similar to that found at the Arai-Bazarǰuł *karavanatun* have been found at Dvin, Garni, and Anberd, as well as at Tille Höyük.[76] Also found was a wrapped or tubular arrowhead in very fragmentary condition; this object is harder to compare with other examples but also suggests a high medieval date based on comparison with finds from Tille Höyük.[77] In one of the gutters, we also found the blade of a long knife, complete with the insertion for a wooden handle, long-since disintegrated. This object is generally similar to another blade found across the Kasakh Valley at the contemporary site of Tełenyacʻ Vankʻ.[78] These metal objects suggest a range of uses and activities by caravan travelers, from daily handiwork to hunting to eating to defense. The Mongol style of the arrowhead we found is no surprise, given that the Kasakh Valley was under Mongol rule from the middle of the thirteenth century onward. Arrowheads were part of the material culture that circulated under these new administrators, similar to the Ilkhanid coins minted at Ani (just to the other side of Aragats) in the latter part of the century. These items were part of everyday (or night) life in this stopping place along the mountain road. This category also includes a variety of other small objects, of which we found only one or two examples during the excavation. These include carnelian and faience beads, fragments of metal trimmings from clothing or harness, and several needles. Rather than the refuse from lavish feasts or long occupancy, the artifact assemblage at Arai-Bazarǰuł speaks of small tools and personal objects lost and left behind.

When an archaeologist is looking at the total assembled artifacts from an excavation, the temptation when looking at a singular, identifiable object is to forensically associate that object with an individual, with one person's story that we can tell. Certainly, some objects make this thinkable if not possible—they are engraved with names, or even found associated with the bodies of buried people. I am going to try to resist this temptation; the scope of my data is too slight, and the tendency to slip into familiar, overly comfortable stereotypes prevents us from potentially saying anything new about the past. For instance, when I think about the delicate carnelian and faience beads found in the caravanserai, I want to resist

FIGURE 16. A reconstructed east-west cross-section of the Arai-Bazarǰuł caravanserai. Drawn by the author.

the old-school archaeological temptation to say, "Ah! there were ladies (jewelry wearers) in the caravanserai, here they are." A major issue with this tendency is that we can see in artistic representations that both men and women in medieval Persia and Byzantium wore jewelry as well as embroidered, beaded clothing. Further, beads of faience and carnelian were kept, carried, and worn by people of various ages and genders for a number of purposes. Perhaps a more interesting story to tell from these few beads is that the "rough space of the road" and the spaces of bodily adornment and protection were not mutually exclusive here, in the Kasakh Valley. And these were not the only worlds that intersected in this arcaded space, full of humans and equids and their breath, food, and dung (see fig. 16).

If we read the excavation sequence "backward" then we can reconstruct a linear narrative of the use-life of the Bazarǰuł caravanserai. This lifespan was relatively brief as monumental structures go—but less so if we think again of medieval caravanserais as "monumental infrastructure." Then the point of comparison isn't the Parthenon, but instead the roadway infrastructure of our modern highways—in which case, a century is pretty impressive. We now regard Soviet-era bus stops as eerie relics of a system of transportation and connectivity built less than a century ago.[79] I remember when I first showed my reconstructions of the Arai-Bazarǰuł caravanserai's floors to Dr. Frina Babayan, excavator of Dvin, Uši, and Harič, among other sites. She was incredulous that a "monumental" building like a caravanserai would have an earthen floor, something associated with quotidian or work spaces in the monastic and urban contexts she was used to. The earthen floor of the Arai-Bazarǰuł caravanserai is emblematic of its double status as monumental infrastructure, as a building that functioned in the registers both of everyday life's mundane tasks and of commemorative politics. Like the world inscribed by

Tigran Honencʻ on the wall at Ani, the caravanserai is therefore a world-building energized by the *care* of its patron, their embodied attention to the capacities and needs of humans, nonhumans, and material things.

To walk into the Arai-Bazarǰuł caravanserai in the thirteenth century was thus to move within intersecting worlds. At its most basic, the experience of hospitality is highly socially freighted. If you have ever experienced hospitable infrastructures when you really needed them, then you can empathize with the experience of medieval travelers: a public water fountain on a hot day, a highway rest stop on a long night drive, public bathrooms in a strange city. And all of these forms are relatively prosaic compared to the politics of hospitality tied up in infrastructures like border control stations (or the deliberate lack thereof), airport customs facilities, or transit waiting rooms. Many of these places, especially airports and other "transit spaces," were summed up and discounted by spatial and social theorists of the later twentieth century. Marc Augé has decried these spaces as "nonplaces," the interchangeable everywhere-nowheres of capitalist modernity and a bane to the modern (western, individual, male) international traveler.[80] Such an idea of nonplace further supports the abstraction of the spacetimes of mobility and commerce into a nondimensional "space of flows" where uniformity stands in for universality.[81] Into this conversation about the phenomena of globalization I would like to push the case of the medieval caravanserai as a reminder of the critical importance of embodied subjectivity in mediating global movements, and of hospitality in housing embodied, mobile subjects. In medieval Eurasia, as today, travel spaces were important because the bodily vulnerabilities, needs, and pleasures of traveling humans (and nonhumans) were important. The regard for or disregard of these needs are part of the construction of differentially permeable boundaries around worlds, whether the world of thirteenth-century power in Armenia or the totalizing power of modern nation-states—and critically, this world-making happens in places, even and especially infrastructural places which serve to tie disparate localities together. As Arturo Escobar has argued contra the discourse on nonplace: "next to the delocalizing effects of translocal forms of power there are also, even if as a reaction to the latter, effects of boundary and ground making linked to places."[82] To use the phrasing from the Noravankʻ monastery caravanserai: for "guests, others and needy," global transit infrastructures are anything but affectless "nonplaces," being rather spaces of surveillance, control, discomfort, relief, or welcome. Medieval caravanserais functioned in a similar mode, transforming potentially alien landscapes into houses for the night, and displaying the capacity of a sovereign—whether Karakhanid, Seljuk, Mamluk, or Armenian—to act as host. I need not go into the extensive literature on the role of hospitality in the traditions of politics to get across how necessary such encounters are, both for knitting together polities and for creating global cultures. As monumental infrastructure, the medieval caravanserai was engineered to tie together the everyday needs of people with the global aspirations of their builders.

Staying a night at the *karavanatun* with their goods and pack animals, travelers would have been surrounded by a space of monumental architecture as well as a place made through the practices of Armenian highway hospitality: fees or charity, taxes on goods, and meals to be eaten inside the caravan hall in the company of other travelers. This place made of architecture and activity situated travelers—as well as the more stationary inhabitants and maintainers of the inn—within a world of practice that entailed both an idea of the local and a perspective on the large-scale. With the door of the *karavanatun* shut and locked for the night (as was common practice during the medieval period), the various projects of travelers and the ecumenes they inhabited would have been contained within the built place of the caravan inn, a concrete argument for the encompassment of these worlds of value within the politics of Vačʿe Vačʿutyan and the Kasakh Valley world—if only for a night. As will be discussed in the next chapter, the material practices of the caravanserai inhabitants—a community of "strangers"—had its own capacity to entail a world of nearness, distance, and particular, embodied politics.

6

The World in a Bowl

Intimate and Delicious Everyday Spacetimes on the Silk Road

Archaeologists are frequently strangers at the mercy of other people's hospitality. One might say that, in general, anthropology is dependent on the cosmopolitanism of others, on the ability to answer questions about one's own world in the paradigmatic language of an outsider, to volunteer as someone else's allegory. It's certainly not a coincidence that much of the foundational writing in anthropology is on the power of hospitality to construct and cement relationships between people: between guest and host, client and patron, insiders and outsiders. A central—though not always appreciated—role in these negotiated relationships is played by exchanges of gifts, and in particular, by the provision of food by a host to their guest. As explored especially by the anthropologist Nancy Munn, the act of welcoming and feasting one's guests wraps both parties (guest and host) in a web of shared spacetime, tying together people's future lives and actions with shared pasts rooted in the ground where the food is nurtured and grown, and in the bodies of those who shared a meal.[1] Drawing a term from her Gawan interlocutors, Munn called this spacetime *skwayobwa*, the shared world made in the sharing of food and hospitality. Earlier in the twentieth century, Mary Douglas explored how the action of sharing food is polyvalent and unpredictable, in that eating a meal warps the scales of social power structures, such that people can literally consume culture.[2] A ramification of the polyvalent sensuousness of food is that the imagination of cooking entails the construction of complex worlds of "place and time, desire and satiety, the longing for home and the lure of the wider world" to the scale of sensual, embodied experience.[3] Decades of anthropological discussion of the role of feasting, or the sharing of food in ritual and public ways, have developed a disciplinary appreciation of meal spacetimes as tournaments of cultural value, zones of transformation.[4] A shared meal is not just an invitation but also an act of

108

cosmopolitics: an injunction to the eater to orient their body within the configured expectations and cosmological orientations of their host.

In this chapter I will examine the role played by eating, but also by preparing and serving food, in mediating the situated experience of a world. Over the course of the previous chapters, I have explored the ways in which the Silk Road is imagined and constructed, both by medieval and by modern people. As I explained at the outset, such an exploration is rooted in understanding how medieval people experienced, thought about, and represented worlds of different scales, and how those imaginaries enable cosmopolitanism, or action-in-worlds. The Silk Road, as it turns out, looks very different at the scale of a single caravanserai than at the scale of a route, or at the scale of a written, literary work. In this chapter I narrow my gaze to one of the most intimate scales available: the span of meals shared within the Arai-Bazarǰuł caravanserai. In doing this, I am taking seriously the possibility that the Silk Road world was a place imagined in everyday actions and casual encounters; I am therefore arguing that the cosmopolitan practice of imagining the space of the Silk Road was possible for not only literate travelers and princely patrons, but also for people who left no historical record of their own. This chapter explores the routine encounters between travelers and hosts, and the construction through these encounters of a shared culture and mutual regard as fellow travelers in the same world. In other words, drawing upon the discussion of the previous chapters I will develop an idea of the caravanserai—and its surrounding village—as a node of *everyday cosmopolitanism*.

A simple meal can be complex. In the summer of 2009, I was in Armenia exploring the territory around Mount Aragats, trying to learn firsthand about medieval landscapes. I was at the time a guest of the Gyumri regional museum, where I made myself a nuisance with my combination of academic and practical ignorance. One morning in an effort to help me learn the topography of early medieval architecture in the surrounding area (and almost certainly to get me out of his hair), Hamazasp Khachatryan, the director of the Shirak museum, dumped me on a bus and told me to ride it to its terminus, the village of Sarakap, where I could find a seventh-century medieval church. Even better, there were the remains of a caravanserai (Jrapi) a few hills over, rescued from the dammed waters of the Akhurean River a few decades previous. I rode a rickety *marshrutka* down the western border until it came to a wide turning stop in front of the fountain and small store that marked the center of Sarakap village; hoisting my pack, I walked among small square houses, sheds, and barns, moving uphill toward the back edge of town, where ruins are frequently to be found. Walking up a side street I passed a woman, who regarded me keenly and then doubled back to ask if I needed help. I asked her where the "old church" was, and she pointed, giving me easy directions to find what once had been a tetraconch chapel, in a small square (really just an opening in the houses) a few streets further on. The church roof had collapsed, and in the Soviet period the church at Sarakap had, like many Armenian churches, been used as a hay barn. At some point in the last few years a corrugated tin roof had been placed over the remaining lintels, the building swept, and candles, icons, and devotion returned to the space.

After collecting my photographs and sketches and notes, I started to wander back through the town toward the road. Suddenly a waving figure popped into the street; it was the same woman, who introduced herself as Ana and demanded that I come into her house for a rest. I quickly found myself in a bright room of a type which I will always associate with small Armenian villages: well-swept wood floor, tall windows lined in long lace curtains, a table with a piece of floral-printed plastic draped over it. As I sat obediently, Ana fetched a pot of just-boiled coffee and one of a pair of teenage girls brought a saucer of wrapped chocolates arranged in a ring; I suspected that a seven-or-so-years-old boy sitting in the next room watching MTV on a flatscreen TV had just been sent to buy them. Ana sat and watched me drink my tiny cup of coffee, nudging fruit and chocolate toward me. She performed a gesture I have since seen many Armenian women practice, where she plucked a chocolate off the plate, unwrapped it, and placed it gently, insistently, next to my coffee cup, as if to finally overcome my frustrating reticence. We talked about my life in Chicago, my parents, and her family; her husband was in Russia for several months working in construction, there was no work in the village or the cities here. As I finally rose to leave she sent one of the girls back to the kitchen, to return with a cellophane bag, which Ana then filled with warm bread and fresh cheese from the plate on the table, certain I could not have eaten enough to sustain me on my imminent one-mile walk. And so it was that two hours later I found myself standing on the edge of the highway waiting to catch a bus back to Gyumri, munching on what is still perhaps my favorite thing to eat in Armenia: fresh chewy bread and a salty crumble of homemade cheese.

In the following years I would eat a lot of meals in a lot of village houses in Armenia and I've cooked my share as well. But I often find myself thinking about this midmorning meal with Ana because of the intimacy of it, and the spontaneity of her hospitality. She opened her house to a young person in weird clothes who had appeared out of nowhere in her town because she felt some conviction that merely giving me directions and setting me on my way was insufficient. Plus she was curious, plus perhaps she was bored and wanted a story to tell later, plus perhaps a hundred other reasons I can't know. But the meal she shared with me transformed me, cementing a memory of that village and of a slice of that woman's life in embodied memory with the taste of thick coffee and too-sweet candy, the smell of a house where fresh cheese and yogurt are stored, where the floor has just been swept with a hand-tied broom and the tan dust hangs in the air. Of course, I was transformed for Ana as well, from a stranger to a guest with a name and parents and a story and strange table manners, whose eyes lit up at the sight of real coffee. It's the mechanics and dynamics of these mutual transformations that sustain my fascination with *everyday eating,* with small rituals and routine gestures that fall under the radar when archaeologists talk about the power of "feasts." By textbook definition, my meal with Ana was the opposite of a feast: it was private, intimate, simple, and ordinary. But I would refer to the recent work of archaeologists interested in the power of cuisine and the everyday and argue that in routine and small rituals the structures of power and normalcy, of culture, are mortared into place.[5] Leading this conversation is archaeologist Christine Hastorf, who has argued through her work on cooking and eating in numerous contexts for the critical significance of intimate cuisine as part of a continuum of transformative practice that also contains feasting. As Hastorf explained, there is a useful analytic distinction between discursive (performed or spoken) and nondiscursive (undiscussed, taken-for-granted) aspects of the social work of practice, that nonetheless is quite blurry for practitioners: "The discursive side of practice includes those performative, commemorative, and semantic processes that actively and consciously draw upon and transmute the long-lived social traditions of a community. In contrast, non-discursive practices include habitual, bodily practices that tend to be unconscious, or at least non-verbal, routinized, and 'natural.'"[6] While people do occasionally draw discursive attention to cultural norms in their daily practice, much of the heavy lifting of culture is done by things that are left unsaid because they are obvious, undisputable, or "the way things have always been done." Cuisine especially is a dense tangle of nondiscursive cultural norms, from the way that vessels, utensils, or even furniture conform to accepted ways of eating, to ideas about who in a community procures, prepares, serves, and eats different kinds of everyday foods. As Hastorf explores in her analysis of cooking, serving, and eating, daily meals combine both discursive and nondiscursive practices in complex ways to reinforce structured relationships of gender, family, community, power, and identity. This is a critical intervention especially for archaeologies of medieval foodways, where approaches to eating have long been directed by understandings of dietary practice (or dietary prohibition) drawn from texts. Recently this conversation has shifted, thanks in particular to the work of members of the POMEDOR working group focused on the materiality of foodways in the medieval Mediterranean.[7] As Yasemin Bagci and Joanita Vroom pointed out, nondiscursive foodways which shaped the lives and worldviews of medieval people are recoverable by interdisciplinary methods, by thinking about the materialities contained in textual accounts, and the capacities of everyday material assemblages to produce and sustain social preferences and cultural worldviews.[8]

FOOD AND EMBODIED WORLDS

Why, then, should we not look to everyday rituals like the making of meals and the feeding of guests for mechanics by which shared cultures like that of the Silk Road were made? Why shouldn't the space created by practices of serving food to travelers, and their eating it, be as significant a world as the architectural spaces of caravanserais or the inscribed and endowed landscapes of local politics? Archaeological approaches to cuisine have demonstrated the capacity for the material artifacts of cooking, serving, and eating to mediate intersections between daily practice and larger-scale social phenomena, thereby framing the experience of travel.[9] Food allows a person to viscerally remember other, distant times and places, and to literally enclose that spatiotemporal vastness within their body.[10] And to return to the argument made by Munn, fed bodies themselves travel, transplanting memories, tastes, and appetites, the cyclical spacetimes of daily meals, into complex mnemo-material worlds.[11] In high medieval Armenia, the link between foodstuffs and the other scalar worlds we have explored so far is made explicit for me in a particular pot form, what archaeologists call the "stamp-belted *karas*." Archaeologists working all over the world make links between ceramic bodies and human bodies. Whether ceramic vessels are made to emulate human forms, or used to contain cremated burials, human beings tend toward an affinity to these round-bellied, strong-shouldered objects. An astoundingly popular form in the Caucasus in the high Middle Ages, the stamp-belted *karas* bears a wide belt along the "shoulder" of the pot, depicting repeating stamped patterns of vegetal, animal, and human figures.[12] These bands mirror, not only the long bands of decoration on the exterior of churches (such as Tigran Honenc''s church of St. Gregory), but also bands of figural *tiraz* embroidery found on medieval elite silken garments across the Silk Road worlds. The *karas*, a glossy red *mise en abyme*, helps me add one more scale to the linked microcosms we have already discussed: the *karas* holds food that is then contained within a human body, itself contained within architecture, contained within the world of imagined life. These scalar worlds—vessels, bodies, buildings—were linked together with common ideas about power, beauty, and desire.[13]

Considering food and the Silk Road, I will think about participation and global culture in two ways. First, I reiterate that cooking and eating was a critical practical means by which material cultures were put into use and transferred over space and time. So much of contemporary emphasis on the ancient Silk Routes has been on the transfer of domesticated crops and artistic styles, modes of dress and music, across vast expanses. Often these analyses produce maps with schematic arrows arcing between the Far East and Europe, along which an ear of millet or a single apple glides like a kid down a waterslide. The spatiotemporal scale of these engagements frequently disregards the work of people who cooked and served foods, who experimented with cooking vessels and spices and ways of preparing meat, grain, and fruit, and who were the technical specialists responsible for whether food cultures "stuck" in particular places. Following on anthropological discussions of practice theory by Ortner and others,[14] but also on theories of practice,[15] I am interested in the ways that making food entails participation within and production of global cultures by agents who aren't necessarily thinking about globality while they are working. This brings us back to an interesting aspect of the multivalency of material cultures. Sometimes drinking tea with sugar (for instance) prompts you to muse on the global chains of human interaction, differential power, and transit that made that everyday beverage possible in your part of the world.[16] More often, however, tea is just tea, or reminds you of any number of other embodied spacetimes and personal worlds; nonetheless, the fact of your global participation remains.

The second way that I want to conceptualize food and global culture is in terms of how hospitality and the sharing of meals were everyday encounters that actually produced the conditions of possibility for global cultures at local scales (and vice versa). In this sense, the cultural practice of welcoming strangers and feeding them (for free or for pay) makes travel, exchange, and interaction possible across large scales. Recently, Oya Pancaroğlu has drawn attention to the significance of hospitality—and especially the feeding of strangers—as an institution for knitting together the multiple, diverse populations of eastern Anatolia and the southern Caucasus in the tumultuous period punctuated by the Seljuk and Mongol invasions.[17] Pancaroğlu focuses on the wording of *waqf* documents (the endowment documentation of Muslim institutions like caravanserai or madrasas) commanding their attendants to feed all "comers and goers," regardless of sect.[18] In an exceptional example, she cites a late thirteenth-century eyewitness account of the serving of honeyed sweets to every guest at the Karatay Sultan Han.[19] The language of the *waqf* documents is very similar to that used in the inscriptions on Armenian caravanserais, committed to the welcoming of "passers-by" and "others." These locally rooted traditions or institutions of hospitality therefore grease the skids of global movements, even if some of the participants in these acts of hospitality are themselves relatively immobile. In thinking about cooking, serving, and eating as necessary practices that make long-distance trade and travel possible, we suddenly have to confront a complexification of the idea of *infrastructure* discussed in the last chapter. If infrastructure is material culture that enables and sustains the transit or movement of people or things, then the complex of skills and assemblages around cooking, serving, and eating is infrastructure as well. Recall the example of the highway systems built in during the New Deal that I mentioned in the last chapter. We habitually conceive of highways, bridges, tunnels and gas stations as infrastructure—but what about the other "services" along the route? Think about motels and restaurants as part of the apparatus of infrastructure that makes a road trip even conceivable in a landscape of highways. I'll be returning to the idea of the roadside restaurant later in this chapter; first, let's get back to Arai-Bazarjuł.

FOOD BY THE SIDE OF THE ROAD: ASSEMBLING A CUISINE AT ARAI-BAZARjUŁ

As I discussed in the previous chapter, the floors of the caravanserai were scattered with the broken remains of ceramic vessels; more critically, the gutters were filled with a dense mix of decomposed human and animal waste as well as ceramics and food waste (animal bones and plant remains) that had been swept off of the nearby floors into the gutters. Though 100 percent of the ceramic artifacts from the excavation were collected when we excavated, only those materials recovered from closed cultural contexts (preserved floors and gutters, covered by a solid layer of collapse which contextually "sealed" the materials) were analyzed.[20] These contexts include the troughs and flagstone barn floors and the clay central gallery floors and flagstone-lined gutter features. From the materials taken from these contexts, I selected out "diagnostic" ceramic fragments. Diagnostic is a relative term in archaeology, meaning that which enables a conclusion to be drawn. A sherd or bone that is very useful to one specialist may be confounding or useless to another, depending on training, experience, or area of research. My definition of "diagnostic" changes constantly as I learn more about medieval ceramics; however, a stable, practical definition combines formal characteristics that allow me to identify the shape of a vessel (such as a rim, a handle, or a base), decorative characteristics that allow me to categorize how the vessel or part of vessel was decorated (both in terms of designs and techniques like burnishing or glazing), and finally, technical characteristics that enable me to say something about how the vessel was made (for instance, temper or marks from fingers or a wheel), or how it was used (pitch deposits for waterproofing, soot deposits from long exposure to fire, drilled holes from repair).

The diagnostic ceramics from Arai-Bazarǰuł were analyzed both through comparison with published corpuses and in collaboration with Frina Babayan at the Armenian National Academy of Sciences Institute of Archaeology and Ethnography. The first thing we established based on the ceramic assemblage from Arai-Bazarǰuł was that, according to comparisons with dated materials from Dvin and other sites, the ceramics from the caravanserai were made during the thirteenth through fourteenth centuries. This finding corroborated the proposed date of the building (1213) and confirmed that we are looking at the remains of meals cooked, served, and eaten when the caravanserai was used by medieval travelers during the Vač'utyan period in the Kasakh Valley. Beyond this general date, it was possible to make a series of more specific observations about the types and forms of ceramic found at the caravanserai. Very quickly: a *type* of ceramic is the general technical and decorative style that a specific fragment might belong to, such as "blue and white porcelain," or "Terra Sigillata ware" or "Fiesta ware"—these names denote particular techniques, time periods, or even places of distribution and use. A ceramic *form* is related to the practical use or capacity of that object: bowl, platter, milk strainer, chamber pot. Archaeologists assign vessels that they find to both types and forms based on techniques of generalization; in other words, these categories can be useful, but are famously slippery in that one person's bowl is sometimes another's cup and so on.[21] So I will endeavor to explain what we found at Arai Bazarǰuł, and, more critically, why this combination of types and forms is important for us. Crucially for the story that this chapter tells, ceramics are the material technology of cooking, serving, and eating food that, when combined with ingredients, practices, and ideas (cooking techniques, table manners, tastes, and norms) constitute a *cuisine*, or an eating culture.

Perhaps unsurprisingly, the fragmented ceramic equipment we found in the road inn was plain by most medievalists' standards. The caravanserai assemblage contains bowls, jars, and pitchers, including fragments of large cooking and storage jars as well as smaller jars and jugs. One lid handle fragment was found on the flagstone floor of one of the stable areas; this style of lid was ubiquitous in medieval Armenia and could have covered anything from a cooking jar to a small oven. The vast majority (98 percent) of the materials recovered from the caravanserai floors and prefloor fills were unglazed red wares.[22] Jars and cooking pots were made of the same clay and generally tempered with the same mixture of micaceous and obsidian sands, and their rims fired to a similar range of medium reds. The bodies (rounded sides and bottoms) of jars could vary in color from grayish to a warm gray-brown, and many body fragments were burned, confirming that they were used for cooking. The similarity of clay color and inclusions indicate that these red ware vessels were made from the same clays, possibly sourced nearby.[23] This finding corroborates the historical suggestions that caravanserais were supported by neighboring villages. Excavations more recently at the Selim caravanserai in Vayots Dzor indicate that the monumental infrastructure of that fourteenth-century building was also rooted in local materiality at the scale of food, drink, and other ceramic practice (see fig. 17).[24]

Bowl Food

The excavations recovered a representative assemblage of fragments of rims from bowls. These bowls varied in their shapes: some of them were *globular*, meaning that their bodies curved smoothly from rim to foot, while others were *carinated*, with a sharp break between a more cylindrical upper body and the curving lower body. Both of these bowl forms probably had ring-form bases and were thrown on a potter's wheel. The bowl rims fell into two large categories: plain round rims (22.4 percent) and flattened-round rims (34.2 percent). Regardless of their styles, the bowl fragments from the inn floors were consistently covered with a redder slip (a paintlike suspension of fine clay in water) and then burnished till they shone. An even brighter red slip was painted along the rims and insides of the bowls. The red slip decoration could vary in consistency or fullness of application—some bowls appear to have been cursorily wiped with the red slip in a single pass, especially in the case of a number of rounded-rim bowl fragments. Other bowls were evenly covered in a bright red slip on exterior and interior and finely burnished to a glossy, enamel-like shine. Looking at these fragments as an assemblage, you start to get a sense of what a "good bowl" looked like in the thirteenth century. Such a bowl would sit in the hand, on the table, or on the ground,[25] with a gleam of bright

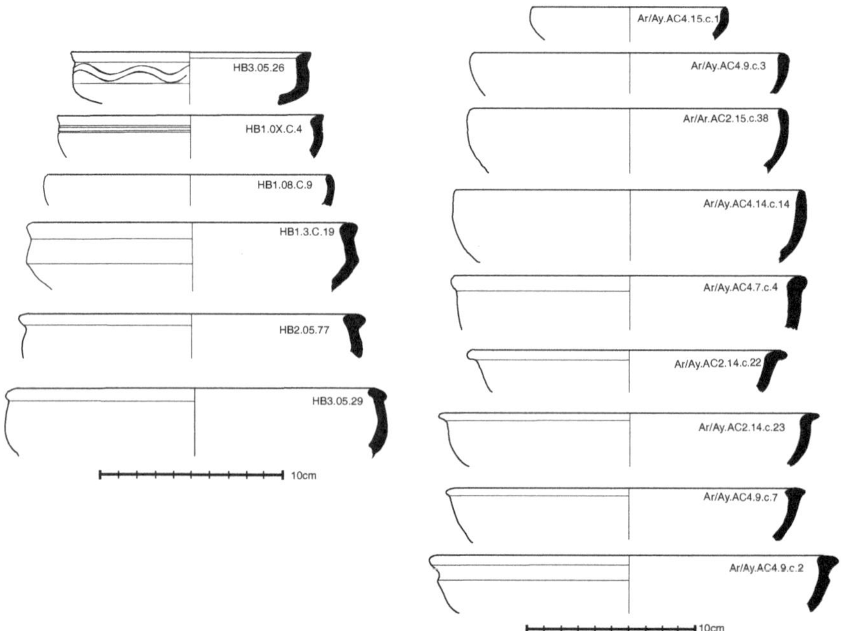

FIGURE 17. Red-slipped redware bowls from Ambroyi village (left) and from the Arai-Bazarǰuł caravanserai (right). Drawn by the author.

red at the rim, and from above would present a shiny red interior to surround the contents. A preference for bowls like this was widespread in the thirteenth to fourteenth centuries, not only in the Kasakh but across Armenia.[26]

Jar Cooking

The assemblage from the caravanserai includes an assortment of rim fragments from cooking jars of similar size, all in the 18–25cm rim diameter range. These jars were produced of red-to-buff clay with sandy inclusions, frequently slipped and burnished on the exterior, and especially on their rims, till they were glossy dark brown or gray. Though no complete vessels were found at Arai-Bazarǰuł, the body fragments recovered in combination with the rim assemblage indicates that these jars had rounded bodies, wide necks, and upright rims like a thick collar. One fragment of such an upright rim included a partial strap handle, which would have attached to the vessel shoulder. The inside of the rim's lip was frequently notched and slanted, so that a lid could be fit snugly onto the jar. While we didn't recover a whole jar from Arai-Bazarǰuł, from the large number of body fragments and from comparisons from finds at other sites we can reconstruct what these jars looked like. It is highly probable that the cooking pots used at the Arai-Bazarǰuł *karavanatun* had thick, coarsely curving and perhaps hand-formed bases, like

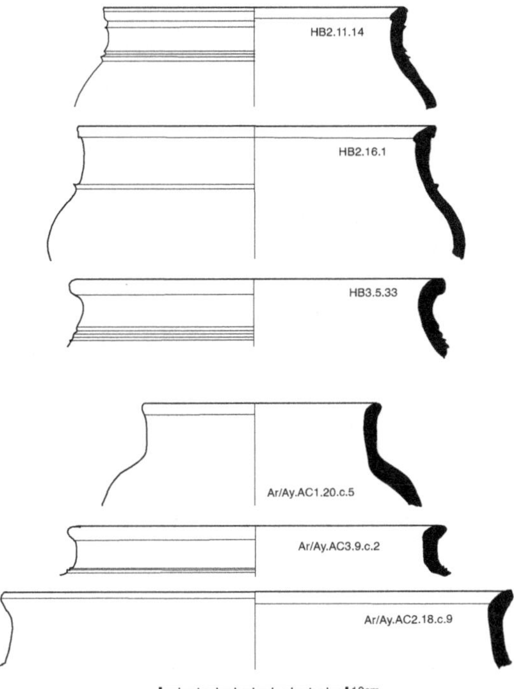

FIGURE 18. Redware cooking jar rims from Ambroyi village (top) and Arai-Bazarǰuł caravanserai (bottom). Drawn by the author.

reconstructed wide-mouth red ware jars which have been found at the high medieval highland site of Yełegis, in Vayots Dzor (see fig. 18).[27]

Not all of the ceramics in the caravanserai were red wares—though most of them were. A considerable portion of the shoulder and neck profile of a decorated white-ware jug was recovered from the fills just above the flagstone floor;[28] jugs like this one are common finds from urban excavations in Armenia, but they have also been found in large quantities at well-connected towns like Arpa, in Vayots Dzor.[29] We also found a literal handful of glazed ceramic bowl fragments; all in all, these outliers rather confirmed the general picture of a relatively utilitarian ceramic assemblage used for serving and eating at the caravanserai.

Eating Space in the Caravanserai

Statistical analyses of the distributions of pottery types within different contexts demonstrate that the red ware assemblage of jars and red bowls was associated with the parts of the building intended for the use of human residents. As mentioned in the previous chapter, a chi-square analysis assessing the occurrence of bowls and jars on the clay floors, versus in gutters or on barn floors, shows strongly nonrandom distribution.[30] Cross-tabular analysis showed that of the diagnostic assemblage of bowl and jar fragments, only 7 percent was found on the clay floors, while 45 percent was recovered from the gutter features. Meanwhile, only 14 percent of the total number of jar and bowl fragments were recovered from the stable areas.[31]

This pattern of deposition of ceramics suggests that the vessels for eating and cooking were largely used in the road inn's central gallery, where travelers could eat at some minimal distance from their animals (and animal waste). That ceramic fragments were largely found in the waste gutters and not pressed into the clay floors suggests as well that food preparation was concentrated within part of the unexcavated portion of the building or, more probably, that cooking occurred in some other location external to the caravan hall itself. This possibility is corroborated by the faunal evidence: very few bone fragments were found on the floors; instead, many small bone fragments were found within the rubbish deposits in the gutters. While the floors may have been swept, this observation also supports the scenario of food being prepared in a single location or in a different context than the caravan hall. In other words, a local cook (or cooks) was preparing food that was then served to travelers, as opposed to each traveler preparing their own meal.

*Complementary Assemblages, Shared Daily Lives: Ceramic
Materials from Ambroyi Village*

Who was cooking in these jars, if not the caravan travelers? In part to answer this question, and to broaden the overly simplistic image of self-sufficient caravans disembedded from local landscapes, in 2013–14 I and a team of colleagues excavated a section of the village of Ambroyi, which in the thirteenth to fourteenth centuries would have abutted and enclosed the Arai-Bazarǰuł caravanserai.[32] This village was a cluster of structures built from undressed stones pulled from the nearby streams, with floors cut into the hard yellow clay of the Kasakh Valley. The greater part of the village was destroyed in the twentieth century by intensive agriculture in the Kasakh Valley; in the preserved section we investigated, we found a dense cluster of ovens and the storage, processing, and garbage pits associated with cooking (see figs. 19a and 19b).[33]

A full account of these excavations is published elsewhere;[34] what is important for this discussion is the evidence we uncovered which suggested that the villagers at Ambroyi and the travelers staying in the caravanserai shared a material world at the level of ceramic assemblages. In particular, the ceramic assemblage at Ambroyi is a "matched set" with that at Arai-Bazarǰuł. We found the same straight-necked cooking jars and red-slipped bowls, indicating that the food eaten at the inn was also cooked and eaten in the village. I vividly remember sitting at a desk in the medieval department in Yerevan in 2015 with Astghik Babajanyan, holding up bowl fragments from the village and road inn and marveling that they could have been from the same vessel.

FIGURES 19A and 19b. Handbuilt clay ovens (*tonirs*) in living and working spaces at Ambroyi. Photos by the author.

These finds required me to rethink the data from the caravanserai. Glazed ceramic types which when found in 2011 in tiny quantities at the road inn were thought to be commodities carried by the travelers,[35] were found in larger fragments and greater quantities in the village. These included bowls decorated with white slip and incised vegetal designs and covered in clear yellow or green glazes, as well as green, yellow, and brown polychrome dishes. This suggests that these sgraffiato and splashware vessels *were* imports, and that the village and inn were connected in complex loops of transit and transfer. The villagers procured serving wares (as well as colored glass bracelets and vessels) through their proximity to the trade routes which connected settlements in the highlands. Then, perhaps, the village cooks used their imported sgraffiato "services" to serve guests in the inn, complicating the directionality of exotic and local material cultures, of foreigners and natives.

Tasty Seeds and Tasty Bones: Macrobotanical and Faunal Data

While the ceramic material gives us a wealth of information about who cooked and how they cooked and served, we are still left with the important question of *what* was cooked in the jars and served into the red burnished bowls. To inform on this question I turn to the plant and animal remains from the gutter features in the caravanserai. The macrobotanical remains from Arai-Bazarǰuł represent a unique source of information about medieval plant economy and diet. So far within the Republic of Armenia, contemporary botanical evidence is published from only two contexts; the settlement of Norabak 1 and medieval layers at Getahovit-2 Cave site.[36] Plant remains from the road inn were recovered using standard floatation and wet-sieving techniques. The first stages of cleaning and analysis of these materials were done by Dr. Roman Hovsepyan in Aparan and in Yerevan, as mentioned in the anecdote at the beginning of the last chapter. Subsequently, the botanical data were studied in detail by Anna Berlekamp.[37] Archaeozoological information from the medieval period in Armenia is even rarer, as most medieval excavations do not retain faunal materials. The faunal data from cultural levels were recovered from unscreened soils and analyzed by Dr. Belinda Monahan in Chicago.

The majority of plant remains from cultivated plants are charred cereal grains, especially wheat and barley.[38] Millet, another common grain, was also found in lesser quantities. Both predominant species of millet, the broomcorn millet (*Panicum miliaceum*) and foxtail or Italian millet (*Setaria italica*) were recorded in the caravanserai assemblage. Millet is a summer grain, while wheat and barley are winter crops requiring more water. Millet was probably cultivated in the lowlands (such as the Araxes River Valley to the south), as the environment of the Kasakh Valley is too severe (though this hypothesis remains to be substantiated for the climatic conditions of the high medieval period). Berlekamp proposed that this data combining summer and winter crops shows us year-round cropping of fields serving the caravanserai.[39] This tells us about the seasonality of agricultural life in the Kasakh Valley (providing detail for the lifeworld described in chapter 4), as well as suggesting that the caravanserai may have been used in winter as well as summer—though it is also possible that travelers were fed stored grain. Charred seeds of various species of legumes (*Fabaceae*) were also recovered. All the recorded cultigens are considered to be traditional crops for the territory of Armenia, and have been recorded since the Iron Age up to the beginning of the previous century.[40] Findings of rose hip, grapes, and plum pits round out the image of plant diet at the *karavanatun*, which seems to be dominated by cereal grains. Presuming that a portion of this charred grain material did not come from sacks of grain stored in the caravanserai, the assemblage suggests a cuisine which incorporated cooked whole grains as well as (or instead of) bread.

The botanical remains also contained traces of plants which were imports to the Kasakh Valley, including figs, pomegranate, olives, and almonds. These were found in the channels, a combination of practice and preservation: travelers ate the fruits and nuts and discarded the pits into the waste channels or onto the floors. Berlekamp noted as well what the nonhuman guests at the caravanserai would have been eating: sorrels (*rumex sp.*) and sedges (*Cyperaceae*) which may have grown in the streams running down the slope of Aragats or along the Kasakh River, as well as small wild legumes, which were common fodder.[41] Berlekamp also points out a crucial aspect of both data and of daily life in the caravanserai: much of the carbonized wild plant material would have been contained in dung which was burned for fuel, a common practice in antiquity as well as in the present.[42] Imagine the interior of the caravanserai lit by small fires built of dung bricks or chips, producing sharp, thick smoke and ashes swept at intervals from the floors into the nearest gutter.

The other hard and durable evidence we have from the various tasty, nourishing, and memorable meals in the caravanserai are fragments of animal bone, remains of meat served and eaten in various forms. This faunal (animal) evidence indicates that the food consumed on the site included a large amount of mutton or goat meat in addition to beef and chicken, as well as a smaller quantity of pork. All of the animal remains found were quite fragmentary, mostly tiny shardlike pieces, which is commensurate with the meat being chopped up and cooked in pots rather than roasted or grilled.[43] Just over 2 percent of the assemblage showed evidence of having been burned, indicating that only a minority of the bone fragments came into direct contact with fire (i.e., further evidence that they were boiled or stewed). The micromorphological study of cut marks on the bone fragments found some evidence for butchery, which was mostly of a chopping nature rather than carving or slicing meat off of bones, and generally gives us the impression that the meat that ended up in the pots served to travelers at the caravanserai was attached to chopped up bones and joints, and perhaps involved a lot of gristle and fatty marrow.

FROM DATA TO CUISINE

The combined ceramic, faunal, and botanical data from the caravanserai therefore provides us with a partial *cuisine assemblage*: a combination of ingredients and instruments which shed light on food practice, enabling us to draw conclusions regarding a number of questions related to cuisine at the caravanserai.

What were they eating? To summarize the above evidence: The gutter contexts of the caravanserai produced charred seeds of cereal grains (wheat and barley) and legumes. The faunal evidence from the Arai-Bazarǰuł *karavanatun* indicated that the food consumed on the site included mutton or goat meat in addition to beef and chicken, as well as pork. All the animal remains found were quite fragmentary, suggesting meat chopped up and cooked in pots rather than roasted or grilled. The majority of the evidence for butchery was evidence for chopping up bones rather than removing meat from bones: this suggests that the food provided to travelers at the inn was a stew of toasted grains and legumes, with occasional scraps of fatty meat and bones. A dish similar to this is still eaten and beloved among Armenians and in the Persian world as well: *herisa*, a greasy, heavy porridge. If you have ever eaten *herisa*, then you can imagine the thick steam that would rise off a pot of this stew as it was placed on the table or floor, and further imagine how such a stew would "stick to your ribs" (as my mother would say). I could thus hypothesize as well, based on our knowledge of the dairying practiced in villages like Ambroyi, that there was probably a hefty dollop of butter or ghee added to the stew as well—though of course this is an ingredient that, like seasonings, leaves few archaeological traces if used in small quantities.

What did they eat it with? The ceramic assemblage from the caravanserai complements the faunal and botanical evidence. We found the set of dishes that you would need to prepare a thick stew of grains and fatty meat, cooking it over a coal fire (perhaps in a *tonir* oven such as those we found at Ambroyi), and to serve it out to a small gathering of guests, each of whom might have received their own red-rimmed bowl. Comparisons with data from other sites help us think about whether travelers eating at the inn would have thought this meal was familiar, tasty, or "comforting." The assortment of ceramic types (wares and forms) found at Ambroyi and used to serve meals to travelers at the *karavanatun* is formally similar to the red ware assemblage that made up a significant portion of dining materiality in castles and monasteries as well as cities in the highlands during the same period. The recovery of a similar combination of wares and forms from sites like Tełenyacʻ Vankʻ, Yełegis, and Daštadem in Armenia, and Gritille in eastern Turkey suggests that such culinary practices were not merely a phenomenon of the caravan hall, but also occurred in other contemporary social contexts.[44] Cooking in rounded, straight-rimmed jars and serving the resulting meal in an assemblage of small (approximately 15cm diameter) footed bowls seems to have been a factor in "local" Anatolian and Caucasian cuisine.[45]

Now we have two of the three components—technology plus ingredients—that make up a cuisine. How can we use the first two plus different kinds of historical evidence to reveal the third: practices? Historical as well as archaeological data suggest that patterns in the ceramic repertoire—such as a strengthened emphasis on deep cooking pots and small serving bowls—might have accommodated a "globalizing" food practice among the administrators, soldiers, traders and travelers who moved through the Near East and Eurasia in the medieval period.[46] Further, recipes preserved from the same period suggest that the cuisine which accompanied the pottery technology found in the caravanserai also bore a significant relationship to medieval imaginations of "comfort food"; that is, cuisine that was associated, not with an exotic place of origin (despite potentially exotic ingredients), but with the imagined and embodied world of wholesome tradition. Muhammad bin Hasan al-Baghdadi wrote *The Book of Dishes* in Baghdad around 1226; this book indicates that canonical or "traditional" cuisine at that time drew on regional influences even while remaining familiar. The recipes in Baghdadi's *Kitab al-ṭabīḫ* were compiled as a work of courtly art; however, the book was not meant as some airy confection, for al-Baghdadi disavowed "strange and unfamiliar dishes" in favor of wholesome foods that were "well known and in common use" in his time and place.[47] In other words, al-Baghdadi's cookbook was not a performance of exoticism but a manual of canonical taste and food practice, a cartography of taste within which the author centrally situated himself, stating essentially "this is what home tastes like."

Discussion of the *Kitab*, as well as of other books of the same title written by medieval Arab authors, frequently focuses on the ingredients of the recipes and their influence on European cuisine,[48] but I am interested also in the implications of the cooking and preparation instructions provided in the *Kitab*—the hints at medieval culinary *practice*.[49] Two of the ten chapters (chapter 2 "Plain Dishes," and chapter 4, "Harisa and Baked Dishes") instruct the aspiring thirteenth-century cook on preparing dishes of grains and meats boiled in stone or clay pots. From this culinary source, it appears that a significant part of medieval Baghdadi "comfort food" was made up of dishes prepared by chopping meat and fat with spices, boiling them with rice, wheat, chickpeas, or lentils, and then serving the settled mixture directly from the pot it was cooked in. Often the cook is instructed to wipe the rim of the cookpot with a clean cloth, in the interest of aesthetics. One could imagine the ceramic repertoire that would accommodate such an everyday cuisine, which was derived in part from Persian and Turkic recipes for classic dishes like *herisa*:[50] a pot big enough for boiling but with a rim narrow enough for a snug lid, with handles for transferring it from fire to table, and bowls for serving the resulting semiliquid food. Perhaps the interior as well as the exterior of the rim of the pot would even be burnished to a ruddy shine, the better to offset the contents as it was set in the midst of hungry diners.

Al-Baghdadi's cookbook is complemented by a manual by Hu Sihui, the title of which (*Yinshan Zhengyao*) translates as *Proper and Essential Things for the Emperor's Food and Drink*. Dated to 1330, this book attests to a shift in culinary worlds: the center of proper and tasty eating is now, according to the author, the table of the Mongol Yuan emperors. The manual contains a record of the recipes recommended to the court of the Mongols and is a testament to the "pretentions of cultural universality" which persisted within the Mongol Empire in the early fourteenth century.[51] Summarized as "a deliberate attempt to represent the Mongolian world order in visible, tangible, edible form," the manual combines nostalgia for comforting traditions as well more exotic cartographies into a single empire of taste.[52] The recipes described in the *Yinshan Zhengyao* represent a fusion of Mongol steppe ingredients with Turkic cooking practices as well as Chinese tastes.[53] Significantly for our purposes, the translators point out that the majority of recipes in this fourteenth-century manual for health are combinations of meat and starches, boiled together in a single pot; while this was foreign to Chinese culinary traditions, such practice aligned with Mongol cosmological health practice.

These recipes illuminate how the cooking of grains and fatty meats together could result in either a cosmologically nutritious Mongol repast or a comforting Baghdadi *herisa* (or both). These dishes also resemble the *dugi* eaten by "Turks" in the Crimea encountered by traveler Ibn Battuta in the 1330s. According to the traveler, the Turks prepared *dugi* by boiling grain in water and adding small pieces of meat (if they had it): "then every man is given his portion in a dish, and they pour over it curdled milk and sup it."[54] All of these simple, stewy, starchy dishes resemble the food which may have been on the standing menu at the Arai-Bazarjuł caravanserai. Notice as well that Ibn Battuta describes the portioning out of the stews into individual bowls, conjuring again the image of travelers sitting together and sharing a common meal served by a local host. While these sources provide links between recipes and material assemblages, numerous textual accounts confirm the central place of *herisa* within medieval and early modern Armenian imaginaries. James R. Russell compiled references to *herisa*, including an episode in the great medieval epic *The Daredevils of Sasun* (*Sasna cṙer*). In the vignette, the hero David steals a huge pot of *herisa* from pious but hypocritical villagers and feeds it to his fellow men.[55] An early modern folk tale further links *herisa* with carnivalesque leveling of heroes and villagers, specifically situated in the courtyard of a caravanserai.[56] By the Ottoman period, *herisa* was eaten as part of Armenian ritual sacrifice (*matał*), and elegized as a Shrovetide food invented by Gregory the Illuminator[57]—a belief that persists into the present.[58]

Returning back to the anthropological discussion of food and embodied politics at the beginning of this chapter, we are presented with a challenge if we try to define the meals served and eaten in the Arai Bazarǰuł caravanserai, or in similar spaces along the Silk Road, in simple terms. The power relations that structure the spacetimes of serving, eating, and embodied memory of these meals—or in the term proposed by Appadurai, their *gastropolitics*—are complicated, challenging the categories of ritual and routine, of ceremonial and domestic.[59] For instance, was the caravanserai, as monumental infrastructure where travelers carried out mundane and intimate practices like eating, sleeping, scratching, eliminating, and so on, a private space or a public space? Does such a categorical distinction between public (politics) and private (daily routines) help us in this case? The stew cooked in a rammed-earth kitchen at Ambroyi and served from an earthenware cook-jar at the caravanserai was greasy, warm, unassuming, and satisfying, but was it *just* an everyday home cooked meal? Or did the fact of hospitality and the architectural space of the caravanserai remind travelers that the food they ate was a "feast" presented by Vačʿe Vačʿutyan, their absent host nonetheless present in the space he had endowed? Is a meal eaten in a caravanserai therefore ceremonial or domestic—or *both/neither*, pointing out the necessity of dissolving the apparent distinction between these concepts in order to analyze the social power of the Silk Road culinary spacetime? Imagined after the example set by Douglas, the complex spatial politics of Silk Road hospitality are encapsulated in the complicated geography of the food itself. How do I "theorize" a tasty stew that was cooked literally in a hole in the Armenian ground, as local as you get, but which was also "comfort food" according to Mongol and Baghdadi cookbooks with cosmographic aspirations, making it something like a cosmopolitan dish? How might the cosmopolitan-ness of a food like *herisa* be further complicated by its folkloric role as a greasy and delicious carnivalesque social lubricant? The space I ultimately found to think through food which is simultaneously here-and-everywhere is the roadside restaurant, and it is that brightly lit, hypermodern space that I will briefly visit before concluding this chapter.

THE SPACE OF *ROAD FOOD*

In the United States we have an academic term for cuisine that is simple to make but hard to forget, which tastes so good that it sparks nostalgia and collapses class distinction. The American gastro-ethnographers Jane and Michael Stern drew this range of culinary experiences in North America under a single heading, calling it *road food*.[60] In their foundational conceptualization of the cuisine concept, Stern and Stern defined road food not in terms of its ingredients per se, but in terms of where it is found and how it is made: "Roadfood means great regional meals along highways, in small towns and in city neighborhoods. It is non-franchised, sleeves-up food made by cooks, bakers, pitmasters, and sandwich-makers who are America's culinary folk artists."[61]

Immediately emerging from this definition and significant for our discussion of scalar worlds and their perception, road food in America according to Stern and Stern is at once resolutely local ("small towns," "non-franchised") but also somehow quintessentially and universally American ("sleeves-up," "folk art"). Road food therefore belongs to no town or region in particular but to the polyglot nation as a whole. To eat road food means that no matter in which highway or neighborhood restaurant a traveler dines, they can know that they are eating something that is both authentically local but also, somehow, reassuringly familiar. This near contradiction between particularity and universality which sits at the heart of road food as a concept dovetails with the imaginary of cosmopolitanism as I am endeavoring to construct it. The capacity of food to enable tactile and concrete co-presence at the same time as participation in other places, times, and wider communities makes road food an apt locus for the cosmographic negotiations of medieval cosmopolitanism. It helps me think about how travelers could enjoy the intimate and comforting pleasure of a simple meal while simultaneously participating in the construction of global culture. As or more importantly, the spacetime-bending capacities of road food means that the people who cook and serve it are themselves critical agents in world-making, are themselves architects of global cultures.

Road Food and a Cosmopolitics of Care

There is a tension in registers in road foods, whether medieval *herisa* or Waffle House hash browns, that points to a critical question of agency, and of subjectivity. In the medieval context, this means questioning what modes of practice are to be considered productive of cosmopolitan spaces, of Silk Road histories. To be road food, a cuisine must be both authentic, culturally true, as well as simple. Road food is made by *cooks*, not chefs—but that doesn't make it any less sublime.[62] Similar to the space of the caravanserai, road food challenges the inherent distinction between domestic and ceremonial, between everyday and ritual, which is supposed to be at the center of the difference between meals and feasts.[63]

Ethnographic description of roadside restaurants stresses the emphasis placed on nourishment, on care of the guest. Barbara Ehrenreich documented the impulse to care on the part of waitresses in a hotel restaurant, even when that care came out of their own minimum-wage salaries, describing how in the middle of a long shift in a tourist restaurant "the service ethic kick[s] in like a shot of oxytocin, the *nurturance hormone.*"[64] The server of road food—whether an all-night truck stop waitress, an urban greasy spoon server, the cook at the back of a dive bar—performs a *work of care* (though it may not appear so), in that this work of culinary world-making and spatial transformation is performed in the course of a labor of making another person at home in a place that is not their home. The work realm of hospitality has only relatively recently been drawn into academic conversations about "care work," or the ways of being and making which used to be called "unproductive labor" or "maintenance labor" under strict Marxist rubrics.[65] This is relevant to our conversation, because it means that making the work of hospitable servers visible as part of the cosmopolitan making of global spaces on par with the construction of buildings or the writing of geography is a bit of an uphill feat. Yet I hope this chapter reveals that the difference between the world-building of a caravanserai and the world-building of a road food meal is not one of significance, but of scale—and even then, the slippery spacetimes of cuisine enable unpredictable embodied shifts across scales of space and memory. Returning again to the work of Nancy Munn and the concept of *skwayobwa*, it is ultimately the practices of hospitality—of welcoming, housing, feeding strangers—that constructs the possibility for people to live in the same future world.

Before reaching the Black Sea coast in 1331–2, Ibn Battuta arrived at the port city of al-Alaya (Alanya), a significant medieval entrepot and the endpoint of an overland route staged with Seljuk-period caravanserais.[66] Ibn Battuta noted the exceptional hospitality of the people of the city, which manifests in open gifts of simple food:

> One of their customs in that country is that they bake bread on only one day each week, making provision on that day for enough to keep them for the rest of the week. Their men used to bring us warm bread on the day it was baked, together with delicious viands to go with it . . . and would say to us, "the women have sent this to you and beg of you a prayer."[67]

What I find remarkable in this account is the parallel in the request of the women bakers providing bread to travelers, and the language of inscriptions left in *karavanatn'ner* by their donors, as well as within the *waqf* documents and inscriptions attached to Seljuk hans and lodges (described in the last chapter).[68] Patrons, princes, and baker women feed the traveling stranger, and ask in return for the gift of their hospitality to be carried forward as their guest moves along their journey and remembers them in prayer and in imagination. This suggests a messiness in the spacetime of hospitality when considered at the scale of cooking, feeding, and eating. It also points to a modality of power: despite the politeness of the request to be remembered, the guest has ultimately little agency in carrying with them a *memento* of their host in the form of a meal eaten, a little world stuck to their ribs.

I found myself thinking about this slippery spacetime at one point in 2015, as we were in the midst of excavations at the Ambroyi village site. My collaborator Frina Babayan had received a request from a *sp'yuřk'ahay* friend in the city to bring them a large quantity of "real *matsoun*"[69]—in other words, authentic, homemade yogurt prepared by a village woman from her own cows and sheep. Homemade yogurt in Armenia is thick and grassy, often with a rich skim of butterfat on the surface; it's delicious and thought to be a cure-all. Ando, one of the team, put Frina in touch with a woman in the village, and the two of them conferred on quantities, modes of delivery, and price. As the *matsoun* was reaching completeness, we stopped by to visit the producer at her house in Arai village; we were welcomed into her front room and seated in our dig clothes on her spotless sofa. Frina and I asked interested questions about how the yogurt was made: What made this woman's product the best in the village? What kind of milk did she use? What vessels? I remember clearly that the woman related an interesting piece of information in an offhand way: the real secret, she said, was not the ingredients but the souring process. As she said: "I have one old garment [*hin šor*] that I always use to cover the milk while it turns. If I don't use that one, it doesn't work out." I remember remarking that the woman definitely said *šor*, referring to something that a person would wear (or a scrap of clothing used as a rag) rather than *ktor*, a more neutral word for a piece of cloth. Reflecting on this later, I realized that the special ingredient in that woman's yogurt was possibly the lactobacillus from *her own body and home*, residual within an old cast-off shirt or skirt. Her repeated cuisine practice therefore mattered at scales both larger and (much) smaller than her own discursive reflection. It still makes me smile thinking of that woman's intimate flora being so famously delicious, and making the trip down the highway to Yerevan, and on a plane back to Los Angeles. This incident also made me think about agency: this literal embodiment of a portable, potable memory was not deliberate on the part of the village woman, and not perceived by the diasporan woman; nonetheless, both were collaborators within the construction of a complex and global shared spacetime enacted in desire, practice, and bodily memory.

These parallels across inadvertently global generosity and explicitly spatiotemporal hospitality demonstrate the centrality of care to the spacetime of medieval Armenian politics—more importantly, however, it shows that the quotidian was political, and the mundane was cosmopolitan. This parallelism—or, I would argue, identity—between the practice of hospitality at the scales of sharing food and of building monumental infrastructure demonstrates that the spaces at the side of the road where food was prepared and served were key to the spacetime of the Silk Road, not a local quotidian apart from it or impacted by it. For the people at Ambroyi, whose houses abutted the ashlar walls of the Arai-Bazarǰuł caravanserai, encounters with travelers *were* everyday occurrences. It is possible that they could get bored of travelers—that the experiences of encounter that for Ibn Battuta or William of Rubruck were profound were, for them, mundane: the arrival of hungry, dusty travelers who needed to be fed and housed along with their animals, and who had similar stories of the road behind them and dreams of the road ahead. The people of Ambroyi contained these linear narratives within the cycles of planting and harvest, pasturing animals and slaughter, dairying, cooking, serving, and cleaning, repair and mending. Reflecting on the cosmopolitics required in the margins of globalization, Owen Sichone discussed the necessity of hospitality to frame the movement of travelers, observing: the "woman who has never left home lives her cosmopolitanism by welcoming the world."[70] Examining the case study of hospitality and power in Armenia as a representative of cultures widespread in the high medieval Silk Road world, it emerges that realms of quotidian and encounter, care and transcendence share overlapping and nested spacetimes, contained in and containing both everyday cycles and the potential for transformation.

Everyday Cosmopolitanisms

Rewriting the Shape of the Silk Road World

The small trickling streams, now running toward the south, and a gradual descent showed that we had crossed the watershed of Central Asia and had reached the valleys of Assyria. Here and there the ruins of a fine old khan, its dark recesses, vaulted niches, and spacious stalls, blackened with the smoke of centuries, served to mark one of the great highways, leading in the days of Turkish prosperity from central Armenia to Baghdad. . . . Commerce has deserted it for many years, and its bridges and caravanserais have long fallen into decay; when with the restoration of order and tranquility to this part of Turkey, trade shall revive, it may become once more an important thoroughfare.

— SIR AUSTIN H. LAYARD, *DISCOVERIES IN THE RUINS OF NINEVEH AND BABYLON* (1853)

Agency can be strange, twisted, caught up in things, passive, or exhausted. Not the way we like to think about it. Not usually a simple projection toward a future. It's what we mean by "having a life" (as in "get a life"). But it's caught up in things. Circuits, bodies, moves, connections. It takes unpredictable and counterintuitive forms.

—KATHLEEN STEWART, *ORDINARY AFFECTS* (2007)

In this book I have tried to tell a different kind of story about the Silk Road, and about Armenia. The result has resembled the way I would tell this story to you if we had been sitting together—perhaps at a small table under a tree on Saryan Street, over a dwindling bottle of wine—in that in telling one story I nest five or six stories together, and start several more to be finished some other time. My starting point has been a story about the floors, arches, and walls of the Arai-Bazarjuł caravanserai, which I can still remember the feel of: cool hard clay, smooth stones, the scrape of gravel, the smear of ashy soil between my thumb and a red-burnished potsherd. To tell the story of the Arai-Bazarjuł caravanserai, I needed to tell you the story of the Kasakh Valley and how it was made a world-in-particular by people like the Vač'utyans, and by people living in villages like Ambroyi, and by archaeologists and historians. But to tell the story of the caravanserai I also needed to tell you about caravanserais in particular and medieval architectures more generally—which ultimately brought me back to the aspirations of princely people like the Vač'utyans to fashion worlds in their own image, to fashion themselves as centers of worlds. And along the way I enumerated the things that made up these worlds, from roads and bridges to candles and prayers, stables, inns, the bones of saints, and the ceramic pots and bowls that set a welcoming table. But I also can't tell the story of those aspirant worlds without crossing their horizons with travelers like William of Rubruck or King Het'um—and in telling their journey stories I cross paths with other travelers in medieval and later times. As I told these stories of the Silk Road at continental scales, I found I had to start again, back up, and tell the story of how it even is that we imagine the worlds of medieval Eurasia as a road of silk. To use Pheng Cheah's words, all these other stories and worlds lie "quivering beneath the surface of the existing world."[1]

This messy snarl of stories contains multiple spacetimes, each with their own protagonists and some with no clear hero. That multiplicity in turn challenges universalist ideas of cosmopolitanism which rely on one story absorbing countless others, on a single protagonist becoming the hero wherever he travels. To draw from Morrison's work on cosmologies of pepper,[2] the reconfiguring webs of encounter and exchange that have been dubbed "the Silk Road" thrived on mutual misrecognition as much as they did on syncretism, on people mistaking centers for edges and vice versa; or as Pollock et al. put it, "centers . . . everywhere and circumferences nowhere."[3] Morrison's original example focused on the mistaking of human labor for wild nature, and resonates with broader challenges of thinking the Silk Road. But I also read misrecognition in the phenomenon by which caravan inns were central to the material practice of politics across some of the apparent cultural seams of the medieval world. Pious Karakhanids, striving for princely and beautiful power, built inns in Central Asia, as did pious Mamluks in the Levant and aspirant Seljuk Turks in Anatolia. Christian princes in Armenia, thinking of their own eternal souls, hired the same stonemasons who built caravan inns for their neighbors. My favorite kind of "misrecognition" is *metaphor*—to see one thing and understand it by way of something else. As we read in inscriptions and texts, warm, safe, hospitable places for travelers to sleep were understood as mutual metaphors for the world, and for the self—as stopping places for the immortal human soul. These institutions—which would also include the blacksmiths, bakers, cooks, millers, and shepherds living in adjoining villages—did more work on the Silk Road than just the very important task of giving tired and hungry travelers a place to sleep. They also provided an opportunity at the levels of political narratives and the experiences of travelers for worlds to come together, if just for the night.

ROADS, STONES, AND STRANGERS: IMAGINING SILK ROAD AGENCY

World-makings in multiple are not exclusive to the Middle Ages, but central to the ways we continue to imagine medieval lifeworlds, and cite them in modern projects (if metaphor is misrecognition, then for what do we misrecognize the metaphor of "the Silk Road"?). As we saw in chapter 2, part of the stickiness of the Silk Road as it has been told is the shape of that story, such that we persist in misrecognizing Marco Polo's East-West list of places as an account of roads traveled, and insist on the Silk Road as a world encountered by a mobile, cosmopolitan subject. This modality of encounter reduces interlocuters, antagonists, and hosts alike to the category of *other*, a group which bleeds as well into the monstrous and marvelous, reducing the rhythms of maintenance and everyday life of all these otherfolk to the status of nature.

Yet, the practice of world-making in in-between places complicates the boundaries between humans and nonhumans, stones and selves and strangers, large and small worlds in other ways. One of the ramifications of this complex and vibrant worlding is recombination across the categories we use to think the past of the Silk Road. These include categories of embodied power, or gender, as they have territorialized our ways of thinking agency in the medieval past. Maintenance labor, cooking, and feeding become central to the making of everyday cosmopolitanisms, to the sustaining of cosmopolitan memories and bodies. And working in the other direction, we must contemplate that the authoring of worlds and the fashioning of self-space-time is not exclusively a masculine or male undertaking.

I like thinking with inscriptions because they frustrate disciplinary divisions between history and archaeology, between architecture and literature. I'll use one final inscription to give a simple example, taking us back to the medieval journey into the Kasakh Valley described in chapter 1. As the high road crosses the shoulder of Mount Aragats, the spires of the monastery of Tełer pierce the horizon overhead.[4] The church, *gavit*, and belltower of the monastery still stand, having been renovated during the Soviet period.[5] As the Soviet-era signage inside informs you, the church was constructed under the patronage of the princess Mamaxatun Vačʻutyan contemporary with the caravan inn at Arai-Bazarǰuł (see fig. 20).

Walking inside the *gavit*, a visitor passes under the dedicatory inscription carved into the delicately arched lintel: "In 681 (1232), in thanks to God I Mamaxatun built the churches, the large and the small and the *gavit*, in my memory and that of my husband Vačʻe, and the inhabitants of this holy monastery offered a mass for us every year at the feast of the Holy Cross of Varaga in all churches with sacrifice and love, and those who may go against my writing, will answer before Jesus Christ (inscribed by Mxitar)."[6] This inscription repeats many of the themes and techniques discussed in the previous chapters; I draw attention to it here because, unlike the majority of the corpus already discussed, this inscription

FIGURE 20. The entrance to the *gavit* at Tełer Vankʻ. The endowment inscription is located in the arched lintel above the door. Photo by the author.

reiterates that the techniques of assembly and epigraphic incorporation even at the architectural level, were not exclusive to male persons in medieval Armenia.[7] Mamaxatun here presents as a cyborg self, knitting her futurity (and that of Vačʻe) with these buildings and the communities which inhabit and sustain them, even as her inscription is written by a male mason-appendage, named as Mxitar. Mamaxatun also situates herself within sacral, feminine lineage: she names the day of her perpetual commemoration with "sacrifice and love" (*matałov ev sirov*) as the feast of the Holy Cross of Varaga. This refers to a fragment of the true cross associated with St. Hripsime, a woman and one of the first Armenian martyrs; the fragment was held in the thirteenth century at Varagavankʻ.[8] Everyday rhythms related to the maintenance of a beautiful world in medieval Armenia were crisscrossed with diverse spacetimes, and active with assembled and assembling bodies which are not easily recognizable as the lonely hero of our old Silk Road stories.

Why We Need New Silk Road Stories

As a story told in twentieth-century Armenian and Soviet historiography, the Silk Road in the Caucasus was a linear tale of progressively developing cosmopolitanism of the rational, modern sort. In the account of high medieval Armenia narrated by the historians and archaeologists Manandyan, Babayan, Marr, and

Arak'elyan, the period of caravanserai- and bridge-building in Armenia signaled a turn away from medieval, locally bound ways of living toward a global future.[9] In Levon Babayan's account, men like Vač'e and K'urd Vač'utan, Tigran Honenc' and Č'esar Orbelyan were "merchant princes," hybrid social actors who mastered the alchemical transformation of movable property into immovable power.[10] The epigraphic and architectural records left by these princes are cited within such narratives as part of a muscular mechanism of place making, as the revenues of trade were fed into engines of patronage and capital investment which churned out the fabric of cities: Kars, Erzerum, Ani, Dvin. These named merchants are thus endowed by this story with the agency to build worlds, straddling medieval provincialism and modern globalism, medieval cyclical time and modern progressive time, like colossi. This story of the Armenian *mecatun* princes joins a compendium of popular tales of Silk Road visionaries, from Alexander the Great to Ghenghis Khan to Shah Abbas I, credited with prioritizing trade through Asia and opening up the Orient to the probing curiosity, desire, and appetites of the West.[11] What all these stories have in common is of course the emphasis on singular human agency over the Silk Road, which in turn is conceived as a landscape that can be brought under control and a source of prosperity that can be channeled.

At the moment, both global cultural heritage organizations and globalizing governments are dreaming along the same lines, drawn East to West. For the last several years, UNESCO and affiliated organizations have been encouraging the nations of Eurasia to align themselves, to make traditions of hospitality and material dreamings and places of transitory stopping into concrete things-in-themselves, places that can be listed, registered, visited, preserved, and made into emblems (or brands) of national character. Silk Road heritage raises a host of questions, enough to fill many other books.[12] All I will do here is raise one big one; if the *universal* of universal cultural heritage and the *universal* of the universal human subject are the same, then who is cultural heritage for? Who is it *not for*? The same question can then be asked of Silk Road line-projects like China's Belt and Road Initiatives, or the United States' sometime Silk Road Strategy, which dream of getting all of Central Asia on the path to some definition of civilization. But as Thorsten put it, "across the territory called the Silk Road can be found competing proprietorship claims over which culture or civilization holds the keys to the best of all possible worlds."[13] In Armenia these competing claims manifest in a clash of worlds: Chinese investment companies fund a route to progress through the heart of the country, six lanes of high speed traffic from Batumi to Bandar Abbas, the dreams of the Seljuks and Safavids rebuilt in concrete and rebar. Meanwhile, the U.S. State Department drives another brand of integration, labeling Silk Road sites across the country, and funding heritage initiatives that help Armenia remember its identity as an outward-looking, Christian (read: nonfundamentalist) post-Soviet state. This is the same Silk Road story written in new media, though one might cynically add that global capitalism, in "buy[ing] the world a Coke" of Silk

Road unity, adds the twist that local stakeholders—meaning the countries of the global south, people living in Yerevan and Aparan—are encouraged to aspire to be nameless, helpful bystanders in their own Silk Road future.

A postcolonial critique might point out that this dream of the Silk Road as a transhistorical pipeline of cosmopolite wealth is an extractive and exploitative story; a feminist critique further argues that it is an androcentric and patriarchal one.[14] I would add that such a story is furthermore simply boring, a barren way to imagine the improbable intricacies of human mobilities, exchanges, miseries, and dignities tangled up in the medieval and early modern world. As John Ganim argues, "there are moments when thinking about the other emerge as ways of thinking about ourselves and therefore about the responsibilities we owe to a world beyond the limits of our social horizon."[15] In the case of the medieval Silk Road, this notion of "others" incorporates both medieval temporal others, as well as the subalterns that modern globalization makes for itself. Our challenge is writing better stories, somehow reconfiguring our habits of thinking to consider world-making as a matter of care shared among humans and nonhumans, across disparate spacetimes and reconfiguring desires. Once that audacious aim is achieved, how do we excavate Silk Road subjectivities that were written but did not write, thus collapsing the apparent contradiction of "everyday medieval cosmopolitanism"? I have found myself attempting to do this by approaching the Other spaces of the Silk Road in other ways. My interest in the institution of the medieval caravan inn, which was a mainstay both of travel experience and also of local Armenian politics, is what drew me first to Armenia and to histories of the Silk Road. My first framing of the caravanserai was as a place of meeting between fellow travelers, of mobile subjects. I tried to write it as a *heterotopia* (essentially a funhouse of transcendent encounter), and as an engine for the subjectification of the travelers who stayed there on one night in their continuing journey. But in 2013–14, as we excavated the adjoining village of Ambroyi, I found my perspective reconfiguring from that of the traveler to those for whom the travelers themselves were transient strangers. I imagined the arrival of the caravaning stranger from the vantage of those for whom such arrivals were part of the quotidian labor of cooking, serving, and cleaning—the maintenance activities of the medieval Silk Road. As work on the role of service workers in mediating the "flows" of globalization continues to show, this infrastructure of accommodation both smooths the frictions of difference and also effects the transformation of both host and guest.[16] The villagers at Ambroyi/Hin Bazarǰuł lived and worked in a full world which contained town, church, castle, road, and travelers. We must however imagine their personhoods using tools other than (or alongside) texts, and think about the ways that the spacetimes of worldview, distance, and difference are intimately built from material things they left, including hearths, shared meals, washed dishes, and, in some cases, small things brought from over the valley horizon: a bead, an arrowhead, or a favorite bowl. And we

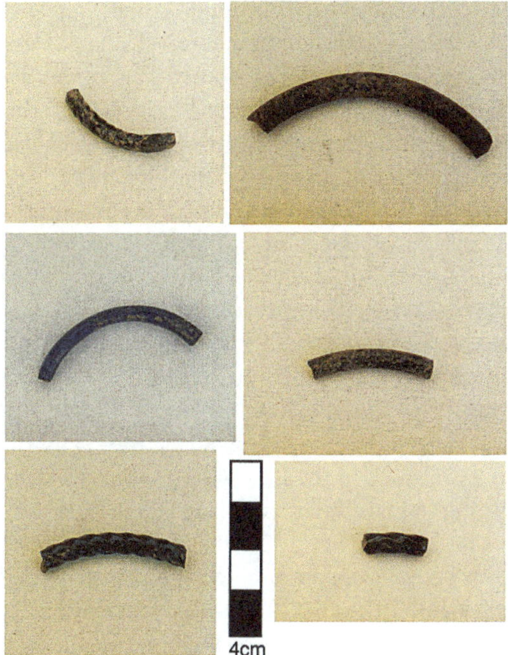

FIGURE 21. Glass bangle bracelet fragments excavated from Ambroyi village. Figure by the author.

can think about the ways that these village spaces abutted and were incompletely overwritten by inscriptions and historical accounts (see fig. 21).

Among the artifacts found at Ambroyi was a series of fragments of bracelets, made from colored glass. The bracelets were all shades of bright blue, ranging from a bold turquoise to a deep cobalt. Bracelets of this type are commonly found across Eurasia in the medieval period, from India to Bulgaria and beyond.[17] While archaeologists have long associated these bracelets with women—to the point of using them to sex otherwise unidentifiable burials—they have not been extensively studied as an artifact category. At Ambroyi we found fragments of these ornaments all around the rooms containing ovens. We even found a fragment inside one of the larger ovens, conjuring up the cringe-inducing scenario of someone reaching their hand in to slap dough against the hot oven wall, only to hear a crack and a tinkle as the bracelet broke and fell into the hot ashes below. In asking whose labor was this cooking and feeding, I find myself unbundling similar assumptions to those challenged by Mamaxatun's inscription discussed above. Were the slender wrists that wore the imported glass bracelets at Ambroyi attached to bodies that thought of themselves as women? Or men? I do think this is an interesting question, but for the moment what I also think is as or more interesting is how these be-bangled bodies in this space—that of routine "women's work" or "maintenance activity"— mattered in a world that contained both ovens and Orient, both the passing of days and the passing of hungry, tired travelers. And to do this requires that I collapse road space and everyday space and let tedium and rhythm into travel, and cosmopolitanism into the quotidian. Seeing the way that stories of medieval spaces are gendered has high stakes in reconfiguring the medieval period in its own terms, as other than the long dark quotidian to which the fleet arrow of the modern can never return. Following Munn, I would work on seeing smaller worlds of the Silk Road as spacetimes run through with local politics that call on the traveler, the outside, and the universal as players in dramas staged in local landscapes. Telling the Silk Road as something more or less than an adventure story read from West to East shapes not only the landscapes that we reconstruct, but also the spaces and times it becomes possible to make.

Feeling the frictions as I tried to construct these other worlds helped me understand how we are wrapped up in stories of the Silk Road as old as Mandeville, and as mystifying. Contemporary approaches to the continent of Eurasia and the peoples living and dreaming within it are stuck in the East-West grooves worn by Marco Polo's adventure story, imagining the Silk Road as a place where time travels backward, more slowly, or not at all. The impact of the shape of Marco Polo's story matters for our own imaginaries because copies of his account were carried by the scholars and travelers who provided the first "scientific" descriptions of the Silk Road, and of our world as a whole. The *Travels* of Polo and Rustichello was required reading for Christopher Columbus in the fifteenth century, for Lord Macartney in the eighteenth, and for travel writer William Dalrymple in the twentieth.[18] In the first years of the twentieth century, the philologist and famous archaeologist Aurel Stein referred to the *Travels* to navigate the human geographies of Central Asia, confident that the peoples and cultures he encountered were the same observed by Polo six hundred years earlier.[19]

This collapsed spacetime remains the desired destination for tourists in Central Asia, as the same narratives are deployed to shape infrastructure and tourism development in the overlapping spheres of UNESCO heritage and the Belt and Road Initiative. In 2020, the *New York Times* travel section ran a series of essays on "The Route That Made the World." Writing on the active practice of silk making in Georgia, Esi Edugyan juxtaposes descriptions of the "particular decay of the Old Soviet republics" with extensive citation of the description of Georgia from Marco Polo's *Travels*.[20] Even while casting aspersions on the authenticity of that text, Edugyan asserts the utility of Marco Polo's "more grounded observations" to help "imagine a past that many people here have managed to keep alive today." All of which is another way of reassuring potential tourists that the Silk Road of Marco Polo is still there, that the people of the Silk Road world have valiantly resisted modernity. I discovered at some point that freelance photographer Michael Yamashita maintains an Instagram account called @thesilkroadjourney, where he juxtaposes excerpts from the travel account of Marco Polo or from references to Zheng He's itinerary with photographs of the "same" places, people, or things in a modern context. This practice of rakish de-temporalization dissolves modern into medieval and vice versa; these exotic peoples have never been modern, but at the same time, the cosmopolitan Silk Road is held up as the medieval world's most modern dream.

If our modern storytellers aren't casting the Silk Road as a spacetime out of time, they frequently recapitulate the East-West polarity defined by Halford John Mackinder in 1904. Mackinder followed Hakluyt in believing in the close link between geographic knowledge and national destiny; he defined Central Asia as a Pivot of History, a golden apple which could only be grasped by the West or the East.[21] The narrative of a mysterious and enticing East giving rich gifts of civilization (but also destruction!) is dangerous because it *seems true*, simply because it's been a story people have been telling for a thousand years.[22] If a feminist critique of science has a point of entry into geopolitics, it is that the total dominance of a logocentric paradigm leads the Authors of Global Destiny to mistake, when reading medieval authored worlds, narrative overlaps for transhistorical confirmations of objective fact. Thus, in the epigram at the head of this chapter Austen Henry Layard, archaeologist and imperial diplomat, seamlessly "reads" the landscape of monumental medieval infrastructure in Anatolia into a narrative of prosperity lost and regained. This narrative was inseparable from the larger human-material-temporal project within which he was at the time enmeshed, the prying of colossal chunks of ancient eastern civilization out of the sands of Iraq to use as a sort of mother dough for the British imperial mission. In musing on the potential for the "revival" of trade under conditions of "order and tranquility," Layard cites the most pernicious imaginary of the Silk Road as a transcontinental stream of abstract desire that irrigates the valleys and roads along which it passes with wealth and the cosmopolitics of profit. Of course, Layard attributes the ruined caravanserais to the failure of global commerce, rather than the disintegration of local practices of world-making and hospitable politics.

In part, I wanted to try to tell a Silk Road at a spatial scale smaller than the continental, and at a timescale shorter than the monumental. I have long been intrigued by a problem in history and archaeology, that we are so reliant on the lives and labors of people that we can't know, and who themselves couldn't know the scope of the phenomena which take center stage in our analyses. Everyday cosmopolitanism is important for me because it widens the angle of the shot, as it were, from the heroic traveler to the lifeways and practices which made roads thinkable, but which also returned the gaze of the road. I continue to be curious about everyday, ordinary, and routine practices which constitute and perpetuate global structures without necessary seeing them for what they are. Anthropology has been concerned with the relationship between structure and individual agency for decades,[23] and my colleagues working at the scales demanded by the Eurasian steppe have been grappling with the question of how to theorize local participation in world-scale cultures in thought-provoking ways.[24] For me what is important is opening up avenues of researching places like Armenia as not just local places or Silk Road places, but as complex spacetimes and resolutely centered worlds-in-themselves, which through intersection of matter, time, and desire become caught up in, as Kathleen Stewart puts it, the agency of "circuits, bodies, moves, connections."[25]

I have maybe written—and am trying to write—a different kind of Silk Road history. In a departure from the general trend I don't want to argue that Armenia or the South Caucasus was the most important part of the Silk Road or the objective center of the world in the thirteenth century (*pace* Ando, Artur, and my other drinking buddies from Arai-Bazarȷ̌uł village). Ongoing research on Indian Ocean trade in the Middle Ages continues to challenge long-standing, land-centered ideas about how the world was connected. But I am fascinated by how the medieval world was knit together from worlds with centers everywhere, and by practices of hospitality and care that treated ordinary people, invisible in historical texts, as if they were important. Hospitality at different scales means that what we call Silk Road cosmopolitanism was a shared project in world making occurring in multiple spacetimes and across plural, overlapping scales.

Ultimately it matters how we tell the story of the Silk Road, how we build that place in things, peoples, and natures, because we (modern archaeologists, dwellers within globalization, earthlings, human denizens of an uncertain global future) are already tangled within its imaginaries. They are already part of the toolset we are using to build our way out of our current problems, whether insecurity, instability, precarity, peripherality, or apathy.[26] In myriad ways, we still live in the world(s) built in the Middle Ages; we literally and figuratively dwell in a storeroom of medieval stuff, from literary tropes to laws, buildings, furniture, foodstuffs, ways of dress, ways of imagining our both our best and worst selves and our most beautiful and barbaric "others." We also live in the worlds built with those medieval things, heirs to the uses of the medieval past to imagine the present. If I might end where I began chapter 2, with Donna Haraway's riff on Marilyn Strathern's still-relevant position that by writing the world differently we write a different world: "it matters what stories we tell to tell other stories with." Or, as Eco wrote in his Silk Road novel, *Baudolino*, in "imagining other worlds, [we] end up changing this one."[27] This argument is I think at the center of feminist work on the Silk Road like Bray's *Technology and Gender*, which complicates the categorical roles of medieval people in making the things that made the world. Medieval weaving women were, for Bray, woven *as* women, and domestic, public, imperial, and global spaces were co-constructed around them.[28] Her analysis requires a scalar shift as we think about medieval global cultures, which are rooted in intimately engaged technologies as well as imperial strategies and continental movements. For my part, I remain fascinated by the history of travel through Eurasia, and I own my romantic imaginaries of travelers moving through the mountains, valleys, and deserts of medieval routes even while possessing firsthand knowledge of how "smelly" a mountain caravanserai might have been. Critically, I do not want the account of hospitality in my narrative to imply that violence, warfare, precariousness, and other dangers were not a real part of medieval life; if anything, they are the topography of the world against which the practices of hospitality are framed. But medieval military adventure is also a story often told, and is a story that loves heroes. My hope is that, after reading this book, you return to the medieval stories of William of Rubruck, of Marco Polo, Ibn Battuta, and others, and find yourself joining me in wondering about the human and nonhuman figures at the margins, the spaces they neglect to describe, the unseen hands that opened doors, made meals, brought fodder, and laid out beds.

If the medieval Silk Road seems like a route out of modern global problems, then a very relevant question to me seems to be, not just how did people in the Middle Ages imagine themselves in relation to broader worlds, but moreover, once they managed that, how did they "matter" those worlds—how did they come to *care* about and for them in the timescale and spatial extent of everyday life and work? I think care is yet another scalar problem; care operates at multiple scales and works to contract spacetimes in unpredictable ways. In thinking about how a global medieval hung together, I am infinitely more curious about care than *control* (a word that most archaeologists can't define anyway). Care in this context is both the sense of caring-for that I described in the last chapter—of labors of care, maintenance work, and the caring of hospitality—but caring for things is also what Maria Puig de la Bellascasa has described as "relating to them, of inevitably being affected by them, and modifying their potential to affect others."[29] This means taking seriously the messy implication of medieval people in the matter of caring: that bodies could be buildings, buildings could be worlds, selves could be spacetimes, meals could be universes encompassed by world-roaming bellies. The version of the medieval world that we might reconstruct using archaeological data is not "more true" than that presented by textual sources. Both medieval written accounts of lives along the Silk Road, and our assemblages of Silk Road things, are interleaved parts of mutually implicated apparatuses for making sense of spacetimes at multiple scales. In other words, they are stories within stories, worlds within worlds—and the more worlds we make of them, the better.

CHAPTER 1. THE SILK ROAD, MEDIEVAL GLOBALITY,
AND "EVERYDAY COSMOPOLITANISM"

1. In defining cosmopolitanism as "action rather than idea," I draw in particular on Pollock 2002: 17.

2. Rezakhani 2010.

3. Stein 1912; Hedin 1938; Wood 2002; Hansen 2012.

4. Manandyan, 1965; Arak'elyan 1958, 1964; there are a number of maps of the silk routes, including impressive interactive versions, as well as numerous digitizations of medieval travelers' routes.

5. E.g., Hansen 2012: 8.

6. Emerson and Floor 1987.

7. Ibn Battuta 1958: 17.

8. Brack 2011; Whitfield 2015: chaps. 4, 5. The accounts of both Ibn Battuta and Marco Polo feature princesses, Khatun Bayalun and Kököchin, who travel great distances—raising the question of how we might imagine the Middle Ages differently if we had the stories of these female agents and not their male cortege. Ongoing work on the fifteenth-century *Book of Margery Kemp* has reiterated that medieval travel was a bodily experience: different bodies traveled differently (e.g., McAvoy 2004).

9. Oxen are recommended by Francesco Pegolotti in his *Merchant's Handbook* (1913: 143–71).

10. Ibn Hawqal is cited by Ter-Ghevondyan (1976: 140). Thanks to Paul Wordsworth for this note from Ibn al-Faqih al Hamadhani; Mirijanyan 2008.

11. St. Clair 2018; Allsen 1997; Whitfield 2018.

12. For discussion of the excavations at Moschevaia Balka, c.f. Knauer 2001; Vorderstrasse 2019; Hansen 2012.

13. Wood 2002.

14. Ganjakec'i 1986. In the thirteenth to fourteenth centuries Cilician Armenia and what is now the Republic of Armenia were two separate polities, united by language and sharing a religion. Most importantly, they were ruled according to shared political traditions by linked branches of the same princely houses, such that medieval texts emphasize the unity between Cilician and Eastern Armenia at the level of aristocratic exploit. Cf. Der Nersessian 1962; Peacock, De Nicola, and Nur Yildiz 2016.

15. Berlekamp 2017 based on work by Roman Hovsepyan; see Franklin 2014b: chap. 5.

16. L. Babayan 1976; Šahnazaryan 2011; Minorsky 1953: 101–3.

17. Ganjakec'i 1986: 302. NB traveling in a disguise, whether as a merchant, or a member of a less conspicuous ethnic group, was common practice in Eurasia from the Middle Ages through the early twentieth century. Cf. Boyle 1964.

18. Kostanyanc' 1913: 76; Ališan 1881: 147. See further discussion in chapter 7.

19. Franklin 2020.

20. Primary sources for these events include Matthew of Edessa, Stepanos Orbelyan, Kirakos Ganjakec'i, the Georgian Chronicle, Samuel Anec'i, and others. An excellent summary of these sources is provided by Robert Bedrosian (1997); he has also provided translations of many sources. The rest of this book will attempt to tell stories of Armenia and the Silk Road using narrative frameworks other than timeline-style recantations of battles and invasions.

21. C.f. Minorsky 1953; Cahen 1968; Peacock 2010, 2015; Peacock et al. 2016.

22. Bedrosian 1997: 243–48.

23. Blessing and Goshgarian 2017. This is a critical counterpoint to a long-standing argument developed by Nikolai Marr, the excavator of Ani, which posited that as nomads the Seljuks had no architecture and thus brought with them no architectural tradition (Marr 1934).

24. Suny 1988: 35–41.

25. Armenians had lived in colonies in and around Trebizond since the seventh century; the Armenian populations in Pontus and Cilicia swelled from the late eleventh century on. See Terian 2009: 100–102.

26. Bedrosian 1997: 256.

27. The Armenian historian Kirakos Ganjakec'i describes the taking of the cities of Khorasan and the lands of Jalal al-din. For a general discussion of the "reception" of the Mongols, see Lane 2012.

28. As Armenia is more immediately involved in European interaction with the Mongols, that is my primary focus here. For a consideration of the Mongol encounter with other Asian societies see for instance Allsen 2001.

29. Peleggi 2001.

30. Sahlins 1976.

31. Specifically, Peleggi cites the seventh-century writer known as Pseudo-Methodius.

32. De Rachewiltz 1971: 34–35.

33. Jackson and Morgan 1990: 122. An interesting aspect of this inclusion by Rubruck, credited by historians as being the most "ethnographic" of thirteenth-century medieval travelers, is that he felt obligated to include references to "fantastical" figures in order to convince his audience (Louis IX and others) of the veracity of his tale.

34. Voegelin 1940; Jackson and Morgan 1990: 24.

35. In Grabar: *žamanaks i verǰ haseal e*. Ganjakecʻi 1961: 231.

36. Pogossian 2012: 173.

37. Aknercʻi 2003: 4.

38. Orbelyan 1859: 208, trans. Robert Bedrosian.

39. Peleggi 2001: 27–33.

40. In using the term *story* I am deliberately referencing Hayden White's landmark observation that historians write histories as *stories*. In particular, the Silk Road as it is told by historians fits into White's category of the Romance, the "drama of self-identification symbolized by the hero's transcendence of the world of experience" (1973: 8). The implications of stories used to write other stories, including history, will be explored in the next chapter.

41. Massey 2004: 10. See also Pollock et al. 2002: 8–9.

42. Ma and ten Grotenhuis 2002; Chin 2013.

43. Hoffman 2001; see also Vernon 2018.

44. This is not a critique: most of these were the product of museum and art historical studies, e.g., Fuxi, Brill, and Shouyun 2009; Kalantaryan et al. 2009; Whitfield, Whitfield, and Agnew 2000; Whitfield 2018; Mair and Hickman 2014; Norell and Patry-Leidy 2011.

45. Moore 2013: 100.

46. Haraway 2016.

47. Munn 1986: 9.

48. Munn 1977, 1983, cited in 1986. See also Munn 1990.

49. Bakhtin 1981: 84.

50. In thinking about how chronotopes structure historical memory I also draw on Raymond Williams's framing of what he refers to as "structures of feeling," which manifest in layers of literary space as "localized dream[s]" about place through time (1975: 12, 26).

51. C.f. Haraway 1991.

52. Barad 2007: 170.

53. Grosz 1995: 100.

54. Thanks to Sarah Ponder for sharing this observation with me. There is a 3D scan of the vellum sheet, with the erased marks over Hereford, visible at www.themappamundi .co.uk/mappa-mundi (last accessed March 17, 2021).

55. Kant 1795: "Since the narrower or wider community of the peoples of the earth has developed so far that a violation of rights in one place is felt throughout the world, the idea of a law of world citizenship is no high-flown or exaggerated notion. It is a supplement to the unwritten code of the civil and international law, indispensable for the maintenance of the public human rights and hence also of perpetual peace" (1795: article 3); Arendt 1973.

56. Brodky-Porges 1981. This is also a central theme in Mary Louise Pratt's 1992 work *Imperial Eyes*. Paul Smethurst and Julia Kuehn have compiled far-ranging discussions on the intersections between perception, expectation and the reception of travel and travel writing (2008).

57. Beck (2002), for instance, argues that the shifted "tactical" everyday cosmopolitanism of global subjects is a completely new sociopolitical phenomenon, even as his definition evokes the "making do" of Levi-Straus's primitive bricoleur.

58. E.g., Pollock et al. 2002; Nava 2002; Sassen 2002; Ehrenreich and Hothschild 2002; Landau and Freemantle 2010; Richard 2013; Moore 2013: 100.

59. Pollock et al. 2002: 585.

60. Ganim 2010: 16. See also Cohen (ed.) 2000; Kinoshita 2007; Lochrie 2009.

61. Derrida 2000; Moore 2013: 102–3.

62. Massey 1994: 12.

63. Bender 2002: S103.

64. Bakhtin 1981: 102. See also Massey 1994: 166–67.

65. For a broader discussion of opposition between the enwalled everyday and realms of adventure in Arthurian romance, and of the effect of these tropes on medieval history and archaeology, see Gilchrist 1999.

66. Massey 1994: 151.

67. Wierling 1995: 154.

68. Brumfiel 1991.

69. Bray 1997.

70. De Beauvoir 1949: 1 (2).

71. Barad 2007; Bennett 2009; Haraway 2016, 1991; Rose 1993; Stewart 1993.

72. Barad 2007: 171.

73. Champion 2017: introduction; Le Goff 1977; Braudel 1981, 1984. Arthur C. Clarke evokes a "superstitious" "dark age" mentality as the enemy of progress-oriented innovation in his 1962 *The Hazards of Prophecy*.

74. Latour 1993: 117.

CHAPTER 2. THE SILK ROAD AS A LITERARY SPACETIME

1. Waugh 2007: 4; Whitfield 2007: 201; Chin 2013: 196; Spengler 2019: 46; Wood 2002: 9.

2. Edwards 2013.

3. This argument has been made many places, but also succinctly in Foucault 1970; Latour 1993. See also Smith and Findlen 2001; Daston and Park 1998.

4. Cf. Walker Bynum 1997.

5. Latour 1993: 98.

6. Thompson 2011; Heuser 2003; Kuehn and Smethurst 2008. See also the extensive discussion in Brewer 2016.

7. This conversation for ethnography and anthropological archaeology was catalyzed by reflections on the literary knowledge production central to both, see Clifford and Marcus (eds.) 1986.

8. C.f. Woolgar 2006: 4.

9. Clifford 1986.

10. Larner 1999; this is an interesting characteristic of attempts to "map" the Silk Road as well, which bump up against the resistance of "fantastical" places to be plotted in Cartesian space alongside "real" places.

11. Daston and Park 1998.

12 It is difficult, in discussing this process, not to fall into a evocation of a monolithic West, even as I work to dismantle the monolithic East (c.f. Kinoshita's 2007 critique of Said). I hope, that in a resolute emphasis on spacetimes, to keep focus on the work of epistemological *mattering*, rather than any singular *being* of "the western imagination."

13. Daston and Park 1998: 23; Le Goff 1985; Walker Bynum 1997.

14. Jackson 2001.

15. Jackson 2001: 347.

16. Al-Muqaddasī 1994.

17. *Harisah* is a savory porridge made from grains (millet or wheat), sometimes involving meat or dairy (see chapter 6); *tharid* is bread in vegetable or meat broth; *aṣidah* is a doughy gruel like hardtack, sometimes with a sauce.

18. Al-Muqaddasī 1994: 74–75.

19. Goshgarian 2011.

20. Larner 1999; Smethurst 2005.

21. Zhou 2009: 11.

22. Kinoshita 2008: 62.

23. Larner 1999: 67.

24. Zhou argued that the *Travels* is not so much a work that defied genre as "an instance that both actualizes and destabilizes various genres to various degrees" (Zhou 2009: 10).

25. Multiple authors have discussed the Mongols as set dressing for landscapes of adventure in Chaucer: see for instance Lynch 1995; chapters in Lynch (ed.) 2002.

26. Polo 1958: 62.

27. Polo 1958: 108.

28. Polo 1958: 177.

29. Larner 1999: 69.

30. Larner 2008: 134, my emphasis.

31. Larner 1999: 73, my emphasis.

32. Mandeville 1953: xxv.

33. For a full discussion of the source material of Mandeville's travels, please see Anthony Bale's 2012 discussion (in Mandeville 2012).

34. Larner referred to Mandeville's purported travel account as "a geographical fantasy" (Larner 2008: 142). Anthony Bale sums up the *Book of Marvels* as a "hybrid thing, mixing fact, error, and fantasy, mostly drawn from the reports of others" (Mandeville 2012: xi).

35. Mandeville 1953: 30.

36. Mandeville 2012: 103.

37. Mandeville 1953: iix.

38. Smethurst 2005: 161.

39. Lochrie 2009.

40. Mandeville 2012: 81.

41. See Le Goff 1985: 27–46 on the politics of wonder.

42. Classen 2002: xxix.

43. Ibn Battuta 2003: 129.

44. Ibn Battuta 2003: 134.

45. Judith Butler (1993) ties all of these practices and their implications up in her definition of "mattering." I like this terminology, which emphasizes that we cannot talk about historical or political subjects prior to the cultural worlds that they make and are made by. See also Moore 1994: 8–27.

46. *Anabasis* 4.1.11.

47. *Anabasis* 4.7.4.

48. *Anabasis* 4.5.25. See also discussion of the longer history of Armenian subterranean architecture in Khatchadourian 2016: 154.

49. E.g., Auge 1992; Castells 1996. I would also include primitivist takes like Ingold's (2016), which categorize the plight of global modernity as seamless networks replacing lived surfaces.

50. Though in this case I am obviously discussing a person (Rubruck) with an exceptional amount of agency, this sense of the messiness of cosmopolitan living draws from the broad conversation on subalterity and differential agency in the context of modern globalization. Specifically, I am interested in the points where worldviews break down (Tsing 2005), the margins where remoteness transforms unpredictably into power (Nordstrom 2007), and where local reconfigurations of globality problematize the easy opposition between local and global (Richard 2013; Pollock et al. 2002; Ehrenreich and Hothschild 2002, Spyer 2000).

51. For instance, when first encountering the wagon trains of Scacatai, between the Black Sea and the Don, Rubruck is annoyed that his Mongol companions tell him to provide a present for Scacatai, and is further perplexed that they keep demanding from him not just food but "some garment or other" (Jackson and Morgan 1990: 100). Rubruck on this and other occasions fails to learn the importance of silken textile gifts, a crucial part of medieval central Asian politics to be discussed in the next chapter.

52. As Vacca (2017) explores, the use of Sasanian-Persian titles such as *shahanshah* (king of kings) by the Armenians (and others in the region such as the Seljuks) was a practice that continued traditions of distinction established in the Sasanian era through the medieval period. In the later medieval period this title was revisited as *išxanac' išxan*, prince of princes.

53. Minorsky 1953: 102.

54. Jackson and Morgan 1990.

55. Of course, in this period the ongoing trade in Eurasia is inextricable from colonial expansion into the Americas. As Wallerstein (1974) most famously argued, this period of exploration, domination, extraction, and innovation transformed imaginaries of the world, even as medieval narratives (of nature, of the political good, of the self and other) were used to make sense of that world.

56. Kotov 1852.

57. Chardin 1811; Tavernier 1678.

58. Herbert 1677.

59. Tavernier 1678: bk. 1, chap. 3: p. 13.

60. That privilege of course came at a cost. Coveting the mercantile networks of the early modern Armenians, Shah Abbas famously transferred the entirety of the Armenian village of Julfa to the backyard of his palace at Isfahan, and maintained the Julfa Armenians (and their trade connections) in the manner of exotic, highly lucrative pets (or as some have stated it, slaves). See Aslanian 2014; Babaie et al. 2004.

61. King 2008: 104.

62. Jackson and Morgan 2009: 201.

63. Layton 1994: introduction.

64. Layton 1994: 16.

65 Layton 1994: 20.

66. This treaty concluded the Russo-Persian War and redrew imperial borders through the Caucasus. At this date Persia ceded the khanates of Erivan, Nakhchevan, and Talysh to the Russian Empire. The border was drawn at the Araxes River, essentially foreshadowing the borders of modern Armenia.

67. Or perhaps, in an imperial future governed by European interests, see the epigram from A.H. Layard and discussion in chap. 7.

68. DeSilvey and Edensor 2013.

69. Bridges and Hair 2010: 18 n. 2; Fuller 2009.

70. The traveler Robert Byron (a descendent of Lord Byron) while traveling through Afghanistan, complained of the illiterate travelers he met who carried no books. He also remarked on the way the style of the novels he read on the road (in this case, Proust's *Remembrance of Things Past*) crept into his travel narrative. Byron 1937: 310.

71. Layard 1853: 14. The *Anabasis* existed in Greek manuscripts in the fourteenth century, and had been translated into English by the latter part of the sixteenth. Nemoianu 1986: 91.

72. Ker Porter 1821: 95.

73. Grossman 2013: 3.

CHAPTER 3. TECHNIQUES OF WORLD-MAKING IN MEDIEVAL ARMENIA

1. The high Middle Ages (locally called the "developed" Middle Ages) in Armenia runs from the ninth century through the first decades of the fourteenth century. My focus is primarily on the latter centuries, but I will discuss cultural practices which cut across the period as a whole.

2. C.f. Toumanoff 1963; Adontz 1970; Ter- Łewondyan 1976; Vacca 2017.

3. C.f. Peacock 2010; Nur Yildiz 2005: 95; La Porta 2011, 2012.

4. Bedrosian 1997: 254; Babayan 1976: 547; Cowe 2016.

5. La Porta 2012; Garsoian 2012; Peacock 2015. See also Beihammer 2016.

6. Babayan 1976: 586.

7. Suny 1993, 2001; Thomson 2013: introduction.

8. Anderson 1983; Hobsbawm and Ranger 1983.

9. Panossian 2006: 102. Panossian notes that the founder of the order, Mkhitar, famously wrote: "I do not sacrifice my nation for my confession or my confession for my nation," paving the way for a explicitly nonsecular Armenian national movement.

10. E.g., Chamchian 1784.

11. Suny 1993. See also Papazian 2019 for a discussion of the negotiated discourse of Soviet Armenia in the context of medieval reconstruction projects.

12. Manjikian 2005: 81. Manjikian also points out that medieval artifacts mediate the "homeland return" experience of diaspora Armenians.

13. While researching for the film Parajanov apparently became enamored with Armenian and Georgian medieval architecture; see Steffen 2013: 120.

14. For Armenia this has long been thought to be a stark change from the early medieval period: see Garsoian 1999 and Ter-Łewondyan 1976. This model of high medieval history was formulated in the commercial-ethic-centered "thesis" of Henri Pirenne (1925) and expounded upon in Malthusian terms by Brenner (1976) and others participating in the subsequent debate on the models according to which the medieval period in Europe gestated capitalism. I want to make clear that it's not so much that I think this idea is "wrong," but that, following on developing traditions of history and historical archaeology in the last few decades, I don't think it helps us tell the most interesting or useful stories about the medieval past. Telling the history of the Middle Ages as the origin story of a modern, capitalist world is a self-centered and ultimately boring way of going about it, and eliminates

the possibility that we might encounter different ways of being, living, and dreaming in the medieval world (and in the present).

15. For instance, the "archipelago of towns" conceived of by Braudel (1984: 30) and applied by Abu-Lughod (1989: 13).

16. Manandyan 1954. English translation by Garsoian cited as Manandyan 1965.

17. Manandyan 1965: 183–84, 187. See also Arak'elyan 1964: 40.

18. Manandyan 1965: 189.

19. Pegolotti 1913: 159; Manandyan 1965: 140.

20. See Franklin, Vorderstrasse, and Babayan 2017 for further discussion of the role of rural-urban dynamics in the history and archaeology of Armenia and Anatolia.

21. Arak'elyan 1964: 16.

22. Arak'elyan 1964: 10.

23. Arak'elyan 1964: 7. All translations are my own unless stated otherwise.

24. In addition to following Marxist models of social development, Armenian historians and medieval historical archaeologists were strongly influenced by canonical works in western European history such as Henri Pirenne, who drew a direct connection between the rise of Christian urbanism and the development of western civilization.

25. Arak'elyan 1964: 18, 40; see also Orbeli 1939: 152.

26. Arak'elyan 1964: 115.

27. Arak'elyan 1964: 22.

28. Arak'elyan 1964: 18.

29. Arak'elyan 1964: 27.

30. Arak'elyan 1964: 29.

31. The Georgian name of the family is Mkhargzeli, I will use the Armenian name consistently throughout.

32. Arak'elyan 1964: 73–74.

33. This is Bedrosian's translation of Ganjakec'i. See also discussion in Arak'elyan 1964: 74–75.

34. Sassen 2001, 2002; Massey 1994; see also Larkin 2013 on infrastructure and politics.

35. Manandyan 1965: 187.

36. Arak'elyan 1964: 46.

37. Arak'elyan 1964: 46.

38. Šahxat'unyan 1842.

39. Chardin 1811.

40. Ker Porter 1821: 172–73.

41. Babayan 1981.

42. Trigger 1989: 212.

43. Marr 1934. The excavations were curtailed by the First World War and the Bolshevik Revolution. The collections from Marr's excavations are distributed in museums in Russia and Armenia and have not been studied as a unified collection since their discovery.

44. T'oramanyan 1942, 1948; Lindsay and Smith 2006: 170.

45. General overviews: Ghafadaryan 1952, 1982; Kalantaryan 1976, 1996; Kalantaryan et al. 2008; Kalantaryan et al. 2009; Areshian and Kalantaryan 2008. Material analyses: Hakopyan 1981, Zhamkochyan 1981; Kocharyan 1991; Babayan 1981.

46. Arak'elyan and Karakhanyan 1962; Harut'yunyan 1978; Karakhanyan and Melk-onyan 1989, 1991; Melkonyan et al. 2017; Babajanyan et al. 2021.

47. My discussion of material culture builds on the typologies which were established based on comparison of the Dvin corpus with materials from contemporary urban sites like Dmanisi in Georgia, and Oren Kala in Azerbaijan. See Babayan 1981; Kalantaryan et al. 2009; Maisuradze 1954; Iessen 1959.

48. Franklin, Vorderstrasse, and Babayan 2017; for a discussion of the impact on heri-tage landscapes and landscape imaginaries, see Franklin and Babajanyan 2018a; this will also be discussed in chapter 4.

49. The tradition of recording buildings as corpuses of epigraphic texts is well estab-lished in Armenia: Ghafadaryan 1948, 1957, 1975; Orbeli 1966; Kostanyanc' 1913.

50. Sargsyan 1977, 1990; Mirijanyan and Babajanyan 2013; Dangles and Proteau 2004, 2007.

51. During the later Soviet period, medieval churches all over Armenia were recon-structed as multicultural monuments to Armenian cultural identity. These include major monuments like the Dvin Cathedral (the foundation of which was reinforced), Hałpat, Sanahin, and Tatev, as well as smaller sites like Haričavank', Sałmosavank' and Hovhan-navank'. Other churches were not renovated, and were used as granaries, barns, or sheds or were left to decay into rubble. In most cases, the materials from these reconstruction excavations were not published except in institute reports. See Hovhannisyan 1982.

52. For Uši: Babayan 2005, Kalantaryan and Babayan 2001.

53. Select Yełegis material published in Kalantaryan et al. 2009.

54. Melkonyan et al. 2017; Bessac 2011.

55. Archaeologies of medieval landscape have a long tradition in the United Kingdom, but primarily served as a way to materially confirm histories of shifts in land use and more general modes of production (e.g., Hoskins 1955). Recently, a focus on perceived landscapes in extraurban places has contributed to a more distributed mode of thinking about medi-eval ideational life, and about the social ways that "town" and "country" were ideologically constructed. This work is also being done in medieval Middle Eastern ("Islamic") archaeol-ogy, which for a long time focused on cities and palaces as the exclusive location of cultural life—but see McPhillips and Wordsworth 2016, and chapters in Anderson, Hopper, and Robinson (eds.) 2018 for new approaches to landscape in the Caucasus.

56. Blessing and Goshgarian 2017: 2.

57. C.f. Vorderstrasse and Roodenberg (eds.) 2009.

58. Goš 2000: 114.

59. During the period of Mxitar Goš's life and writing, Armenia was ruled first by the Seljuks and then by the Georgian Bagratids. Much of the stated intent of the written *Datastanagirk* was to provide a means of juridically defining Armenian self-determinacy in relation to still-active Seljuk legal institutions. Franklin 2019; see also the use of dietary prohi-bitions recorded in the *Datastanagirk'* as a mode of boundary making in Goshgarian 2011: 53.

60. In my emphasis throughout on world-making, I depart from the authorship model of construction posited by Smith (2000), which leans on persuasion as central to legitimacy and subjection. If a prince sets a world in motion, there are no persuadable subject positions that could exist prior to or outside that world.

61. Al-Mulk 1960: 10. See further discussion in Peacock 2015.

62. Eastmond 2015.

63. Goš 2000: 122.

64. Greenwood 2004.

65. Maranci 2008: 28–29.

66. Cf. Maranci 2017: 37. Examples include the seventh-century church at Haŕičavankʿ or the tenth-century church at Karkop. Interestingly, these bands of Armenian inscriptions also parallel techniques of decorative and/or apotropaic inscriptions on other, earlier buildings. Walker (2015) has discussed an interesting corpus of such banded inscriptions carved in pseudo-Kufic, or designs which visually resembles decorative Arabic. The Marmašen inscription replaces the pseudo-Kufic with Armenian. Eva Hoffman (2001), Clare Vernon (2018), and Margaret Graves (2018) discuss the use of Arabic and pseudo-Kufic inscriptions in Christian structures, as well as upon objects and in the hems of embroidered garments—gesturing toward a more broadly shared technique of textual adornment across medieval bodies, objects, and buildings.

67. Dadoyan 2011.

68. Franklin 2015.

69. Marr 1934: 33.

70. The medieval Armenian calendar's year one is the year 552 in the Gregorian calendar. I will note differential dates (Armenian and *hijra* dates) within inscriptions, but otherwise I will use dates a.d. throughout.

71. *Hayrenik* is a polyvalent term in Armenian, meaning inheritance, heritage, or even patrimony. In the medieval case, it referred specifically to inalienable (heritable) properties: thus Tigran Honencʿ is making the point both that he is a person of consequence and that his gift should "stick" to the monastery over time.

72. One dang is a unit of currency equivalent to one sixth of a dahekan, which was in turn equivalent to the Byzantine *nomisma* or solidus (Thomson 1997). The dang was a standard unit of rents collected during the high medieval period.

73. This is my translation via Garsoian's translation of Manandyan (1965, 185–86), and drawing from Mahé (2001). The Grabar inscription is presented in its entirety in Orbeli (1966: 63) and translated in Marr (1934: 35). An updated version is also available in Avagyan (1978). See also Franklin 2015 for more conceptual discussion of this inscription.

74. To use Maria Puig de la Bellacasa's (2011, 2017) phrase; critically, the difference between matters of care and Latour's matters of concern is not just an ontology or epistemology, but more importantly an ethics of assemblage—in other words, what do we owe to the things and humans we assemble?

75. References to farms, smithies, traps, and so on, in medieval endowment inscriptions were understood to be synecdoche for the labors and produce which went on in them. C.f. Trepanier 2014: 31.

76. Dadoyan 2011: 62.

77. Carile 2014. See also Franklin 2015; Khalpakchyan 1980.

78. Guidetti, M. 2017: 155–84.

79. Hakobyan and Mikayelyan 2018: 46, fig. 11. The authors also point out the motifs depicted in Jerusalem MS 2660, shown in figure III.2. See also Marr 1907: fig. 15. The figure is also reproduced in Marr 1934, fig. 190; Marr's caption for this figure is "Fresco ornamentation in the style of a textile." See also Blessing 2019: 233–34.

80. Hoffman 2001.

81. Allsen 1997: see esp. chap. 4.

82. Jones 1996, 2002, 2007.

83. Jones 2002; Eastmond and Jones 2001.

84. See discussion in Jones 1996; Hakobyan and Mikayelyan 2018.

85. Jones 2002: 351.

86. The practice of using silk continues into the Mongol period in Armenia: Stepʻanos Orbelyan (1859) describes the bestowing of robes on princes from Vayots Dzor. Amanda Phillips (2015) has discussed the continuing significance of robing, specifically in gold-figured silk, through the Ottoman period.

87. Arakʻelyan 1964: 182; Ališan 1881: 25.

CHAPTER 4. MAKING AND REMAKING THE WORLD
OF THE KASAKH VALLEY

1. Moore 2013: 108.

2. Bender 2002: S103.

3. Stewart 1993: 17.

4. I discuss my orientation to archaeological landscape in greater detail elsewhere, especially Franklin 2020.

5. The previous names of many of these places are recorded in Soviet topographic maps from the 1950s. According to consensus, many place names in Armenia were changed in connection with the Safavid Persian conquest and major population relocation under Shah Abbas I and his successors. As Petrosyancʻ states, "[d]eprived of their Armenian inhabitants, the places in this region lost their Armenian names" (1988: 20).

6. Petrosyancʻ 1988: 6. For reviews of medieval Armenian architecture see Tʻoramanyan 1942, 1948; V. Harutyunyan 1960; Khalpakchyan 1971, 1980; Yakobson 1950.

7. This enormous and rich archive of images currently exists, to my knowledge, only as prints. These fragile prints are currently stored in stacks on shelves within the Service for the Protection of Historical Environment and Cultural Museum-Reservations SNCO.

8. As I have discussed elsewhere (Franklin, Vorderstrasse, and Babayan 2017), Tʻoramanyan developed a theme that was expanded by his colleagues and successors, that the form of the Armenian church (and by extension, high medieval architecture more broadly) was a linear evolution of the architecture of the traditional Armenian house. In their own manner, scholars developing this argument traced the form of native Armenian architecture back to the subterranean houses described by Xenophon. See Vardanyan 1959: 121; Yakobson 1950: 159–60.

9. Tʻoramanyan 1942: 220–33.

10. The *gavit* or narthex is a particular architectural form in medieval Armenia, especially from the tenth century onward. These spaces are usually square, with a central drum (frequently letting in light) supported by four pillars. The space was used for ritual assembly of nonmonastics, as well as for commemoration and burial of prominent congregants. For architectural discussion, see Mnatsakanyan 1952.

11. This process was recorded by Petrosyancʻ (1988: 26) and also related to me by Dr. Roman Hovsepyan, whose grandparents were born in the village.

12. Also see Ghazarian and Ousterhout (2001) for a discussion of the local design of muqarnas at Astvacnkal.

13. Petrosyancʻ 1988: 6.

14. Petrosyancʻ 1988: 10.

15. Babayan 1976: 547.

16. Petrosyancʻ 1981: 289.

17. Petrosyancʻ 1982; Sargsyan 1977.

18. The Tsaghkahovit plain has hosted a long sequence of archaeological investigations, most recently including those affiliated with the Project for the Archaeology and Geography of Ancient Transcaucasian Societies (ArAGATS); see Smith, Badalyan, and Avetisyan 2005; Badalyan et al. 2008; Smith et al. 2003, 2009; Badalyan, Smith, and Khatchadourian 2018; Lindsay and Smith 2006, Greene and Lindsay 2013, Lindsay 2006; Khatchadourian 2016; Greene 2012; Marshall 2014; Chazin 2016. This body of work has authoritatively framed the landscapes of Aragatsotn for prehistoric and classical periods.

19. This is an extensive list of archaeological places and objects (khachkars and standing stones) maintained over the last several decades and consulted by the heads of departments at the Institute of Archaeology. In 2009 when I began my survey work, excerpts from the Monuments List were "divulged" to me and represented as personal expert knowledge by a senior archaeologist. It was only in 2015 that the list was made available online, and shared widely among junior archaeologists. See discussion in Franklin and Babajanyan (2018a and b) for a discussion of the ramifications of this lack of knowledge sharing in terms of both the cultures of science within the institute, and the relationships within international collaborative projects. The primary upshot of this experience for me is that I completed an intellectual break away from a long-term (masculinist, colonial) habit of thinking of archaeological survey as a process of "discovery" of historically significant or monumental sites which had somehow escaped the notice of local people and scientists working in the region for decades.

20. Petrosyancʻ 1988: 20.

21. Thanks so much to the volunteer survey team: Ray Franklin, Stephen Franklin, and Rick Scupham.

22. A very rough Armenian medieval ceramic periodization applied in this analysis: fourth to seventh century: Early Medieval; seventh to tenth century: Medieval I; tenth to twelfth century: Medieval II; twelfth to thirteenth century: High Medieval I; thirteenth to fifteenth century High Medieval II; sixteenth to nineteenth century: Early Modern. In my unpublished dissertation (Franklin 2014b) I refer to the period between 1200 and 1500 as the "Late Medieval Period," a terminological import. I have since reconfigured the chronology and adopted "high" as a translation of my Armenian colleagues' "developed" medieval.

23. Alan Greene and Ian Lindsay, personal communication.

24. I have a personal affection for the palimpsest metaphor and have frequently deployed it: Franklin and Hammer 2017; Franklin 2019; Franklin and Babajanyan 2018a; Franklin 2020. See Crawford 1918 for an original formulation, Wilkinson 2003 for an expansion, and Johnson 2007 for an extensive genealogy.

25. Hence the invention of a term, building from Wilkinson's *signature landscapes*, of "landscapes of destruction" by Mediterranean archaeologist John Cherry (2014) to describe similarly ameliorated landscapes in southern Armenia. The challenges of amelioration to medieval landscape reconstruction is discussed in Franklin and Babajanyan 2018a, as well as other chapters of Anderson et al. 2018.

26. See Franklin 2014c, 2020.

27. A pyx is a container for the eucharist, often made of precious metals.

28. From Babayan 2005; my trans.

29. Ghafadaryan 1957.

30. Ghafadaryan 1957: 135–36.

31. T'oramanyan 1942: 131, Ghafadaryan 1948: 11.

32. Ghafadaryan 1948: 82–83; my translation.

33. Maranci 2006.

34. Guidetti 2017: 163; Ghazarian and Ousterhout 2001.

35. The village south of the monastery of Hovhannavank'.

36. My translation from a combination of sources: the text of the inscription is recorded in Petrosyanc' 1988: 24. See also Kiesling 2001, Petrosyanc' 1978. I think the recorded text of the inscription is taken from Ghevont Ališan's *Ararat*: under the entry for Apnagegh. Also, a note: in Franklin (2020) I incorrectly locate this inscription on the southern wall of the church. That depicted inscription is in fact from 1207, and commemorated the renovation of the single-naved small church by prominent locals (Petrosyanc' 1988: 23).

37. Petrosyanc' 1988: 23 (drawing on T'oramanyan) Presumably this refers to the fourth-century St. Jacob of Nisibis, said to be the brother of Gregory the Illuminator; relics of St. Jacob abound across the Armenian Christian world.

38. The Hovhannavank' inscription was recorded by Ghafadaryan (1948: 103), the Sałmosavank' inscription was recorded by Manuč'aryan (2015).

39. Manuč'aryan 2015: 47.

40. Pogossian 2012: 172–73.

41. Khalpakchyan 1980 refers to this or a partner inscription, which lists also a daughter, Mamaxatun—named for her builder-grandmother. It is possible that this is part of the degraded section of the inscription which was illegible by the time of Manuč'aryan's visit.

42. Barrett 1999: 255.

43. Badalyan et al. 2008; Khatchadourian 2016.

CHAPTER 5. TRAVELING THROUGH ARMENIA: CARAVAN INNS AND THE MATERIAL EXPERIENCE OF THE SILK ROAD

1. Medieval and early modern caravanserais could be constructed with differential degrees of internal access, such that distinction was preserved within the building. Many "royal" caravanserais have special chambers set aside for regal or princely travelers; see Blessing 2013; Campbell 2011. Also, spatial divisions and distinctions could be created in ways not recorded within the floor plan of a stone building.

2. Foucault 1967: 6.

3. The use of the caravan as an allegory for the journey of human life was also popular within medieval Buddhism: see Whitfield 2018: 85.

4. See discussion in Sauvaget 1940; Hillenbrand 1998; Sims 1978; Crane 1993; Cytryn-Silverman 2010. For a historical discussion of the caravanserai as an institution, see Constable 2003.

5. Dankoff and Kim 2011: 100.

6. Aflaki 2002: 384. This encounter is meant to illustrate the inverted status of worldly and learned knowledge, tropically deploying the levelling effects of the caravanserai space.

7. C.f. Ibn Hawqal 1800: 201.

8. Crane 1993; Constable 2003: 84; Harut'yunyan 1960, Arak'elyan 1964. See also the discussion of *pandoks* donated by Tigran Honenc' in chapter 3.

9. Rogers 1976; Blessing 2013.

10. La Porta 2008–9: 135.

11. Mauss 1999: 41.

12. Derrida and Dufourmantelle 2000: 15.

13. For just one example, one of the indices of Ibn Battuta's fourteenth-century cosmopolitanism was his acceptance of numerous slaves as gifts (as well as splendid robes like those discussed in chapter 3) from welcoming rulers across Central Asia into South Asia.

14. E.g., Manandyan 1965, 1979.

15. Goš 2000: 117–18, 156, 304.

16. De Vinsauf 1965: 155.

17. Ibn Battuta 2003: 157

18. "Tana" refers to the region around the sea of Asov, at the mouth of the Volga. Cathay is the general term used by medieval Europeans to refer to China.

19. Pegolotti 1913: 153.

20. See the excellent discussion in Larkin 2013. A great example of this is the deleterious effect of the 1977 New York blackout on the career of then-mayor Abe Beam, or the appellation by Londoners of the abhorred "Boris Buses" after then-mayor Boris Johnson.

21. See also: *How It Began, with Brad Harris: A History of the Modern World*, https://howitbegan.com/podcasts/episode-105-monumental-infrastructure (accessed February 25, 2021).

22. The mural, commissioned by the Treasury Department, was intended to symbolize the growth of the city and its four great industries: "Sternberg Mural ready," 1938.

23. The fact that the WPA was also deployed in the construction of internment camps for Japanese Americans after the U.S. entry into the Second World War confirms the ambivalence of infrastructures, which act to enforce boundaries even as they construct and accommodate citizens.

24. Harut'yunyan 1960.

25. Harut'yunyan 1960: v.

26. Ogel 2008: 3. Önge (2007) did imply that this pattern may be a result of the differential preservation of caravanserai structures in the Anatolian landscape, as opposed to palaces or other buildings.

27. See further discussion in Yavuz 1997; Crane 1993; Blessing 2013, Peacock 2015, Blessing and Goshgarian 2017.

28. Ogel 2008: 5.

29. Ertug 1991: 76.

30. Ogel 2008: 3, also Önge 2007.

31. By the Ottoman period, private caravanserais were called "manazil"; also, in twelfth-century astronomical terms the word referred to the shift in the moon's phase caused by the corresponding march of one day's darkness across its face.

32. Yavuz 1997: 89; see also chapters in Blessing et al. 2017; and Tavernari 2010.

33. This *han* has been intensively restored and the courtyard excavated but to my knowledge no report is available.

34. C.f. Tavernari 2017.

35. Redford 2016a.

36. Ogel 2008: 2, reiterated by Bektaş 1999: 29–30.

37. Bektaş 1999: 23.

38. Tavernari 2017, Guidetti 2017.

39. Önge 2007: 59, from Oney 1971. See also Eastmond 2016 for discussion of animal forms in broader context.

40. Ogel 2008.

41. Bektaş 1999: 19.

42. Onge 2007: 52, citing work by Yavuz.

43. Crane 1993: 3.

44. Discussing this caravanserai in 2016, Redford stated in fact that it "is the only surviving caravanserai not built by a member of the Seljuk elite" (2016a: 228) essentially committing Harut'yunyan's error in reverse by ignoring the caravanserais in Armenia, including that at Arai, which are contemporary with and structurally similar to Hekim Han.

45. The caravanserai was reconstructed in the seventeenth century; Redford 2016a: 228.

46. Eastmond 2014: 80. See this source for the text of the Syriac version as well.

47. Eastmond 2014: 80. See also Erdmann 1961 vol. 1: 66.

48. Redford 2016a: 228.

49. Erdmann 1961 vol 1: table 6, plates 79–82.

50. Goš 2000: 254.

51. Barxudaryan 1967: 246. English trans. Astghik Babajanyan.

52. The name has been changed in recent years on signage and websites to Orbelian's Caravanserai, presumably to more accurately reflect the builder of the inn; I will stick to the name in longer usage to avoid confusion.

53. Ališan 1883: 164–65.

54. Abu Sa'id Bahadur Khan, ninth ruler of the Ilkhanate (r. 1316–35).

55. I want to deliriously thank Khodadad Rezakhani for translation of this text and discussion of its significance in broader context. Khodadad also pointed out the further addition of the last line, presumably by the mason, as a fascinating appendage request for grace.

56. Ališan erroneously gives this as Smbat.

57. This term *hogetun*, which translates literally as "spirit-house"; Arak'elyan explains this by defining *hogi* as "breath," such that a caravanserai could be thought of as a "breath catching house" (1964: 51).

58. My translation from Ališan 1883: 164–5; see also Barxudaryan 1967: 177–8 for a transcription, Kiesling 2001: 73 for a translation.

59. La Porta 2011: 107.

60. Yavuz (1997) calls this form "shelter hall" in the Seljuk context.

61. By this I mean, included in the corpus of Armenian caravanserais by Harut'yunyan (1960).

62. Harut'yunyan 1960: 62.

63. Blessing and Goshgarian (eds.) 2017; Peker 2014; Eastmond 2015b.

64. Again, separate from the extensive, nearly obsessive interest in caravanserais as architecture, as demonstrated by additional multivolume studies by Kleiss (1996–2001); see also Sauvaget 1939, 1940.

65. For more discussion of this route, its temporalities and landscape, see Franklin 2020.

66. Hillenbrand 1998: 346–49, Tavernari 2017.

67. See discussion of the evidence for this inscription in the previous chapter.

68. Franklin, Vorderstrasse, and Babayan 2017.

69. T'oromanyan 1942; Harut'yunyan 1960.

70. Šahxat'unyan 1842: 168–69, cited in Harut'yunyan 1960: 42.

71. Every minute of digging this building, and every one of my voiced-aloud interpretive musings was in the company of four excavators from Arai-Bazarǰuł: Artur Kocharyan, Ando Sarkisyan, Gev Petrosyan, and Petik Petrosyan.

72. Harut'yunyan noticed what may have been a drain in the east wall of the caravanserai when he visited the site prior to his 1960 publication (1960: 44).

73. By Dr Belinda Monahan, the faunal analyst for this material.

74. These equid shoes are of a type found as well at contemporary medieval sites such as Gritille and Tille Hoyuk, as well as at Dvin. Ghafadaryan 1952, 1982; Redford 1998 et al.: 171; J. Moore 1993: 151.

75. Sargsyan 1990: 184; Medvedev 1967: 57.

76. Dvin: Ghafadaryan 1952: 161; Garni: Arak'elyan and Karakhanyan 1962: 52; Anberd: Harut'yunyan 1978: fig. 59; Tille Hoyuk: J. Moore 1993: 153.

77. J. Moore 1993.

78. Sargsyan 1990.

79. This affect is well represented in the work of photographer Christopher Herwig: http://herwigphoto.com/soviet-bus-stops (accessed February 25, 2021).

80. Augé 1992.

81. E.g., Castells 1996; but see Massey 1994.

82. Escobar 2001: 147.

CHAPTER 6. THE WORLD IN A BOWL: INTIMATE AND DELICIOUS EVERYDAY SPACETIMES ON THE SILK ROAD

1. Munn 1977: 124.

2. Douglas 1966: 51–71.

3. O'Neill 2007; xxi–xxii.

4. Dietler and Hayden (eds.) 2001; Graff and Rodriguez-Alegria (eds.) 2012; Hastorf 2017.

5. Hastorf 2017; Robin 2013; Gilchrist 2012.

6. Hastorf 2012: 216. In this discussion Hastorf cites Butler's 1993 discussion of discursive/nondiscursive/explicit/natural, and emphasizes the space in cooking-as-practice for the negotiation as well as reproduction of cultural tradition. Also note the ways that modalities of cooking/eating are also gendered: feasts are masculinized, and the "natural" cooking of everyday sustenance (maintenance) is feminized.

7. See the recent collection of work from this group: Vroom, Waksman, and Van Oosten (eds.) 2017.

8. Bagci and Vroom 2017.

9. Dietler and Hayden (eds.) 2001; Brumfiel 1991; Russell and Martin 2012; Stein 2012.

10. Sutton 2001; Caldwell 2006.

11. Munn 1977; but also Hastorf 2017: 9.

12. For examples see: Arak'elyan 1958, plates 41 and 42; Babayan 1981; Mirijanyan 2008; Kalantaryan et al. 2009; Marr 1934; Mkrtchyan and Grigoryan (eds.) 2014.

13. For discussion of decoration across registers see chapter 3; see also Eastmond 2016.

14. Ortner 1976.

15. Bourdieu 1972; T. Bray 2003.

16. I am referring to the ur-case in anthropological commodity chain studies, Mintz's *Sweetness and Power*—which demonstrated that it is partly the role of anthropology to reveal the histories and worlds in our everyday things.

17. Goshgarian 2011: 49–68; Pancaroğlu 2013: 48–81.

18. Pancaroğlu 2013: 49. Pancaroğlu is specifically talking about multiple Islamic sects in this case, but discusses the policy of Seljuk caravanserais, recorded in waqf documents, to welcome and serve Christians as well as Muslims. See also Redford 2016b for expanded discussion.

19. Pancaroğlu 2013: 53.

20. Total count for analyzed ceramics from cultural levels including nondiagnostic fragments is n = 524; count of diagnostic rims, handles, and base fragments is n = 161. To compare this to the ceramic totals from a similar area of exposure at the nearby Ambroyi village, see Franklin, Vorderstrasse, and Babayan 2017.

21. These categories are even slipperier when we take into account that ceramic objects traveled in and out of contexts of production and (re)use.

22. These have been termed "red wares" because the bowl colors cluster in the Munsell 2.5YR 5/4 and 6/4 range, as well as around 5YR 6/4: light reds and red (this latter usually referring to burnished slips, not bodies).

23. Inclusions are materials like grit, ground stone, or chaff which are added into clay to affect its plasticity or behavior during firing. We are in the process of testing the assumption of proximity by using comparative quantitative analysis of the chemical makeup of the ceramics from Arai-Bazarǰuł as well as other contemporary sites in the highlands.

24. Zaqyan and Babajanyan 2014.

25. For the medieval Anatolian practice of eating seated on the ground, see Trepanier 2014.

26. Sargsyan 1990; Mirijanyan and Babajanyan 2013; Kalantaryan et al. 2009; Babajanyan and Franklin 2018, Babajanyan et al. 2020: 383.

27. Kalantarian et al. 2009: plate 47. See also Sagona 2010.

28. White wares are made of more finely levigated yellow clays with, presumably, different sources than the volcanic clays in the Armenian red ware. This vessel could have been made, however, from one of the numerous lakebed clay deposits in the Kasakh Valley. See Greene 2012, and analyses by Minc in Smith et al. 2003.

29. Ghafadaryan 1948: 82; Babajanyan and Franklin 2018.

30. $X2 = 89.5625$, $df = 4$, $p < 2.2e\text{-}16$

31. The outputs and details of these statistical analyses are presented in the appendices of Franklin 2014b.

32. Collaborators on this project were: Dr. Frina Babayan, National Academy of Sciences Institute of Archaeology and Ethnography; and Dr. Tasha Vorderstrasse, University of Chicago Oriental Institute. We were assisted by Artur Kocharyan and Ando Sargsyan.

33. Franklin, Vorderstrasse, and Babayan 2017; Babayan et al. 2014.

34. Franklin, Vorderstrasse, and Babayan 2017; see also Babayan et al. 2014, 2015.

35. See ceramic discussion in Franklin 2014a and 2014b.

36. Hovsepyan 2013; Kalantaryan et al. 2012.

37. Dr. Hovsepyan was working at the time in the laboratory of Dr. Joy McCorriston at the Ohio State University. See Berlekamp 2017.

38. The major cereals crops recorded were hulled barley (*Hordeum vulgare*, hulled varieties) and naked wheat (*Triticum aestivum*/turgidum). This latter wheat group consists of various free-threshing species of tetraploid (macaroni wheat, e.g., *T. durum*) and hexaploid (bread wheat, *T. aestivum*) wheat grains (which are more or less indistinguishable especially when charred). In order for plant remains to be preserved for eight centuries, they must be either desiccated and kept dry, waterlogged and kept wet, frozen and kept frozen, or charred (among a few other methods). This means that to archaeologically re-create what plants people in the Middle Ages were eating at any given site we are dependent on accidents of practice as well as preservation.

39. Berlekamp 2017: 31.

40. Hovsepyan 2014, Stoletova 1930.

41. Berlekamp 2017: 32.

42. Miller 1984.

43. To further test this hypothesis, the category of medium mammals, which are the most probable food animals (sheep/goat and pig), was analyzed for average size of bone fragment to assess the pattern of processing these meat foods. The average weight per fragment of medium mammals was 2.72g, indicating a fairly intense degree of fragmentation (e.g., a complete sheep/goat long bone can weigh as much as 40g).

44. Sargsyan 1990; Kalantaryan et al. 2009 (materials from Yełegis); Redford et al. 1998; Babajanyan et al. 2020.

45. Recent finds from Vayots Dzor show that there were "variations" on this cuisine standard, raising the question of how and what kinds of deviations from the norm were considered tasty regional specialties along the highland roads. See Babajanyan and Franklin 2018.

46. Vionis 2009.

47. Rodinson and Arberry 2001.

48. E.g., Freedman 2008.

49. Bagci and Vroom (2017) use a similar method in a parallel analysis of Anatolian contexts.

50. Herisa, not to be confused with the condiment harissa, is still a foodstuff redolent with tradition across Iran, Iraq, and Armenia.

51. Buell and Anderson 2010: 6.

52. Buell and Anderson 2010: 6.

53. Buell and Anderson 2010: 6, 155.

54. Ibn Batutta 2003: 122.

55. Russell 2003: 138; Goshgarian 2011.

56. Russell 2003: 139.

57. Goshgarian 2011: 58–60.

58. Petrosian and Underwood 2006.

59. Appadurai 1981.

60. Stern and Stern 1978. Their term is actually the portmanteau *roadfood*, which I frankly think is hard to pronounce.

61. Stern and Stern 1978: introduction.

62. I chose this word deliberately, to indicate the redolent romanticism and nostalgia (both spatiotemporal concepts) inherent to the concept of road food, especially in the United States. As a UK colleague pointed out, these associations with road meals are not universally shared (the British don't feel the same way about "cafs" as some Americans feel about diners, and the cultural associations are very different). Again, road food is a parochial kind of universalism.

63. On a personal note, I (as it may already be apparent) have a love of diners, where there is frequently a casually ceremonialized celebration of excess. So many road food restaurants used to feature a ceremonial feast for one, the "if you can eat a whole <insert giant local specialty here> it's free and we take your picture for posterity" offer.

64. Ehrenreich 2001: 17 (my emphasis).

65. See an extensive discussion in Sherman 2007.

66. Redford 2016a: 223.

67. Ibn Battuta 2003: 102.

68. Pancaroğlu 2013.

69. *Sp'yurk'ahay* is the term for members of the Armenian diaspora.

70. Sichone 2008: 320–21.

CHAPTER 7. EVERYDAY COSMOPOLITANISMS: REWRITING THE SHAPE OF THE SILK ROAD WORLD

1. Cheah 2008: 38.

2. Morrison 2018.

3. Pollock et al. 2002: 12.

4. See Franklin 2020 for discussion of this route.

5. Hovhannisyan 1982: 52.

6. From Ališan 1881: 147. Translated with help from Astghik Babajanyan.

7. C.f. Redford 2016b; Crane 1993: 11–12; Yalman 2017.

8. For a discussion of the True Cross of Varaga and medieval narratives of its links to Hripsime, see Pogossian 2019.

9. Manandyan 1965; L. Babayan 1976; Arak'elyan 1958; Djanpoladyan and Kalantarian 1988; also I would include the histories written in the late twentieth century: Hovhannisian et al. (eds.) 1997; Panossian 2006; Bournoutian 2006.

10. See also Bedrosian 1997; Franklin 2014b: chap. 2.

11. Matthee 2012a and b.

12. Tim Winter (2019) has an interesting recent take on some of these questions as they affect Central Asia.

13. Thorsten 2005: 309.

14. See for instance Chakrabarty 2000; Haraway 2016; Verges 2019.

15. Ganim 2010: 6.

16. Ehrenreich and Hothschild 2002.

17. Hundreds of bracelet fragments were recently found in test excavations at Indor (Trivedi 2020). See also Giorgieva, Detcheva, and Dimitriev 2010; and Franklin, Vorderstrasse, and Babayan 2017 for a more complete discussion.

18. Wood 2002: 121.

19. E.g., Stein 1912: 66, 133, 318.

20. Edugyan 2020.

21. Mackinder 1904; Dugan 1962.

22. This topographical orientalism was revived by European Romantics in the 1870s, and is enjoying a further revival in neoliberal circles with the rise of China and Central Asia as political and economic powers. C.f. Oldmeadow 2011: 26.

23. Ortner 1976: 126–66.

24. E.g., Chang 2018; Frachetti and Bullion 2018; Hermes et al. 2018, Spengler 2019.

25. Stewart 2007: 86 (see epigram at start of chapter).

26. C.f. Yang et al. 2016. I don't have space in this book to engage with the specter of the Anthropocene more fully, though the process of writing this has oriented my thoughts about futurity, agency, and living across scales.

27. Eco 2002: 99.

28. Bray 1997: 57.

29. Puig de la Bellacasa 2011: 99.

BIBLIOGRAPHY

Abu-Lughod, Janet. 1989. *Before European Hegemony: The Thirteenth-Century World System*. Oxford: Oxford University Press.

Adontz, Nicholas. 1970. *Armenia in the Period of Justinian: The Political Conditions Based on the Naxarar System*. Trans. with partial revisions, a bibliographical note, and appendices by Nina G. Garsoïan. Lisbon: Calouste Gulbenkian Foundation.

Aflaki, Šams-al-dīn. 2002. *The Feats of the Knowers of God (Manāqeb Al-ʿārefin)*. Trans. John O'Kane. Leiden: Brill.

Akbari, Suzanne C., and Amilcare Iannucci, eds. 2008. *Marco Polo and the Encounter of East and West*. Toronto: University of Toronto Press.

Aknerc'i, Grigor. 2003. *History of the Nation of Archers*. Trans. Robert Bedrosian. Available at archive.org.

Ałayan, Tsatur, et al., eds. 1976. *History of the Armenian People*. Vol. 3, *Armenia in the Period of Developed Feudalism (Second Half of the Ninth Century until the Mid-Fourteenth Century)*. Armenian SSR Academy of Sciences Institute of History. Yerevan: Armenian SSR Academy of Sciences Publishing. In Armenian.

Alcock, Susan. 1993. *Graecia Capta: The Landscapes of Roman Greece*. Cambridge: Cambridge University Press.

Ališan, Łevond. 1881. *Ayrarat*. Venice: Mxit'arean Publishing. In Armenian.

———. 1883. *Sisakan: Topography of the World of Syunik*. Venice: Mxit'arean Publishing . In Armenian.

Allsen, Thomas. 1997. *Commodity and Exchange in the Mongol Empire*. Cambridge: Cambridge University Press.

———. 2001. *Culture and Conquest in Mongol Eurasia*. Cambridge: Cambridge University Press.

Anderson, Benedict. 1983. *Imagined Communities*. London: Verso.

Anderson, William, Kristen Hopper, and Abby Robinson, eds. 2018. *Landscape Archaeology in Southern Caucasia: Finding Common Ground in Diverse Environments*. Vienna: Austrian Academy of Sciences, Institute for Oriental and European Archaeology (OREA) series.

Appadurai, Arjun. 1981. Gastro-Politics in Hindu South Asia. *Symbolism and Cognition* issue. *American Ethnologist* 8(3): 494–511.

Arak'elyan, Babken. 1958. *Cities and Crafts in Armenia, IX–XIII Centuries*. Vol. 1. Yerevan: Armenian SSR Academy of Sciences Publishing. In Armenian.

———. 1964. *Cities and Crafts in Armenia, IX–XIII Centuries*. Vol. 2. Yerevan: Armenian SSR Academy of Sciences Publishing . In Armenian.

———. 1976. The New Rise of Cities in the 12th–13th centuries. In *History of the Armenian People*, vol. 3, *Armenia in the Period of Developed Feudalism (Second Half of the Ninth Century until the Mid-fourteenth Century)*, ed. Tsatur Ałayan et al., 558–78. Armenian SSR Academy of Sciences Institute of History. Yerevan: Armenian SSR Academy of Sciences Publishing. In Armenian.

Arak'elyan, Babken, and Grigor Karakhanyan. 1962. *Garni I: Excavations*. Yerevan: Armenian SSR Academy of Sciences Publishing. In Armenian.

Arendt, Hannah. 1973. *The Origins of Totalitarianism*. New edition with added preface. New York: Harcourt Brace Jovanovich.

Areshian, Gregory, and Aram Kalantaryan. 2008. Return to a Great Excavation of the Past: A New Joint Project in Armenia. *Backdirt: Annual Review of the Cotsen Institute of Archaeology at UCLA*: 50–59.

Aslanian, Sebouh. 2014. *From the Indian Ocean to the Mediterranean: The Global Trade Networks of Armenian Merchants*. Berkeley: University of California Press.

Augé, Marc. 1992. *Non-places: Introduction to an Anthropology of Supermodernity*. London: Verso.

Avagyan, S.A. 1978. *Investigation of Stone Inscriptions*. Yerevan: Yerevan University Press. In Armenian.

Babaie, Sussan, et al. 2004. Slaves of the Shah: New Elites of Safavid Iran. London: I.B. Tauris.

Babajanyan, Astghik, and Kathryn Franklin. 2018. Everyday Life on the Medieval Silk Road: VDSRS Excavations at Arpa, Armenia. *Aramazd: Armenian Journal of Near Eastern Studies* 12(1): 154–82.

Babajanyan, Astghik, et al. 2021. A View on Life in the Medieval Fortress at Dashtadem: Results of the 2015 and 2018 Campaigns. In *Archaeology of Armenia in Regional Context: Proceedings of the International Conference dedicated to the 60th Anniversary of the Institute of Archaeology and Ethnography*, ed. Pavel Avetisyan and Arsen Bobokhyan, 371–93. Yerevan: Publishing House of the Institute of Archaeology and Ethnography.

Babayan, Frina. 1981. *Designs of Fine Art Ceramics in Medieval Armenia*. Yerevan: Armenian SSR Academy of Sciences Publishing. In Armenian.

———. 2005. *Sourb Sargis Vankʻ at Uši*. Yerevan: Gitutyun Press. In Armenian.

Babayan, Frina, Kathryn Franklin, and Tasha Vorderstrasse. 2014. Preliminary Excavations at Ambroyi Village, Armenia: A House on the Silk Road. *Oriental Institute Annual Reports, 2013–2014*: 12–21.

———. 2015. The Project for Medieval Archaeology of the South Caucasus (MASC): Ambroyi, Armenia. *Oriental Institute Annual Reports, 2014–2015*: 14–20.

Babayan, Levon. 1976. The Development of Zak'arid Power and New Armenian Feudal Houses. In *History of the Armenian People*, vol. 3, *Armenia in the Period of Developed Feudalism (Second Half of the Ninth Century until the Mid-fourteenth Century)*, ed. Tsatur Ałayan et al., 541–56. Armenian SSR Academy of Sciences Institute of History. Yerevan: Armenian SSR Academy of Sciences Publishing. In Armenian.

Badalyan, Ruben, Adam T. Smith, and Lori Khatchadourian. 2018. Project Aragats: 10 years of Investigations into Bronze and Iron Age Sites in the Tsaghkahovit Plain, Republic of Armenia. *TUBA-AR* 13(13): 263–76.

Badalyan, Ruben, et al. 2008. Village, Fortress, and Town in Bronze and Iron Age Southern Caucasia: A Preliminary Report on the 2003–2006 Investigations of Project ArAGATS on the Tsaghkahovit Plain, Republic of Armenia. *Archäologische Mitteilungen aus Iran und Turan* 40: 45–105.

Bagci, Yasemin, and Joanita Vroom. 2017. Dining Habits at Tarsus in the Early Islamic Period: A Ceramic Perspective from Turkey. In *Medieval MasterChef*, ed. Joanita Vroom et al., 63–94. Turnhout: Brepols.

Bakhtin, Mikhail. 1981. Forms of Time and of the Chronotope in the Novel. In *The Dialogic Imagination*, trans. Michael Holquist, 84–258. Austin: University of Texas Press.

Barad, Karen. 2007. *Meeting the Universe Halfway: Quantum Physics and the Entanglement of Matter and Meaning*. Durham, NC: Duke University Press.

Barrett, John C. 1999. The Mythical Landscapes of the British Iron Age. In *Archaeologies of Landscape: Contemporary Perspectives*, ed. Wendy Ashmore and A. Bernard Knapp, 253–65. Oxford: Blackwell.

Barxudaryan, Sedrak. 1967. *Corpus of Armenian Inscriptions. Vol. 3, Yeghegnadzor and Azizbekov Regions*. Yerevan: Armenian SSR Academy of Sciences Institute of Archaeology and Ethnography. Armenian SSR Scientific Publishing. In Armenian.

b. Battuta, Shams al-Din. 1958. *The Travels*. Trans. Sir Hamilton Alexander Roskeen Gibb. Cambridge: Cambridge University Press for the Hakluyt Society.

———. 2003. *The Travels of Ibn Battutah*. An abridgement of the Gibb translation for the Hakluyt Society, by Tim Mackintosh-Smith. London: Picador.

Beck, Ulrich. 2002. The Cosmopolitan Society and Its Enemies. *Theory, Culture, and Society* 19(1–2): 17–44.

Bedrosian, Robert. 1997. Armenia in the Seljuk and Mongol Periods. In *The Armenian People from Ancient to Modern Times*, ed. Richard Hovhannisian, vol. 1, *The Dynastic Periods: From Antiquity to the Fourteenth Century*, 241–71. London: Palgrave Macmillan.

Beihammer, Alexander D. 2016. Christian Views of Islam in Early Seljuq Anatolia: Perceptions and Reactions. In *Islam and Christianity in Medieval Anatolia*, ed. Andrew C.S. Peacock, Bruno De Nicola, and Sara Nur Yildiz, 51–76. London: Routledge.

Bektaş, Cengiz. 1999. *A Proposal Regarding the Seljuk Caravanserais, Their Protection and Use*. Harbiye, İstanbul: Building Information Center (YEM) Publishing.

Bender, Barbara. 2002. Time and Landscape. *Current Anthropology* 43, supplement (August–October): S103–S112.

Bennett, Jane. 2009. *Vibrant Matter: A Political Economy of Things*. Durham, NC: Duke University Press.

Berlekamp, Anna. 2017. Paleobotanical Analysis of Arai-Bazarjuł: A Late Medieval Armenian Caravanserai. Bachelor's thesis, Ohio State University.

Bessac, Jean-Claude. 2011. Observations on Monumental Construction in the Northwest of the Republic of Armenia. *Syria* 88: 379–415. In French.

Blessing, Patricia. 2013. Allegiance, Praise, and Space: Monumental Inscriptions in Thirteenth-Century Anatolia as Architectural Guides. In *Calligraphy and Architecture in the Muslim World*, ed. Mohammad Gharipour and İrvin Cemil Schick, 431–46. Edinburgh: Edinburgh University Press.

———. 2019. Silk Road without Fabrics: Ani at the Crossroads of Trade and Textile Motifs in Architecture. In *Ani at the Crossroads*, ed. Zaza Shkirtladze, 229–54. Tbilisi: Ivane Javakhishvili Tbilisi State University Press.

Blessing, Patricia, and Rachel Goshgarian, eds. 2017. *Architecture and Landscape in Medieval Anatolia, 1100–1500*. Edinburgh: Edinburgh University Press.

Bourdieu, Pierre. 1972. *Outline of a Theory of Practice*. Cambridge: Cambridge University Press.

Bournoutian, George. 2006. *Concise History of the Armenian People*. Costa Mesa, CA: Mazda.

Boyle, John A. 1964. The Journey of Het'um I, King of Little Armenia, to the Court of the Great Khan Mongke. *Central Asiatic Journal* 9: 175–89.

Brack, Yoni. 2011. A Mongol Princess Making Hajj: The Biography of El Qutlugh Daughter of Abagha Ilkhan (r. 1265–82). *JRAS*, series 3, 21(3): 331–59.

Bradley, Richard. 1998. *The Significance of Monuments: On the Shaping of Human Experience in Neolithic and Bronze Age Europe*. London: Routledge.

Braudel, Fernand. 1981. *Civilization and Capitalism, 15th–18th c.* Vol. 1, *Structures of Everyday Life*. Berkeley: University of California Press.

———. 1984. *Civilization and Capitalism, 15th–18th c.* Vol. 3, *The Perspective of the World*. New York: Harper and Row.

Bray, Francesca. 1997. *Technology and Gender: Fabrics of Power in Late Imperial China*. Berkeley: University of California Press.

Bray, Tamara. 2003. Inca Pottery as Culinary Equipment: Food, Feasting, and Gender in Imperial State Design. *Latin American Antiquity* 17(1): 1–22.

Breckenridge, Carol, et al., eds. 2000. *Cosmopolitanism*. Durham, NC: Duke University Press.

Brenner, Robert. 1976. Agrarian Class Structure and Economic Development in Pre-industrial Europe. *Past and Present* 70: 30–75.

Brewer, Keagan. 2016. *Wonder and Skepticism in the Middle Ages*. London: Routledge.

Bridges, Roy C., and Paul E.H. Hair. 2010. *Compassing the Vaste Globe of the Earth: Studies in the History of the Hakluyt Society, 1846–1996*. Surrey: Ashgate.

Brodky-Porges, Edward. 1981. The Grand Tour as Educational Device. *Journal of Tourism Research* 8(2): 171–86.

Brumfiel, Elizabeth. 1991. Weaving and Cooking: Women's Production in Aztec Mexico. In *Engendering Archaeology: Women and Prehistory*, ed. Joan Gero and Margaret Conkey, 224–54. Oxford: Blackwell.

Buell, Paul, and Eugene Anderson. 2010. *A Soup for the Qan: Chinese Dietary Medicine of the Mongol Era as Seen in Hu Sihui's Yinshan Zhengyao*. Leiden: Brill.

Butler, Judith. 1990. *Gender Trouble*. New York: Routledge.

———. 1993. *Bodies That Matter*. New York: Routledge.

Byron, Robert. 1937. *The Road to Oxiana*. New York: Penguin Classics.

Cahen, Claude. 1968. *Pre-Ottoman Turkey*. Trans. J. Jones-Williams. New York: Taplinger.

Caldwell, Melissa. 2006. Tasting the Worlds of Yesterday and Today: Culinary Tourism and Nostalgia Foods in Post-Soviet Russia. In *Fast Food/Slow Food: The Cultural Economy of the Global Food System*, ed. Richard Wilk, 97–114. Lanham, MD: Altamira.

Campbell, Jennifer. 2011. Architecture and Identity: the Occupation, Use, and Reuse of Mughal Caravanserais. PhD diss., Department of Anthropology, University of Toronto.

Carile, Maria C. 2014. Buildings In Their Patrons' Hands? The Multiform Function of Small Size Models between Byzantium and Transcaucasia. Monograph issue edited by Patricia Blessing. *Architectural Models, Mobility, and Building Techniques: Modes of Transfer in Medieval Anatolia, Byzantium, and the Caucasus. FUNUN/Kunsttexte.de* 3: 1–14.

Castells, Manuel. 1996. The Space of Flows. In *The Rise of the Network Society*, 407–59. London: Wiley Blackwell.

Chakrabarty, Dipesh. 2000. *Provincializing Europe: Postcolonial Thought and Historical Difference*. Princeton, NJ: Princeton University Press.

Chamchian, Mikayel. 1784. *The History of the Armenians from the Beginning of the World until Modern Times*. Venice: Mxit'arean Publishing. In Armenian.

Champion, Matthew. 2017. *The Fullness of Time: Temporalities of the Fifteenth-Century Low Countries*. Chicago: University of Chicago Press.

Chang, Claudia. 2018. *Rethinking Prehistoric Central Asia: Shepherds, Farmers, and Nomads*. Abingdon and New York: Routledge.

Chardin, Jean. 1811. *Voyages du Chevalier Chardin en Perse*. Paris: Le Normant.

Chazin, Hannah. 2016. The Life Assemblage: Rethinking the Politics of Pastoral Practices. In *Incomplete Archaeologies*, ed. Emily Miller Bonney, Kathryn Franklin, and James Johnson, 28–47. Oxford: Oxbow.

Cheah, Pheng. 2008. What Is a World? On World Literature as World-Making Activity. *Daedalus* 137(3): 26–38.

Cherry, John. 2014. Archaeological Landscapes, Pushed toward Ruination. In *Of Rocks and Water: Toward an Archaeology of Place*, ed. Ömur Harmansah, 204–12. Oxford: Oxbow.

Chin, Tamara. 2013. The Invention of the Silk Road, 1877. *Critical Inquiry* 40(1) (Autumn 2013): 194–219.

Clarke, Arthur C. 1962. Hazards of Prophecy: The Failure of Imagination. In *Profiles of the Future: Enquiry into the Limits of the Possible*, 19–39. London: Gollancz.

Classen, Albrecht. 2002. The Self, the Other, and Everything in Between. Introduction to *Meeting the Foreign in the Middle Ages*, xi–xxvi. New York: Routledge.

Clifford, James. 1986. On Ethnographic Allegory. In *Writing Culture*, ed. James Clifford and George Marcus, 98–121. Berkeley: University of California Press.

Clifford, James, and George Marcus, eds. 1986. *Writing Culture: The Poetics and Politics of Ethnography*. Berkeley: University of California Press.

Cohen, Jeffrey J., ed. 2000. *The Postcolonial Middle Ages*. New Middle Ages Series. London: Palgrave.

Constable, Mary. 2003. *Housing the Stranger in the Mediterranean World*. Cambridge: Cambridge University Press.

Cowe, Peter. 2016. Patterns of Armeno-Muslim Interchange on the Armenian Plateau in the Interstice Between Byzantine and Ottoman Hegemony. In *Islam and Christianity in Medieval Anatolia*, ed. Andrew C.S. Peacock, Bruno De Nicola, and Sara Nur Yildiz, 77–106. London: Routledge.

Crane, Howard. 1993. Notes on Saldjūq Architectural Patronage in Thirteenth Century Anatolia. *Journal of the Economic and Social History of the Orient* 36(1): 1–57.

Crawford, Osbert G.S. 1918. *Archaeology in the Field*. London: Phoenix House.

Cytryn-Silverman, Katia. 2010. *The Road-Inns (Khans) of Bilad al-Sham*. BAR Series 2130. Oxford: ArchaeoPress.

Dadoyan, Seta. 2011. *The Armenians in the Medieval Islamic World*. Vol. 3, *Medieval Cosmopolitanism and Images of Islam*. New Brunswick, NJ: Transaction.

Dangles, Philippe, and Nicolas Proteau. 2004. Sondages Archéologiques sur l'Enceinte Nord d'Ani. *Revue des Études Arméniennes* 29 (2003–4): 503–33.

———. 2007. Observations sur quelques Fortresses de la Région d'Ani. *Revue des Études Arméniennes* 30 (2005–7): 273–99.

Dankoff, Robert, and Sooyong Kim. 2011. *An Ottoman Traveller: Selections from the Book of Travels by Evliya Çelebi*. London: Eland.

Daston, Lorraine, and Katharine Park. 1998. *Wonders and the Order of Nature*. Princeton, NJ: Zone.

De Beauvoir, Simone. 1953. *The Second Sex*. New York: Knopf.

de Rachewiltz, Igor. 1971. *Papal Envoys to the Great Khans*. Great Travelers. London: Faber and Faber.

de Vinsauf, Geoffrey. 1965. Itinerary of Richard I and Others, to the Holy Land. Translation in *Chronicles of the Crusades*, reprint ed. Roy C. Cave and Herbert H. Coulson, 155. New York: Biblo & Tannen.

Der Nersessian, Sirarpie. 1962. The Kingdom of Cilician Armenia. in *A History of the Crusades*, vol. 2, ed. Kenneth M. Setton, 630–31. Philadelphia: University of Pennsylvania Press.

Derrida, Jacques, and Anne Dufourmantelle. 2000. *Of Hospitality*. Palo Alto, CA: Stanford University Press.

DeSilvey, Caitlin, and Tim Edensor. 2013. Reckoning with Ruins. *Progress in Human Geography* 37(4): 465–85.

Dietler, Michael, and Brian Hayden, eds. 2001. *Feasts: Archaeological and Ethnographic Perspectives on Food, Politics, and Power*. Tuscaloosa: University of Alabama Press.

Djanpoladian, Hripsime, and Aram Kalantaryan. 1988. *The Trade Connections of Medieval Armenia, VI–XIII Centuries (According to glass-work data)*. Monuments of Armenian Archaeology 14. Institute of Archaeology and Ethnography; ed. by Babken Arak'elyan. Yerevan: Armenian SSR Academy of Sciences Publishing. In Armenian.

Douglas, Mary. 1966. *Purity and Danger*. New York: Routledge.

Dugan, Arthur B. 1962. Mackinder and His Critics Reconsidered. *Journal of Politics* 24(2): 241–57.

Eastmond, Antony. 2014. Inscriptions and Authority in Ani. In *Der Doppeladler: Byzanz und die Seldschuken in Anatolien vom späten 11. bis zum 13. Jahrhundert*, ed. Neslihan Asutay-Effenberger, and Falko Daim, 71–84. Mainz: Verlag des Römisch-Germanischen Zentralmuseums.

———. 2015a. Textual Icons: Viewing Inscriptions in Medieval Georgia. In *Viewing inscriptions in the Late Antique and Medieval World*, ed. Antony Eastmond, 76–98. Cambridge: Cambridge University Press.

———, ed. 2015b. *Viewing inscriptions in the Late Antique and Medieval World*. Cambridge: Cambridge University Press.

———. 2016. Other Encounters: Popular Belief and Cultural Convergence in Anatolia and the Caucasus. In *Islam and Christianity in Medieval Anatolia*, ed. Andrew C.S. Peacock, Bruno De Nicola, and Sara Nur Yildiz, 183–214. New York: Routledge.

Eastmond, Antony, and Lynn Jones. 2001. Robing, Power, and Legitimacy in Armenia and Georgia. In *Robes and Honor: The Medieval World of Investiture*, ed. Stewart Gordon. London: Palgrave.

Eco, Umberto. 2002. *Baudolino*. Trans. William Weaver. New York: Harcourt Brace.

Edugyan, Esi. 2020. How Silk-Making Represents a More Hidden Side of Georgia's Past. *New York Times*, May 11.

Edwards, Robert. 2013. Cosmopolitan Imaginaries. In *Cosmopolitanism and the Middle Ages*, ed. John Ganim, 163–80. London: Palgrave.

Ehrenreich, Barbara. 2001. *Nickel and Dimed: On Getting By in America*. New York: Henry Holt.

Ehrenreich, Barbara, and Arlie Russell Hothschild 2002. *Global Woman: Nannies, Maids, and Sex Workers in the New Economy*. London: Granta.

Emerson, John, and Willem M. Floor. 1987. Rahdars and Their Tolls in Safavid and Afsharid Iran. *Journal of the Social and Economic History of the Orient* 30(3): 318–27.

Erdmann, Kurt. 1961. *The Anatolian Caravanserai in the Thirteenth Century*. Vols. 1–2. Berlin: Verlag Gebr. Mann. In German.

Ertug, Ahmet. 1991. *The Seljuks: A Journey through Anatolian Architecture*. Trans. Timur Bragner. Istanbul: Ahmet Ertug.

Escobar, Arturo. 2001. Culture Sits in Places: Reflections on Globalism and Subaltern Strategies of Localization. *Political Geography* 20: 139–47.

Foucault, Michel. 1967. Of Other Spaces: Utopias and Heterotopias. Trans. Jay Miskowiec. *Architecture/mouvement/continuite*. Paris: Groupe Moniteur.

———. 1970. *The Order of Things: An Archaeology of the Human Sciences*. Routledge.

Frachetti, Michael D., and Elissa Bullion. 2018. Bronze Age Participation in a Global Ecumene: Mortuary Practice and Ideology across Inner Asia. In *Globalization in Prehistory: Contact, Exchange, and the "People without History,"* ed. Nicole Boivin and Michael Frachetti, 102–30. Cambridge: Cambridge University Press.

Franklin, Kathryn. 2014a. A House for Trade, a Space for Politics: Excavations at the Arai-Bazarjugh Late Medieval Caravanatun. *Anatolica* 40: 1–21.

———. 2014b. "This world is an inn": Cosmopolitanism and Caravan Trade in Late Medieval Armenia. PhD diss., Department of Anthropology, University of Chicago.

———. 2014c. Early Results of Research into Trade Routes and Political Economy of Medieval North Armenia. In *Habitus: Studies in Anthropology and Archaeology*, ed. Harut'yun Marut'yan et al. 304–16. Yerevan: National Academy of Sciences Gitutyun Press.

———. 2015. Assembling Subjects: World Building and Cosmopolitics in Late Medieval Armenia. In *Incomplete Archaeologies: Assembling Knowledges in the Past and Present*, ed. Emily Miller Bonney, Kathryn Franklin, and James A. Johnson. Oxford: Oxbow.

———. 2019. Making Worlds at the Edge of Everywhere: Politics of Place in Medieval Armenia. In *The Archaeology of Medieval Islamic Frontiers: From the Mediterranean to the Caspian Sea*, ed. A. Asa Eger, 195–224. Louisville: University Press of Colorado.

———. 2020. Moving Subjects, Situated Memory: Thinking and Seeing Medieval Travel on the Silk Road. *International Journal of Historical Archaeology*. Special issue, *Beyond (within, through) the Grid: Mapping and Historical Archaeology* 24: 852–76.

Franklin, Kathryn, and Astghik Babajanyan. 2018a. Towards a Landscape of Infrastructure: the First Season of the Vayots Dzor Silk Road Survey. In *Landscape Archaeology in Southern Caucasia: Finding Common Ground in Diverse Environments,* ed. William Anderson, Kristin Hopper and Abby Robinson, 131–44. Vienna: Austrian Academy of Sciences, Institute for Oriental and European Archaeology (OREA) series.

———. 2018b. The Power of Making Places: Collaborative Heritage and Working with ARISC in Armenia. *Journal of Eastern Mediterranean Archaeology and Heritage Studies* 6(3). 205–16.

Franklin, Kathryn, Tasha Vorderstrasse, and Frina Babayan. 2017. Examining the Late Medieval Village from the Case at Ambroyi, Armenia. *Journal of Near Eastern Studies* 76(1): 113–38.

Frankopan, Peter. 2015. *The Silk Road.* London: Bloomsbury.

Freedman, Paul. 2008. *Out of the East: Spices and the Medieval Imagination.* New Haven, CT: Yale University Press.

Fuller, Mary. 2009. Richard Hakluyt's Foreign Relations. In *Travel Writing, Form, and Empire,* ed. Julia Kuehn and Paul Smethurst, 38–52. New York: Routledge.

Fuxi, Gan, Robert Brill, and Tian Shouyun, eds. 2009. *Ancient Glass Research along the Silk Road.* London: World Scientific.

Ganim, John. 2010. Cosmopolitanism and Medievalism. *Exemplaria* 22(1):5–27.

Ganjakec'i, Kirakos. 1961. *History of the Armenians.* Ed. Karapet Aghabegi Melik-Ohandžanyan. Matenadaran. Yerevan: Armenian SSR Academy of Sciences Publishing. In Armenian.

———. 1986. *History of the Armenians.* Trans. from Classical Armenian by Robert Bedrosian. New York: Sources of the Armenian Tradition.

Garsoian, Nina G. 1999. *Church and Culture in Early Medieval Armenia:* London: Variorum.

———. 2012. A Sketch of the Evolution of the Armenian Naxararut'iwn during the Interregnum of the 2nd–9th Centuries. *Revue des Études Arméniennes* 34: 41–71. In French.

Ghafadaryan, Karapet G. 1948. *Hovhannavank' and its Inscriptions.* Yerevan: Armenian SSR Academy of Sciences Publishing. In Armenian.

———. 1952. *The City of Dvin and Its Excavations.* Vol. 1. Armenian SSR Academy of Sciences Archaeological Expeditions, 1937–1950. Work Results Yerevan. In Armenian.

———. 1957. *Sanahin Monastery and Its Inscriptions.* Armenian SSR Academy of Sciences and the Armenian State History Museum. Armenian Academy of Sciences Publishing. In Armenian.

———. 1975. *Yerevan: Medieval Monuments and Lapidary Inscriptions.* Armenian SSR Academy of Sciences Institute of Archaeology and Ethnography. Yerevan: Armenian SSR Academy of Sciences Publishing. In Armenian.

———. 1982. *The City of Dvin and Its Excavations.* Vol. 2 of *Armenian SSR Academy of Sciences Archaeological Expeditions, 1951–72.* Work Results Yerevan. In Armenian.

Ghazarian, Armen, and Robert Ousterhout. 2001. A Muqarnas Drawing from Thirteenth-Century Armenia and the Use of Architectural Drawings during the Middle Ages. *Muqarnas* 18: 141–54.

Gilchrist, Roberta. 1999. The Contested Garden. In *Gender and Archaeology: Contesting the Past*, 109–45. London: Routledge.

———. 2012. *Medieval Life: Archaeology and the Life Course*. Woodbridge: Boydell.

Giorgieva, Ralitsa, Albina Detcheva, and Yanko Dimitriev. 2010. Chemical and Technological Characterization of Medieval Glass Bracelets from South-East Bulgaria. *Open Chemistry* 12(11): 1169–75.

Goš, Mxitar. 2000. *The Lawcode (Datastanagirkʻ) of Mkhitar Goš*. Trans. with commentary and indices by Robert W. Thomson. Amsterdam: Rodopi.

Goshgarian, Rachel. 2011. Blending In and Separating Out: Sixteenth Century Anatolian Armenian Food and Feasts. In *Starting with Food: Culinary Approaches to Ottoman History*, ed. Amy Singer, 49–68. Princeton, NJ: Weiner.

Graff, Sarah, and Enrique Rodriguez-Alegria, eds. 2012. *The Menial Art of Cooking: Archaeological Studies of Cooking and Food Preparation*. Louisville: University Press of Colorado.

Graves, Margaret. 2018. Say Something Nice: Supplications on Medieval Objects, and Why They Matter. In *Studying the Near and Middle East at the Institute for Advanced Study, Princeton, 1935–2018*, ed. Sabine Schmidtke, 322–30. Piscataway, NJ: Gorgias.

Greene, Alan. 2012. Where Pottery and Politics Meet: Mundane Objects and Complex Political Life in the Late Bronze Age South Caucasus. In *The Archaeology of Power and Politics in Eurasia: Regimes and Revolutions*, ed. Charles W. Hartley, G. Bike Yazicioğlu, and Adam T. Smith, 302–22. Cambridge: Cambridge University Press.

Greene, Alan, and Ian Lindsay. 2013. Mobility, Territorial Commitments, and Political Organization Among Late Bronze Age Polities in Southern Caucasia. *Archaeological Papers of the American Anthropological Association*. Special issue, *Territoriality in Archaeology*: 54–71

Greenwood, Timothy. 2004. A Corpus of Early Medieval Armenian Inscriptions. *Dumbarton Oaks Papers* 58: 27–91.

Grossman, Vasily. 2013. *An Armenian Sketchbook*. Trans. Robert and Elizabeth Chandler. New York: New York Review of Books.

Grosz, Elizabeth. 1995. *Space Time and Perversion: Essays on the Politics of Bodies*. New York: Routledge.

Guidetti, Mattia. 2017. The "Islamicness" of Some Decorative Patterns in the Church of Tigran Honencʻ in Ani. In *Architecture and Landscape in Medieval Anatolia, 1100–1500*, ed. Patricia Blessing and Rachel Goshgarian, 155–84. Edinburgh: Edinburgh University Press.

Hajib, Yusuf Khāṣṣ. 1983. *Wisdom of Royal Glory: a Turko-Islamic Mirror for Princes*. Trans. and with an introduction by Robert Dankoff. Chicago: University of Chicago Press.

Hakobyan, Nura. 1981. Medieval Armenian Fine Art Metalwork. *Medieval Monuments of Armenia 10. Medieval Monuments*, vol. 3. Armenian SSR Academy of Sciences Institute of Archaeology and Ethnography. Yerevan: Armenian SSR Academy of Sciences Publishing. In Armenian.

Hakobyan, Zaruhi, and Lilit Mikayelyan 2018. The Senmurv and Other Mythical Creatures with Sasanian Iconography in the Medieval Art of Armenia and Transcaucasia. In *Fabulous Creatures and Spirits in Ancient Iranian Culture*, ed. Matteo Compareti, 39–76. Bologna: Paolo Emilio Persiani.

Hansen, Valerie. 2012. *The Silk Road: A New History.* Oxford: Oxford University Press.

Haraway, Donna. 1991. *Simians, Cyborgs, and Women: The Reinvention of Nature.* New York: Routledge.

———. 2016. *Staying with the Trouble.* Durham, NC: Duke University Press.

Harut'yunyan, Smbat. 1978. *Anberd.* Armenian SSR Academy of Sciences Institute of Archaeology and Ethnography. Yerevan: Armenian SSR Academy of Sciences Publishing. In Armenian.

Harut'yunyan, Varazdat. 1960. *Caravan Inns and Bridges in Medieval Armenia.* Yerevan: Armenian SSR Academy of Sciences Publishing . In Armenian.

Hastorf, Christine. 2012. Steamed or Boiled: Identity and Value in Food Preparation. *eTOPOI: Journal for Ancient Studies,* special volume, 2: 213–42.

———. 2017. *The Social Archaeology of Food: Thinking about Eating from Prehistory to the Present.* Cambridge: Cambridge University Press.

b. Hawqal, Muḥammad Abū'l-Qāsim. 1800. *The Oriental Geography of Ebn Haukal. An Arabian Traveller of the Tenth Century.* Trans. and ed. William Ouseley. London: Printed by Wilson for T. Cadell, and W. Davies.

Hedin, Sven. 1938. *The Silk Road.* Translated by Francis Hamilton Lyon. New York: Dutton.

Heffernan, Carol. 2003. *The Orient in Chaucer and Medieval Romance.* Studies in Medieval Romance. Cambridge: Brewer.

Herbert, Thomas. 1677. *Some Yeares Travels into Africa and Asia the Great.* Tempe: ACMRS (Arizona Center for Medieval and Renaissance Studies).

Hermes, Taylor, et al. 2018. Urban and Isotopic Niches Reveal Dietary Connectivities along Central Asia's Silk Roads. *Scientific Reports* 8 (1): 5177.

Heuser, Sabine. 2003. *Virtual Geographies: Cyberpunk at the Intersection of the Postmodern and Science Fiction.* Amsterdam: Rodopi.

Hillenbrand, Robert. 1998. *Islamic Architecture: Form, Function, and Meaning.* New York: Columbia University Press.

Hobsbawm, Eric, and Terrence Ranger, eds. 1983. *The Invention of Tradition.* Cambridge: Cambridge University Press.

Hoffman, Eva. 2001. Pathways of Portability: Islamic and Christian Interchange from the Tenth to the Twelfth Century. *Art History* 24(1): 17–50.

Hoskins, William G. 1955. *The Making of the English Landscape.* Hodder and Stoughton.

Hovhannisyan, Constantin. 1982. *Restoration of Monuments in the Armenian SSR (Album).* Yerevan: Hayastan. In Russian and Armenian.

Hovhannisian, Richard, et al., eds. 1997. *The Armenian People from Ancient to Modern Times.* Vol. 1, *The Dynastic Periods: From Antiquity to the Fourteenth Century.* London: Palgrave.

Hovsepyan, Roman. 2013. First Archaeobotanical Data from the Basin of Lake Sevan. *Veröffentlichungen des Landesamtes für Denkmalpflege und Archäologie Sachsen-Anhalt.* Vol. 67. *Archäologie in Armenien* 2: 93–104.

———. 2014. Archaeobotanical Investigations at Iron Age III Tsaghkahovit (Appendix 1), 152–53, 163–64. In *Empire in the Everyday: A Preliminary Report on the 2008–2011 Excavations at Tsaghkahovit, Armenia,* ed. Lori Khatchadourian. *American Journal of Archaeology* 118(1): 137–69.

Iessen, Alexander A. 1959. *Proceedings of the Azerbaijani (Oren-Kala) Archaeological Expedition.* Materials and Research of the Archaeology of the USSR, 67. Moscow: Scientific Press. In Russian.

Ingold, Timothy. 2016. *Lines: A Brief History*. New York: Routledge.

Jackson, Peter. 2001. Medieval Christendom's Encounter with the Alien. *Historical Research* 74(186): 347–69.

Jackson, Peter, and David Morgan. 1990. Introduction and translated text. *The Mission of Friar William of Rubruck: His Journey to the Court of the Great Khan Mongke, 1252–1255*. Indianapolis, IN: Hackett.

Johnson, Matthew. 2007. *Ideas of Landscape*. London: Blackwell.

Jones, Lynn. 1996. The Church of the Holy Cross and the Iconography of Kingship. *Gesta* 33 (2):104–17.

———. 2002. The Visual Expression of Bagratuni Kingship: Ceremonial and Portraiture. *Revue des Études Arméniennes* 28: 341–98.

———. 2007. *Between Islam and Byzantium: Aghtamar and the Visual Reconstruction of Medieval Armenian Rulership*. Aldershot: Ashgate.

Kalantaryan, Aram. 1976. *Dvin I: Excavations in the Central Quarter, 1964–1970*. Archaeological Excavations in Armenia 13. Yerevan: Armenian SSR Academy of Sciences Publishing. In Armenian.

———. 1996. *Dvin: History and Archaeology of the City*. Civilisations du Proche-Orient: 2. Paris: Neuchâtel, Recherches et publications. In French.

Kalantaryan, Aram, and Frina Babayan. 2001. The Lapidary Inscriptions of Uši Sourb Sarkis Vankʿ. *Historical-Philological Journal* 2: 169–99. In Armenian.

Kalantaryan, Aram, et al. 2008. *Dvin IV: The City and Its Excavations*. Yerevan: NAS RA Institute of Archaeology and Ethnography. "Gitutʿyun" Publishing. In Armenian.

———. 2009. *Armenia in the Cultural Context of East and West: Ceramics and Glass (4th–14th Centuries)*. Joint Research Project of the Swiss National Science Foundation. Republic of Armenia National Academy of Sciences Institute of Archaeology and Ethnography. Yerevan: NAS RA Institute of Archaeology and Ethnography. "Gitutʿyun" Publishing. In Armenian.

Kalantaryan, Irina, et al. 2012. The Archaeological Investigations of Getahovit-2 cave (Armenia) in 2011–2012: The Preliminary Results. *Aramazd: Armenian Journal of Near Eastern Studies* 7 (1): 7–23.

Kant, Immanuel. 1795. Perpetual Peace: A Philosophical Sketch. Available at Mount Holyoke website, www.mtholyoke.edu/acad/intrel/kant/kant1.htm (accessed July 29, 2019).

Karakhanyan, Grigor, and Husik Melkonyan. 1989. Vardenut: Excavation Results. In *Republic of Armenia, 1987–1988: Archaeological Fieldwork Results Academic Dedicated Scientific Session*, 80–82. Yerevan: Armenian SSR Academy of Sciences Institute of Archaeology and Ethnography Press. In Armenian.

———. 1991. Results of Excavations at Anberd and Vardenut. *Republic of Armenia, 1989–1990 Archaeological Fieldwork Results Academic Dedicated Scientific Session* , 111–12. Yerevan: Armenian SSR Academy of Sciences Institute of Archaeology and Ethnography Press. In Armenian.

Ker Porter, Robert. 1821. *Travels in Georgia, Persia, Armenia, Ancient Babylonia, &c. &c.: During the Years 1817, 1818, 1819, and 1820*. London: Longman, Hurst, Rees, Orme, and Brown.

Khalpakchyan, Hovhannes Kh. 1971. *Civil Architecture of Armenia (Dwelling and Public Buildings)*. Moscow: Construction Literature Publishing. In Russian.

———. 1980. *Architectural Ensembles of Armenia*. Moscow: Isskustvo. In Russian.

Khatchadourian, Lori. 2016. *Imperial Matters*. Berkeley: University of California Press.

172 BIBLIOGRAPHY

Kiesling, Brady. 2001. *Rediscovering Armenia: An Archaeological/Touristic Gazetteer and Map Set for the Historical Monuments of Armenia.* Ed. Raffi Kojian. Yerevan: Tigran Mets.

King, Charles. 2008. *The Ghost of Freedom: A History of the Caucasus.* Oxford: Oxford University Press.

Kinoshita, Sharon. 2007. Deprovincializing the Middle Ages. In *The Worlding Project: Doing Cultural Studies in the Era of Globalization,* ed. Rob Wilson and Christopher Leigh Connery, 75–89. Santa Cruz, CA: New Pacific.

———. 2008. Marco Polo's *Devisement dou Monde* and the Tributary East. In *Marco Polo and the Encounter of East and West,* ed. Akbari, Suzanne C. and Amilcare Iannucci, 60–86. Toronto: University of Toronto Press.

Kleiss, Wolfram. 1996–2001. *Karawanenbauten in Iran.* Vols. 1–6. Berlin: Deitrich Reimer Verlag.

Knauer, Elfriede R. 2001. A Man's Caftan and Leggings from the North Caucasus of the Eight to Tenth Century: A Genealogical Study. *Metropolitan Museum Journal* 36: 125–54.

Kocharyan, Grigor. 1991. *Dvin III: Dvin in the Classical Period.* Armenian SSR Academy of Sciences Institute of Archaeology and Ethnography. Yerevan: Armenian SSR Academy of Sciences Publishing. In Armenian.

Kostanyanc', Karapet. 1913. *Epigraphic Annal.* Bibliotheca Armeno-Georgica 2. St. Petersburg: Press of the Imperial Academy of Sciences. In Armenian.

Kotov, Fedot. 1852. *About the Journey to the Persian Kingdom and from Persia to the Turkish Land and to India and to Hormoz, Where Ships Arrive.* Moscow: Annals of the Imperial Moscow Society for Russian History and Antiquity 15. In Russian.

Kuehn, Julia, and Paul Smethurst. 2008. *Travel Writing, Form, and Empire: The Poetics and Politics of Mobility.* Routledge Research in Travel Writing. New York: Routledge.

Landau, Loren B., and Iriann Freemantle. 2010. Tactical Cosmopolitanism and Idioms of Belonging: Insertion and Self-Exclusion in Johannesburg. *Journal of Ethnic and Migration Studies* 36(3): 375–90.

Lane, George. 2012. The Mongols in Iran. In *The Oxford Handbook of Iranian History,* ed. Touraj Daryaee, 243–70. Oxford: Oxford University Press.

La Porta, Sergio. 2008–9. Lineage, Legitimacy and Loyalty in Post-Seljuk Armenia: A Reassessment of the Sources of the Failed Orbelean Revolt against King Giorgi III of Georgia. *Revue des Études Arméniennes* 31: 127–65.

———. 2011. Conflicted Coexistence: Christian-Muslim Interaction and Its Representation in Medieval Armenia. In *Contextualizing the Muslim Other in Medieval Christian Discourse,* ed. Jerold C. Frakes, 103–23. London: Palgrave.

———. 2012. The Kingdom and the Sultanate Were Conjoined: Legitimizing Land and Power in Armenia during the 12th and Early 13th Centuries. *Revue des Études Arméniennes.* 34: 73–118.

Larkin, Brian. 2013. The Politics and Poetics of Infrastructure. *Annual Review of Anthropology* 42: 327–43.

Larner, John. 1999. *Marco Polo and the Discovery of the World.* New Haven, CT: Yale University Press.

———. 2008. Plucking Hairs from the Great Chams Beard: Marco Polo, John de Langhe, and Sir John Mandeville. In *Marco Polo and the Encounter of East and West*, ed. Suzanne C. Akbari and Amilcare Iannucci, 133–55. Toronto: University of Toronto Press.

Latour, Bruno. 1993. *We Have Never Been Modern*. Trans. Catherine Porter. Cambridge, MA: Harvard University Press.

Layard, Austen H. 1853. *Discoveries in the Ruins of Nineveh and Babylon; with Travels in Armenia, Kurdistan and the Desert: Being the Result of a Second Expedition Undertaken for the Trustees of the British Museum*. New York: Putnam.

Layton, Susan. 1994. *Russian Literature and Empire*. Cambridge: Cambridge University Press.

Le Goff, Jacques. 1977. *Time, Work, and Culture in the Middle Ages*. Chicago: University of Chicago Press.

———. 1985. *The Medieval Imagination*. Chicago: University of Chicago Press.

Lindsay, Ian. 2006. Late Bronze Age Power Dynamics in Southern Caucasia: A Community Perspective on Political Landscapes. PhD diss., Department of Anthropology, University of California, Santa Barbara.

Lindsay, Ian, and Adam T. Smith. 2006. A History of Archaeology in the Republic of Armenia. *Journal of Field Archaeology* 31: 165–84.

Lochrie, Karma. 2009. Provincializing Medieval Europe: Mandeville's Cosmopolitan Utopia. *PMLA* 124(2): 592–99.

Lynch, Kathryn L. 1995. East Meets West in Chaucer's Squire's and Franklin's Tales. *Speculum* 70(3): 530–51.

———, ed. 2002. *Chaucer's Cultural Geography*. New York: Routledge.

Ma, Yo-Yo, and Elizabeth ten Grotenhuis. 2002. Along the Silk Road. *Asian Art and Culture* 6. Seattle: University of Washington Press.

Mackinder, Halford J. 1904. The Geographical Pivot of History. *Geographical Journal* 23 (4): 421–37.

Mahé, Jean-Pierre . 2001. The Testament of Tigran Honenc': The Fortune of an Armenian Merchant in Ani in the 12th–13th Centuries. *Comptes rendus des séances de l'Academie des Inscriptions et Belles-Lettres* 145(3): 1319–42. In French.

Mair, Victor, and Jane Hickman. 2014. *Reconfiguring the Silk Road: New Research on East West Exchange in Antiquity*. Philadelphia: University of Pennsylvania Museum of Archaeology and Anthropology.

Maisuradze, Zacharias. 1954. *Georgian Fine Art Ceramics, XI–XIII Centuries. (Slipped-Ware Ceramics from Dmanisi)*. Academy of Sciences of the Georgian SSR, Institute of Art History. Tbilisi: Georgian SSR Adacemy of Sciences Publishing. In Russian.

Manandyan, Hakob. 1954. *The Trade and Cities of Armenia in Relation to Ancient World Trade*. Yerevan: Yerevan University Press. In Russian.

———. 1965. *The Trade and Cities of Armenia in Relation to Ancient World Trade*. Trans. Nina Garsoian. Lisbon: Livraria Bertrand.

———. 1977. *Collected Works II*. Armenian SSR Academy of Sciences, Institute of History. Yerevan: Armenian SSR Academy of Sciences Publishing. In Armenian.

———. 1979. *Collected Works III*. Armenian SSR Academy of Sciences, Institute of History. Yerevan: Armenian SSR Academy of Sciences Publishing. In Armenian.

Mandeville, Sir John. 1953. *Mandeville's Travels: Text and Translation*. With an introduction by Malcolm Letts. London: Hakluyt Society.

———. 2012. *The Book of Marvels and Travels*. A new trans. and intro. by Anthony Bale. Oxford: Oxford World's Classics.

Manjikian, Lalai. 2005. Collective Memory and Diasporic Articulations of Imagined Homes: Armenian Community Centres in Montreal. Master's thesis, Department of Communication Studies, McGill University.

Manuč'aryan, Ashot. 2015. Deciphering of Two Inscriptions by K'urd I Vač'utyan. *Bulletin of Yerevan University: Armenian Studies* 2(17): 41–49. In Armenian.

Maranci, Christina. 2006. Building Churches in Armenia: At the Edge of Empire and the Edge of the Canon. *Art Bulletin* 88(4): 656–75.

———. 2008. Performance and Church Exterior in Early Medieval Armenia. In *Medieval Performance: Perspectives, Histories, Contexts*, ed. Elina Gertsman, 17–32. New York: Routledge.

———. 2017. The Great Outdoors: Liturgical Encounters with the Early Medieval Armenian Church. In *Aural Architecture in Byzantium: Music, Acoustics, and Ritual*, ed. Bissera Pentcheva, 32–51. Abingdon on Thames: Taylor and Francis.

Marr, Nikolai. 1907. Summary of Excavations at Ani in the Summer of 1906 *Themes and Discussions on the Subject of Georgian Philology*. St Petersburg: n.p. In Russian.

———. 1934. *Ani: Literary History of the City and Excavations within the Citadel*. National Academy of Material Culture History. Moscow: State Social-Economic Publishing. In Russian.

Marshall, Maureen. 2014. Subject(ed) Bodies: A Bioarchaeological Investigation of Lived Experiences and Mobile Practices in Late Bronze-Early Iron Age (1500–800 b.c.) Armenia. PhD diss., Department of Anthropology, University of Chicago.

Massey, Doreen. 1994. *Space, Place, and Gender*. Minneapolis: University of Minnesota Press.

———. 2004. Geographies of Responsibility. *Geografiska Annaler*. Series B, special issue, *The Political Challenge of Relational Space, Human Geography* 86(1): 5–18.

Matthee, Rudi. 2012a. Safavid Iran through the Eyes of European Travelers. In *From Rhubarb to Rubies: European Travels in Safavid Iran (1550–1700). Harvard Library Bulletin* 23(1–2): 10–24.

———. 2012b. The Safavid Economy as Part of the World Economy. In *Iran and the World in the Safavid Age*, ed. Willem Floor and Edmund Herzig, 18–47. New York: I.B. Tauris and the Iran Heritage Foundation.

Mauss, Marcel. 1999. *The Gift: The Form and Reason for Exchange in Archaic Societies*. Trans. W.D. Halls. New York: Norton.

McAvoy, Liz Herbert. 2004. Authority and the Female Body in the Writings of Julian of Norwich and Margery Kempe. London: Boydell and Brewer.

McPhillips, Stephen, and Paul Wordsworth, eds. 2016. *Landscapes of the Islamic World: Archaeology, History, and Ethnography*. Philadelphia: Pennsylvania University Press.

Medvedev, Alexander F. 1967. Tatar-Mongol Arrowheads in Western Europe. *Soviet Archaeology* (2): 50–60. In Russian.

Melkonyan, Husik, et al. 2017. The Excavations of Dashtadem Fortress: Preliminary Report of 2015 Fieldwork Activity. *Aramazd: Armenian Journal of Near Eastern Studies* 11(1–2): 263–92.

Miller, Naomi F. 1984. The Use of Dung as Fuel: an Ethnographic Example and an Archaeological Application. *Paléorient* 10: 71–79.

Minc, Leah. 2009. A Compositional Perspective on Ceramic Exchange among Late Bronze Age Communities of the Tsaghkahovit Plain. In *The Archaeology and Geography of Ancient Transcaucasian Societies*, vol. 1, *The Foundations of Research and Regional Survey in the Tsaghkahovit Plain, Armenia*, ed. Adam T. Smith et al., 381–92. Oriental Institute Publications 134. Chicago: Oriental Institute, University of Chicago.

Minorsky, Vladimir. 1953. *Studies in Caucasian History*. London: Taylor's Foreign Press.

Mintz, Sidney. 1985. *Sweetness and Power*. New York: Penguin.

Mirijanyan, Diana. 2008. A Fragment of a Stamp-Decorated Vessel from Armavir. *Culture of Ancient Armenia* 14 (Yerevan): 307–11. In Armenian.

Mirijanyan, Diana, and Astghik Babajanyan. 2013. Ceramics from Tełenyac' Vank'. *Historical-Philological Journal* 192: 134–50. In Armenian.

Mkrtchyan, Iveta, and Anelka Grigoryan, eds. 2014. *Armenian Ceramics 9th–13th Centuries: Dvin, Ani*. Yerevan: History Museum of Armenia. In Armenian and English.

Mnatsakanyan, S.X. 1952. *Architecture of Armenian Narthexes*. Yerevan. National Academy of Sciences Press. In Russian.

Moore, Henrietta. 1994. *A Passion for Difference*. Cambridge: Polity.

———. 2013. The Fantasies of Cosmopolitanism. In *After Cosmopolitanism*, ed. Rosi Braidotti, 97–111. New York: Routledge.

Moore, John. 1993. *Tille Hoyuk I: The Medieval Period*. Ankara: British Institute at Ankara Monograph.

Morrison, Kathleen. 2018. Christians and Spices: Hidden Foundations and Misrecognitions in European Colonial Expansion to South Asia. In *Globalization in Prehistory: Contact, Exchange, and the "People without History,"* ed. Nicole Boivin and Michael Frachetti, 283–307. Cambridge: Cambridge University Press.

al-Muqaddasī, Muḥammad ibn Aḥmad Shams al-Dīn. 1994. *The Best Divisions for Knowledge of the Regions: A Translation of Ahsan al-taqasim fi marifat al-aqalim*. Trans. Basil Anthony Collins. Reading: Centre for Muslim Contribution to Civilisation and Garnet Publishing.

al-Mulk, Nizam. 1960.*The Book of Government; or, Rules for Kings*. Trans. H. Darke. New Haven, CT: Yale University Press.

Munn, Nancy. 1977. The Spatiotemporal Transformations of Gawa Canoes. *Journal de la Société des Océanistes* 54–55(33): 39–53.

———. 1983. Gawan kula: Spatiotemporal Control and the Symbolism of Influence. In *The Kula: New Perspectives on Massim Exchange*, ed. E. and J. Leach, 277–308. Cambridge: Cambridge University Press.

———. 1986. *The Fame of Gawa. A Symbolic Study of Value Transformation in a Massim (Papua New Guinean) Society*. Cambridge: Cambridge University Press.

———. 1990. Constructing Regional Worlds in Experience: Kula Exchange, Witchcraft, and Gawan Local Events. *Man* 25 (1): 1–17.

Nava, Mira. 2002. Cosmopolitan Modernity: Everyday Imaginaries and the Register of Difference. *Theory, Culture, and Society* 19(1–2): 81–99.

Nemoianu, Virgil 1986. Picaresque Retreat: From Xenophon's *Anabasis* to Defoe's *Singleton*. *Comparative Literature Studies* 23(2): 91–102.

Nordstrom Carolyn. 2007. *Global Outlaws: Crime, Money, and Power in the Contemporary World*. Berkeley: University of California Press.

Norell, Mark, and Denise Patry-Leidy. 2011. *Travelling the Silk Road: Ancient Pathways to the Modern World*. American Museum of Natural History. New York: Sterling.

Nur Yildiz, Sara. 2005. Reconceptualizing the Seljuk-Cilician Frontier: Armenians, Latins, and Turks in Conflict and Alliance during the Early Thirteenth Century. In *Borders, Barriers, and Ethnogenesis: Frontiers in Late Antiquity and the Middle Ages*, ed. Florin Curta, 91–120. Turnhout: Brepols.

Ogel, Semra. 2008. *The Seljuk Face of Anatolia: Aspects of the Social and Intellectual History of Seljuk Architecture*. Foundation for Science Technology and Civilization: FSTC Ltd Online Publication. See https://muslimheritage.com/the-seljuk-face-of-anatolia (last accessed March 20, 2021).

Oldmeadow, Harry. 2011, *Ex Oriente Lux:* Eastern Religions, Western Writers. *Literature and Aesthetics* 21(1): 23–42.

O'Neill, Molly. 2007. Introduction to *American Food Writing: An Anthology with Classic Recipes*, ed. Molly O'Neill. New York: Penguin Putnam.

Oney, Gönül. 1971. Lion Figures in Anatolian Seljuk Architecture. *Anatolia* 13: 1–64.

Önge, Mustafa. 2007. Caravanserais as Symbols of Power in Seljuk Anatolia. In *Power and Culture: Identity, Ideology, Representation*, ed. Jonathan Osmond and Ausma Cimdina, 49–69. Pisa: Pisa University Press.

Orbeli, Iosef A. 1939. The Problem of Seljuk Art. In *Second International Congress on Armenian Art and Archaeology: Papers*, 150–55. Leningrad: September 1935. Moscow: Armenian SSR Scientific Publishing. In Russian.

———. 1966. *Corpus of Armenian Inscriptions*. Vol. 1, *The City of Ani*. Yerevan: Armenian SSR Scientific Academy Press. In Armenian.

Orbelyan, Stepʻanos. 1859. *History of Syunik*. Paris: K. V. Šahnazaryan. In Armenian.

Ortner, Sherry. 1976. Theory in Anthropology since the Sixties. *Comparative Studies in Society and History* 26(1): 126–66.

Pancaroğlu, Oya. 2013. Devotion, Hospitality, and Architecture in Medieval Anatolia. *Studia Islamica* 108: 48–81.

Panossian, Razmik. 2006. *The Armenians: From Priests and Kings to Merchants and Commissars*. New York: Columbia University Press.

Papazian, Sabrina. 2019. Armenia across Borders: Heritage Revitalization from the Soviet Era to the Present. PhD diss., Department of Anthropology, Stanford University.

Peacock, Andrew C.S. 2010. *Early Seljuq History: A New Interpretation*. New York: Routledge.

———. 2015. *The Great Seljuk Empire*. Edinburgh: Edinburgh University Press.

Peacock, Andrew C.S., Bruno De Nicola, and Sara Nur Yildiz, eds. 2016. *Islam and Christianity in Medieval Anatolia*. New York: Routledge.

Pegolotti, Francesco B. 1913. *Practica della Mercatura*. Excerpted in *Cathay and the Way Thither, Being a Collection of Medieval Notices of China*, vol. 3, ed. and trans. Henry Yule and Henri Cordier, 143–76. London: Hakluyt Society.

Peker, Ali U. 2014. Architectural Transformations in Medieval Anatolia (with Special Reference to Central Asia). In *Byzantine Culture. Papers from the Conference "Byzantine Days of Istanbul,"* ed. Dael. Sakel, 279–91. Ankara: Turkish Historical Society.

Peleggi, Maurizio. 2001. Reconfiguring Alterity: the Mongol in the Visual and Literary Culture of the Late Middle ages. *Medieval History Journal* 4(1): 15–33.

Petrosian, Irina, and David K. Underwood 2006. *Armenian Food: Fact, Fiction, and Folklore.* Bloomington, IN: Yerkir Publishing and Lulu.

Petrosyancʻ, V.M. 1978. Astvacnkali Vankʻ. *Ejmiatsin: Official Journal of the Mother See of Holy Ejmiatsin* 35(3): 57–61. In Armenian.

———. 1981. Astvacacin Church and Inscriptions of Mravyan Village. *Historical-Philological Journal* 3: 289–94. In Armenian.

———. 1982. Tełenyacʻ Vankʻ as a Cultural Center. *Historical-Philological Journal* 1: 121–29. In Armenian.

———. 1988. *Nig Aparan Historical-Architectural Monuments.* Armenian SSR Historical and Cultural Monuments Protection Society. Yerevan: Hayastan Press. In Armenian.

Phillips, Amanda. 2015. Ottoman Hilʾat: Between Commodity and Charisma. In *Frontiers of the Ottoman Imagination: Studies in Honor of Rhoads Murphey*, ed. Marios Hadhian-astasis, 111–38. Leiden: Brill.

Pirenne, Henri. 1925. *Medieval Cities: Their Origins and the Revival of Trade.* Princeton, NJ: Princeton University Press.

Pogossian, Zaroui. 2012. Armenians, Mongols, and the End of Times: An Overview of 13th Century Sources. In *The Caucasus during the Mongol Period*, ed. Jurgen Tubach, Sophia Vashalomidze, and Manfred Zimmer, 169–98. Wiesbaden: Reichert Verlag.

———2019. Relics, Rulers, Patronage: The True Cross of Varag and the Church of the Holy Cross on Ałtamar. In *The Holy Cross of Ałtamar: Politics, Art, Spirituality in the Kigdom of Vaspurakan*, ed. Zaroui Pogossian and Edda Vardanyan, 126–206. Leiden: Brill.

Pollock, Sheldon. 2002. Cosmopolitan and Vernacular in History. In *Cosmopolitanism*, ed. Carol Breckenridge et al., 15–53. Durham, NC: Duke University Press.

Pollock, Sheldon, et al. 2002. Cosmopolitanisms. In *Cosmopolitanism*, ed. Carol Breckenridge et al., 1–14. Durham, NC: Duke University Press.

Polo, Marco. 1958. *The Travels.* Trans. and intro. Ronald Latham. New York: Penguin.

Pratt, Mary Louise. 1992. *Imperial Eyes: Travel Writing and Transculturation.* New York: Routledge.

Puig de la Bellacasa, Maria. 2011. Matters of Care in Technoscience: Assembling Neglected Things. *Social Studies of Science* 41(1): 85–106.

———. 2017. *Matters of Care: Speculative Ethics in More-Than-Human Worlds.* Minneapolis: University of Minnesota Press.

Redford, Scott. 2005. A Grammar of Rum Seljuk Ornament. *Mesogeios* 25–26: 283–310.

———. 2016a. Reading Inscriptions on Seljuk Caravanserais. In "A mari usque ad mare" Cultura visuale e materiale dall'Adriatico all'India a cura di Mattia Guidetti e Sara Mondini. *Eurasiatica* 4: 221–34.

———. 2016b. The Rape of Anatolia. In *Islam and Christianity in Medieval Anatolia*, ed. Andrew C.S. Peacock , B. De Nicola, and S. Nur Yildiz, 107–16. New York: Routledge.

Redford, Scott, et al. 1998. *The Archaeology of the Frontier in the Medieval Near East: Excavations at Gritille, Turkey.* Philadelphia: University Museum Publications, University of Pennsylvania.

Redgate, Anne E. 2000. *The Armenians.* Peoples of Europe Series. Malden, MA: Blackwell.

Rezakhani, Khodadad. 2010. The Road That Never Was: The Silk Road and Trans-Eurasian Exchange. *Comparative Studies of South Asia, Africa, and the Middle East* 30(3): 420–33.

Richard, Francois. 2013. Thinking through "Vernacular Cosmopolitanisms": Historical Archaeology in Senegal and the Material Contours of the African Atlantic. *International Journal of Historical Archaeology* 17: 40–71.

Robin, Cynthia. 2013. *Everyday Life Matters: Maya Farmers at Chan.* Gainesville: University Press of Florida.

Rodinson, Maxime, and Arthur J. Arberry 2001. *Medieval Arab Cookery.* London: Prospect.

Rogers, John Michael. 1976. Waqf and Patronage in Seljuk Anatolia: The Epigraphic Evidence. *Anatolian Studies* 26: 69–103. British Institute at Ankara.

Rose, Gillian. 1993. *Feminism and Geography: On the Limits of Geographical Knowledge.* Cambridge: Polity.

Rosenzweig, Melissa. 2016. Cultivating Subjects in the Neo-Assyrian Empire. *Journal of Social Archaeology* 16(3): 307–34.

Russell, James. R. 2003. The Praise of Porridge. *Le Muséon* 116(1): 137–79.

Russell, Nerissa, and Louise Martin. 2012. Cooking Meat and Bones at Neolithic Çatalhöyük, Turkey. In *The Menial Art of Cooking,* ed. Sarah Graff and Enrique Rodríguez-Alegría, 87–98. Louisville: University Press of Colorado.

Sagona, Antonio. 2010. Sos Höyük: An Ancient Settlement Near Erzurum. In *Geleceğe Armağan: Arkeolojik, Kültürel ve Estetik Yansımaları,* ed. Mehmet Işıklı, Erhat Mutlugün, and Mine Artu, 42–49. Erzurum: Ataturk Üniversitesi.

Sahlins, Marshall. 1976. *Islands of History.* Chicago: University of Chicago Press.

Sargsyan, Gagik. 1977. Inscription from Tełenyac' Monastery. *Herald of the Social Sciences* 8: 100–107. In Armenian.

———. 1990. Tełenyac' Monastery Excavations (1979–1989 Results). *Historical-Philological Journal* 3: 174–90. In Armenian.

Sassen, Saskia. 2001. *The Global City.* 2nd ed. Princeton, NJ: Princeton University Press.

———. 2002. Global Cities and Survival circuits. In *Global Woman: Nannies, Maids. and Sex Workers in the New Economy,* ed. Barbara Ehrenreich and Arlie Russell Hothschild, 254–74. London: Granta.

Sauvaget, Jean. 1939. Medieval Syrian Caravanserais. *Ars Islamica* 6(1): 48–55. In French.

———. 1940. Medieval Syrian Caravanserais II: Mamluk Caravanserais. *Ars Islamica* 7(1): 1–19. In French.

Šahxat'unyan, Yovhannes. 1842. *Account of the Church of Ejmiatsin and Five Provinces of Ararat.* Vol. 2. Ejmiatsin, Armavir, Armenia: Press of the See of Ejmiatsin. In Armenian.

Šahnazaryan, Armen. 2011. Zakarid Armenia in the First Era of the Ilkhanate. *Historical-Philological Journal* 1: 129–40. In Armenian.

Sherman, Rachel. 2007. *Class Acts: Service and Inequality in Luxury Hotels.* Berkeley: University of California Press.

Sichone, Owen. 2008. Xenophobia and Xenophilia in South Africa: African Migrants in Cape Town. In *Anthropology and the New Cosmopolitanism: Rooted, Feminist, and Vernacular Perspectives,* ed. Pnina Werbner, 309–24. Oxford: Berg.

Sims, Eleanor. 1978. Trade and Travel: Markets and Caravanserais. In *Architecture of the Islamic World: Its History and Social Meaning,* ed. George Michell, 80–111. London: Thames and Hudson.

Smethurst, Paul. 2005. The Journey from Modern to Postmodern in The Travels of Sir John Mandeville and Marco Polo's Devisement dou Monde. In *Studies in Medievalism*, special issue, *Postmodern Medievalism*, 159–79. Cambridge: Brewer.

Smethurst, Paul, and Julia Kuehn. 2015. *New Directions in Travel Writing Studies*. London: Palgrave.

Smith, Adam T. 2000. Rendering the Political Aesthetic: Political Legitimacy in Urartian Representations of the Built Environment. *Journal of Anthropological Archaeology* 19: 131–63.

———. 2012. "Yerevan, My Ancient Erebuni": Archaeological Repertoires, Public Assemblages, and the Manufacture of a (Post-)Soviet Nation. In *The Archaeology of Power and Politics in Eurasia: Regimes and Revolutions*, ed. Charles. W. Hartley, G. Bike Yazicioğlu, and Adam T. Smith, 57–77. Cambridge: Cambridge University Press.

———. 2016. *The Political Machine: Assembling Sovereignty in the Bronze Age Caucasus*. Princeton, NJ: Princeton University Press.

Smith, Adam T., and Karen Rubinson. 2004. *Archaeology in the Borderlands: Investigations in Caucasia and Beyond*. UCLA Monographs 47. Los Angeles: Cotsen Institute of Archaeology Press.

Smith, Adam T., Ruben S. Badalyan, and Pavel S. Avetisyan. 2005. Southern Caucasia during the Late Bronze Age: An Interim Report on the Regional Investigations of Project ArAGATS in Western Armenia. In *Anatolian Iron Ages: Proceedings of the fifth Anatolian Iron Ages Colloquium Held at Van, 6–10 August 2001*, ed. Altan Çilingiroglu and Gareth Darbyshire, 175–85. Ankara: British Institute at Ankara.

Smith, Adam T., et al. 2003. Early Complex Societies in Southern Transcaucasia: A Preliminary Report on the 2002 Investigations of Project ARAGATS on the Tsaghkahovit Plain, Republic of Armenia. *American Journal of Archaeology* 108(1): 1–41.

———. 2009. *The Archaeology and Geography of Ancient Transcaucasian Societies*. Vol. 1, *The Foundations of Research and Regional Survey in the Tsaghkahovit Plain, Armenia*. Oriental Institute Publications 134. Chicago: Oriental Institute, University of Chicago.

Smith, Pamela, and Paula Findlen. 2001. *Merchants and Marvels: Commerce, Science, and Art in Early Modern Europe*. New York: Routledge.

Spengler, Robert. 2019. *Fruit from the Sands*. Berkeley: University of California Press.

Spyer, Patricia. 2000. *The Memory of Trade: Modernity's Entanglements on an Eastern Indonesian Island*. Durham, NC: Duke University Press.

St. Clair, Kassia. 2018. The *Golden Thread*. London: Hodder & Stoughton.

Steffen, James. 2013. *The Cinema of Sergei Parajanov*. Madison: University of Wisconsin Press.

Stein, Gil. 2012. Food Preparation, Social Context, and Ethnicity in a Prehistoric Mesopotamian Colony. In *The Menial Art of Cooking: Archaeological Studies of Cooking and Food Preparation*, ed. Sarah Graff and Enrique Rodriguez-Alegria, 47–63. Louisville: University Press of Colorado.

Stern, Jane, and Michael Stern. 1978. *Roadfood: The Coast-to-Coast Guide to 800 of the Best Barbecue Joints, Lobster Shacks, Ice Cream Parlors, Highway Diners, and Much, Much More*. New York: Clarkson Potter.

Sternberg Mural Ready: Work Depicting Chicago's Rise to Hang in Postoffice There. *New York Times*, February 3, 1938, 21.

Stewart, Kathleen. 1993. *A Space on the Side of the Road*. Princeton, NJ: Princeton University Press.

———. 2007. *Ordinary Affects*. Durham, NC: Duke University Press.

Stoletova, Ekaterina A. 1930. Field and Garden Crops of Armenia. *Bulletin of Applied Botany and Genetic Plant Breeding* 23(4): 1–376.

Suny, Ronald. 1988. *The Making of the Georgian Nation*. 2nd ed. Bloomington: Indiana University Press.

———. 1993. *Looking towards Ararat: Armenia in Modern History*. Bloomington: University of Indiana Press.

———. 2001.Constructing Primordialism: Old Histories for New Nations. *Journal of Modern History* 73(4) (December 2001): 862–96.

Sutton, David. 2001. *Remembrance of Repasts: An Anthropology of Food and Memory*. New York: Berg.

Tavernari, Cinzia. 2010. Medieval Road Caravanserais in Syria: An Archaeological Approach. In *Proceedings of the 6th International Congress on the Archaeology of the Ancient Near East, May 5th–10th, 2009*, vol. 3, *Islamic Session*, 191–205. Rome: Università di Roma, Sapienza.

———. 2017. Stones for the Travelers: Notes on the Masonry of Seljuk Road Caravanserais. In *Architecture and Landscape in Medieval Anatolia (1100–1500)*, ed. Patricia Blessing and Rachel Goshgarian, 59–94. Edinburgh: Edinburgh University Press.

Tavernier, Jean Baptiste. 1678. *The Six Voyages of John Baptiste Tavernier*. Trans. John Phillips. London: Printed for R.L. and M.P. Available at archive.org.

Ter-Łewondyan, Aram. 1976. *The Arab Emirates in Bagratid Armenia*. Trans. Nina Garsoian. Lisbon: Calouste Gulbenkian Foundation Armenian Library.

Terian, Abraham. 2009. The Armenian Ties to Medieval Trebizond. In *Armenian Pontus: The Trebizond Black Sea Communities*, ed. Richard Hovannisian, 93–113. Costa Mesa, CA: Mazda.

Thompson, Carl. 2011. *Travel Writing*. New York: Routledge.

Thomson, Robert. 1997. Mxitar Goš and His Lawcode. In *Armenian Perspectives: 10th Anniversary Conference of the Association Internationale Des Etudes Armeniennes, School of Oriental and African Studies, London*, ed. Nick Awde, 119–27. London: Psychology Press.

———. 2013. *Ełiše: History of Vardan and the Armenian War*. Cambridge, MA: Harvard University Press.

Thorsten, Marie. 2005. Silk Road Nostalgia and Imagined Global Community. *Comparative American Studies: An International Journal* 3(3): 301–17.

T'oramanyan, T'oros. 1942. *Materials for Armenian Architectural History*. Vol. 1. Yerevan: ArmFAN Publishing. In Armenian.

———. 1948. *Materials for Armenian Architectural History*. Vol. 2. Yerevan: ArmFAN Publishing. In Armenian.

Toumanoff, Cyril. 1963. *Studies in Christian Caucasian History*. Washington, DC: Georgetown University Press.

Trepanier, Nicholas. 2014. *Foodways and Daily Life in Medieval Anatolia: A New Social History*. Austin: University of Texas Press.

Trigger, Bruce. 1989. *A History of Archaeological Thought*. Cambridge: Cambridge University Press.

Trivedi, Mudit. 2020. The Archaeology of Virtue: Tradition, Islam, and the Materiality of Conversion in Medieval North India. PhD diss., Department of Anthropology, University of Chicago.

Tsing, Anna. 2005. *Friction: An Ethnography of Global Connection*. Princeton, NJ: Princeton University Press.

Vacca, Alison. 2017. *Non-Muslim Provinces under Early Islam: Islamic Rule and Iranian Legitimacy in Armenia and Caucasian Albania*. Cambridge: Cambridge University Press.

Vardanyan, Solomon. 1959. *Architecture of Armenian Popular Dwelling Houses*. Yerevan: Haypethrat. In Armenian.

Vergès, Francoise. 2019. Capitalocene, Waste, Race, and Gender. *E-flux* 100. See www.e-flux.com/journal/100/269165/capitalocene-waste-race-and-gender (accessed March 20, 2021).

Vernon, Clare. 2018. Pseudo-Arabic and the Material Culture of the First Crusade in Norman Italy: The Sanctuary Mosaic at San Nicola in Bari. *Open Library of Humanities* 4(1): 36: 1–43.

Vionis, Athanasios. 2009. Material Culture Studies: The Case of the Medieval and Post-Medieval Cyclades, Greece (a.d. 1200–1800). In *Medieval and Post-Medieval Greece: The Corfu Papers*, ed. John Bintliff and Hannah Stöger, 177–97. BAR Series 2023. Oxford: Archaeopress.

Voegelin, Eric. 1940. The Mongol Orders of Submission to European Powers, 1245–1255. *Byzantion* 15: 378–413.

Vorderstrasse, Tasha. 2019. Buddhism on the Shores of the Black Sea: North Caucasus; Frontier between the Muslims, Byzantines, and Khazars. In *The Archaeology of Medieval Islamic Frontiers: From the Mediterranean to the Caspian Sea*, ed. A. Asa Eger, 168–94. Louisville: University Press of Colorado.

Vorderstrasse, Tasha, and Jacob Roodenberg, eds. 2009. *Archaeology of the Countryside in Medieval Anatolia*. Uitgaven van het Nederlands Instituut voor het Nabije Oosten te Leiden 113. Leiden: Brill.

Vroom, Joanita. 2009. Medieval Ceramics and the Archaeology of Consumption. In *Archaeology of the Countryside in Medieval Anatolia*, ed. Tasha Vorderstrasse and Jacob Roodenberg, 235–58. Leiden: Nederlands Institut voor het Nabije Oosten.

Vroom, Joanita, Yona Waksman, and Roos Van Oosten, eds. 2017. *Medieval Masterchef: Archaeological and Historical Perspectives on Eastern Cuisine and Western Foodways*. Turnhout: Brepols.

Walker, Alicia. 2015. Pseudo-Arabic "Inscriptions" and the Pilgrims Path at Hosios Loukas. In *Viewing Inscriptions in the Late Antique and Medieval world*, ed. Antony Eastmond, 99–123. Cambridge: Cambridge University Press.

Walker Bynum, Carolyn. 1997. Wonder. *American Historical Review* 102(1): 1–26.

Wallerstein, Immanuel. 1974. *The Modern World-System I: Capitalist Agriculture and the Origins of the European World-Economy in the Sixteenth Century*. New York: Academic Press.

Waugh, Daniel. 2007. Richthofen's "Silk Roads": Toward the Archaeology of a Concept. *Silk Road* 5(1) (Summer 2007): 1–10.

White, Hayden. 1973. *Metahistory: The Historical Imagination in Nineteenth-Century Europe*. Baltimore: Johns Hopkins University Press.

Williams, Raymond. 1975. *The Country and the City*. New York: Oxford University Press.

Winter, Tim. 2019. *Geocultural Power: China's Quest to Revive the Silk Roads for the Twenty-first Century*. Chicago: University of Chicago Press.

Whitfield, Roderick, Susan Whitfield, and Neville Agnew. 2000. *Cave Temples of Mogao: Art and History on the Silk Road*. Los Angeles: Getty Conservation Institute and the J. Paul Getty Museum.

Whitfield, Susan. 2007. Was There a Silk Road? *Asian Medicine* 3: 201–13.

———. 2015. *Life along the Silk Road*. Berkeley: University of California Press.

———. 2018. *Silk, Slaves, and Stupas: Material Culture of the Silk Road*. Berkeley: University of California Press.

———, ed. 2019. *Silk Roads: Peoples, Cultures, Landscapes*. Berkeley: University of California Press.

Wierling, Dorothy. 1995. The History of Everyday Life and Gender Relations: On Historical and Historiographical Relationships. In *The History of Everyday Life*, ed. Alf Lüdtke, trans. William Templer, 149–68. Princeton, NJ: Princeton University Press.

Wilkinson, Anthony. 2003. *Archaeological Landscapes of the Near East*. Tuscon: University of Arizona Press.

Wood, Frances. 2002. *The Silk Road*. London: Folio Society.

Woolgar, Christopher M. 2006. *The Senses in Late Medieval England*. New Haven, CT: Yale University Press.

Xenophon. *The Anabasis*. Accessed at the Perseus Digital Library, Tufts University, http://perseus.tufts.edu (last accessed March 20, 2021).

Yakobson, Anatoliy L. 1950. *A Study in the History of Armenian Architecture, 5–17th centuries*. Moscow: State Press of Architecture and Urban Planning. In Russian.

Yalman, Susan. 2017. The "Dual Identity" of Mahperi Khatun: Piety, Patronage, and Marriage across Frontiers in Seljuk Anatolia. In *Architecture and Landscape in Medieval Anatolia, 1100–1500*, ed. Patricia Blessing and Rachel Goshgarian, 224–52. Edinburgh: Edinburgh University Press.

Yang, Duwei, et al. 2016. New Road for Telecoupling Global Prosperity and Ecological Sustainability. *Ecosystem Health and Sustainability* 2(10).

Yavuz, Aysil Tükel. 1997. The Concepts That Shape Anatolian Seljuq Caravanserais. *Muqarnas* 14: 80–95.

Zaqyan, Artavazd, and Astghik Babajanyan. 2014. Results of Archaeological Excavations of the Selim Caravanserai. *VEM Pan-Armenian Journal* 4(48): 125–34. In Armenian.

Zhamkochyan, Aghavni. 1981. Fritwares of Medieval Armenia, IX–XIVth Centuries. *Archaeological Monuments of Armenia 10: Medieval Monuments*. Vol. 3. Armenian SSR Academy of Sciences Institute of Archaeology and Ethnography. Yerevan: Armenian SSR Academy of Sciences Press. In Armenian.

Zhou, Gang. 2009. Small Talk: A New Reading of Marco Polo's Il Milione. *MLN* 124(1): 1–22.

Zimansky, Paul. 1985. *Ecology and Empire: The Structure of the Urartian State*. Studies in Ancient Oriental Civilization 41. Chicago: Oriental Institute Press.

INDEX

Founded in 1893,
UNIVERSITY OF CALIFORNIA PRESS
publishes bold, progressive books and journals
on topics in the arts, humanities, social sciences,
and natural sciences—with a focus on social
justice issues—that inspire thought and action
among readers worldwide.

The UC PRESS FOUNDATION
raises funds to uphold the press's vital role
as an independent, nonprofit publisher, and
receives philanthropic support from a wide
range of individuals and institutions—and from
committed readers like you. To learn more, visit
ucpress.edu/supportus.